Radioman:
Twenty-Five Years
in the Marine Corps

For Kanik

Radioman: Twenty-Five Years in the Marine Corps

From Desert Storm to Operation Iraqi Freedom

Andrew Hesterman and Robert Einaudi

GREEN COVE LIBRARY,
THANK FOR ALL YOU DO! WISHING YOU
CONTINUED SUCCESS
S/F HESTY,

Pen & Sword
MILITARY

First published in Great Britain in 2022 by
Pen & Sword Military
An imprint of
Pen & Sword Books Ltd
Yorkshire – Philadelphia

ISBN 978 1 39909 075 9

Typeset by Mac Style
Printed and bound in the UK by CPI Group (UK) Ltd, Croydon, CRO
4YY

Pen & Sword Books Limited incorporates the imprints of Atlas,
Archaeology, Aviation, Discovery, Family History, Fiction, History,
Maritime, Military, Military Classics, Politics, Select, Transport, True
Crime, Air World, Frontline Publishing, Leo Cooper, Remember
When, Seaforth Publishing, The Praetorian Press, Wharncliffe Local
History, Wharncliffe Transport, Wharncliffe True Crime
and White Owl.

For a complete list of Pen & Sword titles please contact

PEN & SWORD BOOKS LIMITED
47 Church Street, Barnsley, South Yorkshire, S70 2AS, England
E-mail: enquiries@pen-and-sword.co.uk
Website: www.pen-and-sword.co.uk

Or

PEN AND SWORD BOOKS
1950 Lawrence Rd, Havertown, PA 19083, USA
E-mail: Uspen-and-sword@casematepublishers.com
Website: www.penandswordbooks.com

Contents

Preface

When you're in the military, you tend to get a lot of questions from family, friends, even curious strangers.

"What's it like?"

"Are you glad you signed up?"

"Have you ever killed anyone?"

As my fellow veterans know, the answers to these questions are never easy.

There have been many books written about the Gulf War, and more still about Iraq and Afghanistan. What could I possibly add?

I'm not special. I'm not a Navy Seal. I didn't kill Bin Laden. And I didn't discover the meaning of life.

But, in my twenty-five years in the Marine Corps, I experienced some things.

I saw more action than most in the Gulf War.

I went to flight school and learned to fly a cool old helicopter.

And I had a unique role and vantage point in Fallujah.

I also stuck around long enough to see the US military go from low-tech to high-tech, from post-Vietnam to post-9/11. I went from Private to Major, from grunt to aviator. In the middle of all this I met a beautiful helo pilot and married her, and together we raised a family.

Rob reached out to me about writing a book shortly after I retired in 2013. I've known Rob since high school. He was one of the first people I told that I'd enlisted. We met up for drinks the night I came back from the Gulf War in 1991, and he still remembered some of my crazy stories from Kuwait (including some of the stories I'd tried to forget).

Like lots of guys retiring from the military, I'd thought about writing a book. So I agreed to give it a shot. Rob and I tossed around lots of ideas about how we might structure the book, but we quickly decided to keep it simple and just tell it like it happened.

It took four years to write. We both have families and jobs and time-consuming hobbies. Some parts went fast and were easy. Other parts were difficult and dragged on for weeks or months. We wrote a lot and rewrote a lot. Rob cut most of my jokes.

I don't have an axe to grind or an agenda to push. For my fellow veterans, maybe you'll find some laughs or understanding here. For those of you who enjoy military history, or like helos, maybe you'll learn a thing or two (heck, I could write a lot more about helos if anyone is interested). And for those who are just curious or perhaps interested in joining, maybe this will spark your interest, or at least entertain you for a bit.

I make no claims to historical accuracy. If my memories are inaccurate, my apologies. This is all real to me, a life not programmed or planned. I am proud of my accomplishments, but I'm not proud of everything revealed in these pages. A few of these stories were difficult or downright embarrassing to put on paper.

I changed the names of many of the people in this book. Some I couldn't reach to get their permission. Some are still involved in active duty, security, or law enforcement careers. In a few rare occasions, stories or characters were tweaked or combined to simplify the readability of the story. No disrespect or dishonesty is intended.

The lawyers wanted this point clear: No classified sources were used in the preparation of this book. It was screened thoroughly to ensure no classified information was included.

So, back to the original questions:

"What's it like?"

"Are you glad you signed up?"

"Have you ever killed anyone?"

Turn the page and find out.

Prologue

My conversion to the Orthodox Christian Church happened during the eight months I was home between two tours to Iraq. This was in late 2005 and I was living near Twentynine Palms, California, with my wife and our two small children. Father David, with permission from the Bishop, made an abbreviated catechism with an accelerated schedule to enable me to be chrismated before I returned to theater.

Kneeling before an icon of Christ, with Father David next to me, I began confessing my sins back as far as I could remember. I had spent a week preparing for my initial confession into Orthodoxy, which had to cover my entire life. I had made notes on everything from swiping a Twinkie in second grade to watching porn to killing men in combat. But now I was finding it very hard to proceed.

Every time I was involved in the death of a man, I put it in a mental box and stuffed it to the back of my mind. As a self-defense mechanism, I purposely avoided those boxes. But now I had to open all those boxes, along with other boxes containing memories of things I wish I had handled differently or not done. It was exhausting and humbling.

Father David listened to my confessions in silence. When I confessed things like losing my temper with my wife and kids or thinking about other women, I could feel his spiritual support. When I confessed to not always following the proper "habit of prayer," I sensed his understanding. But when I confessed to sliding a knife under a man's ribs during the Gulf War, he uttered a slight "hmmm." When I confessed to watching one of my guided bombs explode among a group of men in Iraq and then cheering as the bodies and debris flew out of the fire and smoke, I could feel him stiffen slightly. But he urged me to continue.

After I finished my confessions, Father David seemed to hesitate. He did not place the stole over my head and begin absolutions as is the custom. The growing silence was almost unbearable. Finally, he began to question me about the rather extreme circumstances I had described. He asked if any of my actions could be considered war crimes or violations of the Geneva Conventions. Confessions are privileged, but if a priest hears of a crime or believes an individual presents a danger to himself or others, the rules are a little different.

I explained that every time I applied deadly force, I attempted to do so using the law of war and rules of engagement. This includes principles of positive identification, proportionality, proper escalation of force, and minimizing collateral damage. I realize that to a civilian these words may sound callous, like jargon, but they have very real meaning and real consequences to those of us in the service.

Hindsight always makes you wonder "What if I tried this?" or "I should have thought about that," but I am confident that I took appropriate action and executed justified strikes in each case. Chances are better than good that each individual who died would have done the same to me or my comrades had they been given the opportunity. Some of them had already fired or struck friendly forces. The wrongdoing was that I should not have enjoyed the strike, savored the drama, or celebrated the kill.

Father David was not a military chaplain, but he was familiar with military challenges. He seemed to understand what I was trying to describe. After some more talk, we continued to absolutions and discussions of how to handle the temptations and habit corrections. Father David's advice was comforting and at the same time, difficult. I was amazed this man could understand so completely.

When we were finished I felt as if I had just run the longest endurance race of my life. I was totally spent. But Father David had led me through the experience, encouraging me and comforting me with assurances that I was forgiven in the eyes of the Lord. I felt as if I was emotionally held up by strong arms, preventing me from collapsing.

Part I

Enlistment and Early Years (1985–1990)

Chapter 1

Suburban Punk or Lethal Weapon?

I drove north on Highway 101, my old Pinto wagon mingling with the late afternoon traffic. Fishbone was blasting from the speakers:

> *Party at ground zero*
> *A "B" movie starring you*
> *And the world will turn to flowing*
> *Pink vapor stew…*

It was 1985. I was a junior in high school and on my way to the Navy recruiting office in San Mateo. Picture me wearing imitation Vuarnet sunglasses, jeans, Chuck Taylors, and a faded Army jacket from a thrift store. I'm sure I had a funny haircut, too – I always had a funny haircut. Picture a young Thompson Bickle, but more goofy than psycho.

I got off on East Hillsdale Boulevard and took a right onto El Camino Real. The recruiting office was another quarter mile on the right-hand side, just past the furniture outlet and across from a sporting goods store. I swung into the empty parking lot, shut off the motor, and got out.

This is a story about my twenty-five years with the United States Marine Corps, but back then I barely knew anything about the Marines. At that time I wanted to be a pilot, and Navy pilots seemed much cooler than Air Force pilots. So I was at the San Mateo Navy recruiting office, testing the waters.

I was nervous as I stepped in through the glass doors. No one knew I was doing this. Not my friends, certainly not my parents. I was on my own here. I paused in the entryway long enough to notice that the rug was worn and that the potted plants needed watering. Then I took a deep breath and opened the door to the Navy office.

The recruiter looked up when I walked in. I had talked to him briefly on the phone, but now he seemed surprised to see me. He stood up. "Can I help you…?"

Back then I didn't know much about uniforms or being "squared away," but he was wearing properly fitted and pressed service dress whites. He was a black man, middle-age, with a receding hairline. There hadn't been many black people in my life up to that point. I was going to school with the children of doctors, Stanford professors, and Hewlett-Packard engineers. Most everyone I knew was white or Asian.

What did we say? What was that conversation like? I remember him spouting a lot of buzzwords, as if he had done a poor job of memorizing a recruiting pamphlet. Things like:

"Launch your career for advancement!"

"Outstanding fiscal benefits!"

"You'll be promoting your own professional potential!"

"Earn upstanding character!"

It was somewhat amusing, but his sales pitch didn't instill confidence. He didn't get me excited about the service. My thoughts drifted. I made some noncommittal remarks and collected some pamphlets. Ten minutes later I stepped back outside into the California sun.

I got back into my faded blue Pinto, which I had recently purchased for $100. I wasn't given a new BMW or Audi like some of my rich classmates. And I wasn't driving my parents' Volvo or Mercedes. No, I'd bought the junk Pinto myself with my own money, earned working after school at a bike shop. I'd added tinted windows and an aftermarket steering wheel and wired up a new stereo. I'd even installed a roof-mounted bike rack worth more than the car.

Can you remember being sixteen? You have your first taste of freedom but you are still totally powerless and dependent. You are sick of being stuck in one place. A lot of my friends were talking about college, but I wasn't ready, not yet. I was looking at the military as my ticket out, a way to see the world and have adventures.

Can you remember 1985? We weren't worried about terrorists back then. We were at the tail end of the Cold War. Reagan was in office. The Berlin Wall was still standing. Two years before, I'd watched a made-for-TV movie called *The Day After* – about life after a major nuclear attack. Like the Fishbone lyric, we all worried about being nuked. We still had drills at school practicing proper reactions to a nuclear attack. Very few people thought of joining the military. That just wasn't something anyone did back then. Or anyone I knew.

As I got back on 101 headed south, I popped my Fishbone cassette into the tape deck and cranked it.

> *Johnny, go get your gun*
> *For the commies are in our hemisphere today*
> *Ivan, go fly your MIG*
> *For the Yankee imperialists have come to play*
>
> *Johnny goes to Sally's house to kiss her goodbye*
> *But Daddy says to spend the night*
> *They make love till the early morning light*
> *For tomorrow Johnny goes to fight...*

When I got home I made no mention to my parents of my trip to the recruiting office. We lived just twenty minutes away, in Los Altos. My parents still live in the same modest ranch house today, and it doesn't look much different. But the area has changed a lot since I was a kid. Back then there were no Google billionaires.

I love my parents, but I think I was a little much for them at that time. I was the last of four children. My brother and two sisters were all good students and generally behaved themselves. Me? Not so much.

My parents are religious people. I have become more religious as I have gotten older, but at that time religion for me meant church on Sunday plus a Wednesday night youth group.

I was the only one of my siblings still living at home. That is, besides the foster kids. My mother is something of a saint, and had started taking in children from troubled homes a few years earlier. The only problem was, I often had to share my room with them. It sucked to come home from school and find that I had a new roommate. Oftentimes I had to share my bunk bed with kids several years younger, who would wet the bed or cry out at night. Once I came home to discover that the twin boys we had living with us had broken all my model airplanes.

Between school, sports, and work, I wasn't home much. Back then I was into bicycles, motorcycles, and cars – anything that could make me go fast. I worked at a bike shop. I also ran cross country and track – I was a strong runner and did well, but I didn't always make it to practice.

I didn't pay attention to school and my studies suffered. I mostly got Cs. Despite all this, there never seemed to be any doubt that I was going to college – it just wasn't clear how it was going to happen.

I didn't know much about my parents' finances but I had a sister who just graduated from Stanford, a brother at UC Davis, and another sister at UC Berkeley. I overheard my parents talking about the troubles they were having paying for school-related expenses. I don't remember my parents ever directly telling me they would or would not pay for school, but my impression was that they didn't have the money.

During my senior year I applied to and was accepted at a few very nice schools. The University of Colorado accepted me, but when it came down to it, I was intimidated by the move and the cost. My brother and plenty of other people I knew had gone to community college and then transferred to "real" schools, so it seemed like a reasonable and economical way to start. So the local Foothill Junior College became my plan.

Graduating from high school was a big anti-climax. I was still living at home. I was eighteen now, a "man," but still sleeping in a bunk bed with a foster kid below me.

Through much of high school I had worked at a bike shop but got fired for being late too many times. So I started working at Safeway.

Remember the cult movie *Repo Man*? I was like Otto, the white suburban punk working at the grocery store. Except Safeway made me take out my earring (I wore two small hoops in my left ear at the time). I also had to buy black shoes to wear with the uniform.

I remember a former Marine who worked at Safeway with me. He didn't speak much. I thought the Marine Corps had turned him into a sullen, depressed shell who didn't have any fun. I definitely didn't want to end up like that. I felt my energy was the only thing I had going for me at the time.

Meanwhile, my mother and I weren't getting along. Mostly I wasn't following her rules – I wasn't letting her know where I was at all times. She'd give me that "I didn't know if I should expect you for dinner" kinda thing, which really meant "I didn't know where you were."

I confided my problems in my sister Anne, who was married and living near Santa Cruz. Anne was very non-judgmental, and it felt good to have a family member on my side. I remember her telling me that I would never be able to comply with all of Mom's rules and that I should just move out.

So that's what I did. A month later I moved in with my friend Paul's mom in Mountain View. Paul had gone off to college in San Diego and his mom was living alone in a good-sized house.

The rules were strict but fair. I wasn't allowed to have visitors, so if someone came over I had to talk to them on the street outside. I had a phone of my own in the room and slept on a mattress on the floor. I could pay the rent or work some of it off by doing chores.

Going to Foothill College was kind of déjà vu – even the campus at Foothill is architecturally the same as my old high school. But the size and the lack of direction made it seem worse to me. I should have been excited about the autonomy and the ability to direct my own future, but I didn't feel that way. I wasn't disciplined enough or smart enough to work up my own plan.

I remember going for long walks at night around the Earle's neighborhood. It felt like I was in exactly the same place I'd been for the last four years. I was depressed, not doing well, always tight for money, and still a nobody. Just another nameless, faceless minion slaving away to get nowhere.

All of this led me right back to the military. I went to the recruiting center in Mountain View that had Army, Navy, Marines, and Air Force. I was already turned off by the Navy, wasn't interested in the Air Force, and didn't know anything about the Marine Corps, so I went to the Army recruiter to look into being a grunt. My idea of the military was the infantry. I wanted to shoot machine guns and go camping and hiking. The thought of a real war for me and everyone else I knew at that time was pretty remote – the last conflict of any kind had been Grenada a few years earlier, and that had been kind of a joke.

The recruiting center was in a strip mall with the typical glass front and a small entry area shared by the four services; each had their own section separated by glass walls. The recruiters watched each other and their candidates through the glass partitions. The Army recruiter looked up my information on the computer and immediately started telling me about being a tank mechanic. I wasn't interested and got kind of frustrated with him. He was more energetic than the Navy recruiter had been, but I didn't want to be a tank mechanic. I wanted to be the big, bad mofo who walked through the jungle with a machine gun.

The Army recruiter showed me several videos on a small TV with a built-in VCR. The videos were typical recruiting tools with amped-up music and images showing how exciting working on tanks could be. I still wasn't impressed.

During the conversation, there was a commotion in the Marine office. The Army recruiter mentioned that the Marines were all crazy. He told me that they were always doing pushups and pullups, yelling and calling cadence even at five in the morning. This piqued my interest a little. I liked to think that I had a reputation for being a little bit crazy and felt some connection.

The Army recruiter gave me some pamphlets and a card and asked me to come back again sometime. As I was leaving, one of the Marine recruiters subtly slid into the entryway and asked me if I'd ever considered the Marine Corps. When I said no, he invited me into the Marine recruiting office.

The energy in the Marine office was different. I got the distinct feeling that they were all happy to be there and much more enthusiastic about life in general. There were a few other recruiters at other desks and several other candidates hanging around. There was a pullup bar in the back, posters of Marines doing physical training everywhere, and lots of camouflage.

We sat down and the recruiter taught me a little bit about the Marine Corps. He talked about Corps history in a way that connected with my limited knowledge of history. He talked about high standards and the reputation of Marines. It all interested me. He didn't mention anything about bonuses, educational benefits, or what jobs it would train me for when I returned to civilian life. It was just about the Marine Corps, how tough Marines were, and how they held the highest standards. I dug his approach.

I was still in research mode and not considering signing up, and he was very understanding about it. It felt more like education and sharing than pressure to join. I gave him my contact information and off I went.

One day I was at my parents' house working on the dead Pinto when my mom said I had a call. That seemed odd because no one ever called me, and even less so at my parents' house.

It was the Marine recruiter. He said, "Have you thought about our conversation? Why don't you come by and we'll talk some more." I still hadn't told my parents I was considering the military and I didn't mention it to them then, either.

So I went back to the recruiter's office, and after that I started to hang out there from time to time. The recruiters ran a mini-boot camp on Saturdays to prepare their candidates for the rigors of boot camp. It was basically a physical training session with a formation run calling cadence, plus calisthenics and pullups at the park down the street. Sometimes our session would follow the format of the Marine Corps physical fitness test (PFT). The recruiters would play Drill Instructor and yell at us and berate us for being weak and lazy. Then when it was done, the game was over and we went back to the office and drank Gatorade.

I enjoyed these sessions. Their ploy was working. I was really starting to envision myself as a Marine. We did a field trip to the reserve unit on Treasure Island one Saturday. That was the first time I saw the new High Mobility Multi-Wheeled Vehicles (Humvees). I was in love!

The Marine recruiter was SSgt Reavy but we all just called him Staff Sergeant. He used big words and lots of Marine jargon. But our discussions were tailored to me and he seemed to be interested in what I thought.

Still, I was hesitating. I felt fairly certain that I would sign up, but was nervous about it. SSgt introduced me to the idea of the Reserves. He sold me on the idea that the Reserves were every bit as much of the Marine Corps as active duty, but it was just one weekend a month and two weeks in the summer. He could give me a four-year contract and guarantee me the military occupational specialty (MOS) of machine-gunner. I would be stationed with a unit in San Jose but could still finish college. The paycheck and the GI Bill would even help pay for school, and I could switch to active duty at any time if I wanted. That seemed like an easy way to test the waters.

I created a list of pros and cons to help me decide. The thing that ultimately pushed me over the top was the fact that I didn't want to spend the rest of my life wondering what would have happened if I had joined the Marine Corps. I wanted to do something exciting. I wanted to be a hero.

On February 18, 1987, I signed a contract for four years in the Marine Corps Reserve. SSgt gave me a white T-shirt with a big red Eagle Globe and Anchor and the letters USMC across the chest. Like a little kid that never takes off his favorite shirt, I wore that T-shirt all the time. It was a double win because I was proud of it and it felt like an f-you to the rich, entitled kids I knew in Palo Alto. I felt like I was sticking it to the man in a reverse sort of way.

A few weeks later I was at my parents' house again, working on the Pinto again. No one was home and I was underneath the car on my dad's creeper, wearing my USMC T-shirt. And I had the haircut, too. My parents didn't know I was even thinking about the military and had not seen me since I had cut my hair short. I always had a difference of opinion with my mother about how I wore my hair, and I knew she didn't like really short hair.

I heard her car pull in. She got out and walked around the Pinto toward the front door. When she saw my legs sticking out from beneath the car she said, "Oh, hi, Andy."

I said, "Hi, Mom! I need to talk to you about something."

I rolled back from underneath the car and sat up on the creeper. Immediately she was looking at my hair.

"I joined the Marine Corps!"

She blinked at me for a second. "Andrew!" she said. "You did what?"

"I joined the Marine Corps," I said. "I go to boot camp May 5th."

She looked shocked. "You are already committed? You have to go?" Then she said, "Wait till your father gets home."

But when my father got home, he didn't know what to say, either. He just stammered a bit when I told him. Then we all went into the kitchen. Mom had already cleared off the round table. We took our usual places.

"You should have asked us about this," my mother said. "I wish you would have at least mentioned you were thinking about it. Don't you agree, Vic?"

"Yes, you should have at least mentioned it," my father said.

My parents really didn't know anything about the military, let alone the Marine Corps. My mom's brother was in the Army for three or four years and she didn't really seem to approve of it. My dad's brother flew J-3s (Piper Cub) in the Air Force but we never talked about that, either. Neither of those uncles came up in the discussion.

"I'm just shocked that you would do something like this," my mother said. "Vic, say something. Aren't you just shocked?"

"Yes, I am, Andy. You should have told us you were considering something like this."

They talked some more about how I should have told them and asked me several more times if I really was obligated, or if there was a way I could get out of it. I hadn't thought about getting out of it because I didn't want to, and I believed that since I had signed the contract, I was legally obligated. I didn't know at the time that you can refuse to ship to boot camp and no adverse actions are taken.

Ultimately, though, it was my decision to make, and I had made it. My parents had little power over me anymore. Eventually I used the excuse that it was getting dark and that I had to ride my bike back to the Earle's. We never talked about it again.

My contract had me going to boot camp on May 5, 1987, to be followed by the School of Infantry (SOI) and then an assignment to the unit in San Jose. It must have been around March when my recruiter called early one morning to ask me to switch my contract to be a radioman. I wasn't interested because I wanted to be a machine-gunner. The new contract would also move boot camp up to April instead of May. I didn't think a comm guy was a grunt. He assured me that I would be just a radio-powered grunt and it would be actually harder because I would have to carry radios and batteries. I didn't know at the time that an M-60 and a bunch of ammo is heavier than a radio and spare batteries. Radios and batteries are heavy, though – twenty-five to thirty pounds for the radio, plus the batteries are about the size and weight of a brick.

His boss, a captain, called me shortly after and gave me the "your country needs you, son" speech. It was a used car salesman technique and I wasn't buying it. I told him no, that I wanted to be a machine-gunner. SSgt called me back again and said they really needed this switch. I asked him what I would get out of it. He told me I would get promoted to private first class (PFC) when I graduated boot camp. I didn't know it at the time but that was a common and fairly easy incentive. So I agreed. This meant I had to go back up to the Military Entrance Processing Station (MEPS) in Oakland to change my contract and redo my physical.

Everyone in the military has stories from MEPS. It is a real cattle herding, nonpersonal kind of place. Sort of what you would expect from a "you signed the contract, now we own you" kind of operation. They probably process one hundred candidates at a time. You get broken down into groups of twenty-five or so and are herded around the station getting eye exams, rectal exams, shots, blood drawn, all kinds of stuff. Picture twenty-five teenagers in their underwear standing in a very sterile hospital-type room and a heavyset woman with a German accent yelling to drop your drawers, bend at the waist, and spread your cheeks. "Wider, spread them wider," she yelled as she paced behind you, peering into places no one else had ever looked.

Toward the end of the day, we were all herded back into a large waiting room and told to stand on the number on the floor that corresponded with the number we had been assigned for the day. Then, with no softening or compassion, they announced:

"Number twelve, you fail, you have scoliosis."

"Number seventeen, fail, you have syphilis, you can come back when you are cured."

"Number twenty-two, fail, you are pregnant."

Those of us who passed were too embarrassed to rejoice so we all just wandered back to the chairs and waited to be collected and bussed home.

The MEPS station was the first place I started to recognize the differences between the types of people that the various services attract. First off, I noticed that all the cute girls were going to the Air Force. The Army candidates seemed to have some sense of entitlement. I also noticed that the Marine candidates didn't seem to expect anything other than the treatment they were receiving.

In the weeks leading up to boot camp, I determined that if I quit my job two weeks prior to leaving, I would have just enough food, clean laundry, and money left to get me through to the day I left. So when the day came, I promptly quit and then had nothing required of me for almost two weeks!

One of my favorite things to do back then was to see movies at the Century Theaters 12 Cineplex. The complex was so large, I could get in at the matinee price and then theater hop all afternoon and into the evening. I'd bring a couple of sandwiches in my jacket pocket and I'd buy a small pack of Red Vines and ask for glasses of water.

Back then I was a big Mel Gibson fan from his early movies like *Attack Force Z*, *Gallipoli*, and of course the *Mad Max* series. So when *Lethal Weapon* came out, I was super excited and watched the movie at least four times in one day. I thought the character Martin Riggs was the coolest ever and wanted to be him. I can still quote him to this day: "When I was nineteen, I did a guy in Laos from a thousand yards out, rifle shot in high winds. Maybe eight or even ten guys in the world could've made that shot."

Between *Lethal Weapon* showings, I remember standing in the atrium area, sipping on a Pepsi. The atrium was fairly crowded in the early afternoon. I was wearing my Marines T-shirt and had the short haircut. It was as close to a Marine "high and tight" as Supercuts could manage. I was less than a week away from doing the first important thing in my life that I had decided to do all on my own.

Suddenly a Marine recruiting commercial came on the big-screen TV. It was the standard cheezy stuff, but the spirit hit me and I started to growl and "ooh-rah" at the commercial like I had learned at the mini-boot camps at the recruiter's office. And I wasn't quiet about it, either – my chants echoed across the arcade and the concessions stand.

After a few moments I noticed that everyone had taken a couple of steps back from me. People were openly staring. But it didn't temper my enthusiasm. If anything, it made me growl and "ooh-rah" louder.

When the commercial ended, I calmly took a sip of my Pepsi and walked off to watch another showing of *Lethal Weapon*.

Chapter 2

Boot Camp

I swear I had just closed my eyes to sleep when there was an explosive crash of trash can lids being slammed together. An empty can was kicked down the squad bay and the strange but scary voices of the drill instructors filled the room.

"GET UP! GET OUTTA THE RACK! GET UP GET UP MOVE MOVE MOVE! GET ON LINE, GET ON LINE!"

My body started to move before my mind had climbed out of the darkness. I was doing something and going somewhere but I didn't fully comprehend where I was. All around me olive drab wool blankets flew. Recruits tumbled out of the top bunks and stumbled out of the bottom bunks.

I stood on line with about forty-five other recruits. Behind us were two rows of twenty-five steel bunk beds with wooden footlockers placed against the end of the racks. The lights seemed particularly bright in the spartan room of white cinderblock walls, khaki floor tiles, and white ceiling. Everyone was blinking and trying to wake up and focus. We stood at attention, not moving, heels against the end of our assigned footlocker, feet at a forty-five-degree angle, back straight, chest out, hands along our sides, looking dead ahead.

Without moving, I glanced left and right. I didn't recognize a soul. The shaved, pasty-white heads from our visit to the barber the previous night made everyone look foreign, and a bit dopey. As the drill instructors paced up and down, yelling at everyone individually, the reality of my situation started to sink in. I had been at the Marine Corps Recruit Depot San Diego for thirty-six hours.

The shitstorm had started as soon as our buses pulled up in front of the yellow stucco, Spanish-style buildings on Friday evening. With their tall archways, red tile roofs, meticulously groomed grounds, and palm trees swaying in the breeze off the bay, it seemed like a striking, idyllic place. But that impression lasted for only moments. DIs yelled for us to get off the bus and form up with our feet on the yellow footprints painted on the sidewalk.

Immediately there was a blur of cataloging everything we had brought with us, including every coin and dollar bill, then locking it all away, getting shots – lots and lots of shots – an initial physical, signing paperwork, then getting issued our first Marine Corps gear: boots, socks, cammies, skivvies, and a canteen. Next we were instructed how to properly wear our newly issued clothes. There was instruction on the importance of hydration, with constant drills to guzzle water from our canteens. And then the mandatory postcard home saying we had arrived safely.

What the hell had I gotten myself into? How could I survive this for three more months? I felt the acid dumping into my stomach and a tightening knot of fear. I was in Marine Corps boot camp. On paper, I seemed like a great candidate. I had been training and preparing. But at that moment, I wondered if I had the intestinal fortitude and thick skin necessary to get through this.

The DIs continued up and down the "highway," berating each recruit. They each had a very unique and loud vocal method. I wouldn't describe it as screaming or yelling, but their worn-out vocal cords still growled at such a decibel level that it was very intimidating – worse than simply being yelled at. They sounded like they had all smoked since they were infants.

One recruit didn't manage to get his shower shoes on before getting on line, and he got it from all three DIs. Another recruit didn't manage to tuck himself away and had his junk hanging out of his boxers. Several recruits had the unfortunate morning erection, and the DIs rolled in on them for being "nasty," with comments like "You like me, boy?" and "Do I turn you on?" Another recruit shuffled a little, so he got a verbal dose. And so it continued for what seemed like an hour, but in reality was probably just a few minutes.

As time went on, it got more and more difficult to stand still. We had all been forced to drink large amounts of water throughout the previous day and had to piss something fierce.

Then came the dreaded command of, "Count off!"

How is it that eighteen-year-olds cannot manage to count in order from one to forty-five? We were lined up in alphabetical order. On command, the first recruit was supposed to yell, "ONE!" and turn his head to the left. The next would yell, "TWO!" and turn his head, and so on. And when someone screwed up, you had to start back at the beginning and so the process got more and more painful. Finally we finished and had our accountability.

The senior DI hollered, "SHIT AND SHAVE AND GET BACK ON LINE IN SIXTY SECONDS!" What the hell? I couldn't even get the lock off my footlocker in sixty seconds! But you had to try!

Off we went, a flurry of activity, with twenty guys trying to shave in just five sinks while the rest relieved themselves with three or four to a urinal. Shaving in a hurry is rarely a good idea, especially when many of us had never really shaved before. When the countdown began out in the squad bay, forty-five recruits came running. There wasn't a single recruit that wasn't bleeding or who didn't have dribbles on his shorts. As we rounded the corner to get back on line a recruit bounced off a DI, who unleashed hell. Meanwhile, three or four footlockers had been dumped and the contents had been kicked up and down the squad bay.

"DON'T EVER LEAVE YOUR FOOT LOCKER UNLOCKED AND UNATTENDED!"

Immediately two recruits were locked up, their bodies at the position of attention while being instructed, "DON'T YOU EVER FREAKING TOUCH ME!" The other two DIs had several recruits locked at attention and were chewing them out for leaving their gear unsecured. The rest of us frantically tried to collect our crap and get it back in our footlockers.

If I hadn't been scared for my life, I would have been laughing my ass off at this situation: a bunch of fuzzy-headed, bleeding recruits running around like headless chickens. And that is pretty much how the next few weeks went.

The squad bay that would be our home for the next thirteen weeks was a rectangular room about fifty by twenty feet with two rows of racks. The racks ended about twenty feet from each end of the room so that there was a small open area. These were referred to as the back classroom and the front classroom. There was a small room with a wooden door off the front classroom called the duty hut. It had two desks, two racks, and several wall lockers. This was the drill instructors' space. Recruits were not allowed there, unless they were specifically instructed to enter.

The first weeks were simply chaos in the morning, but after that everyone started to understand the routine. We got up, got dressed, made our rack. Racks were made tight with forty-five-degree folds on the corners and a two-inch fold by the pillow. To make the rack tight, we learned to pull the blanket taught underneath by reaching through the wire springs under the mattress and pulling it snug all the way around the rack. This was easier on the top rack because you didn't have to lie on the floor on your back to reach in through the wire springs.

Next came morning cleanup. Each squad had a duty and the recruit squad leader was expected to direct his squad to accomplish the task efficiently. Generally one squad would have the head, one squad would clean the main portion of the squad bay, and one squad would clean the front and back classrooms. The entire process probably took ten minutes but it seemed like an hour.

To swab the floor, we were taught a technique called deck toweling. With a wet towel folded to four by eighteen inches on the floor in front of you, you placed your hands on the towel and pushed it around the floor. Your knees were not allowed to touch the floor so you were almost in a push-up position as you slid the towel around. It was a serious butt and leg workout. At random points throughout boot camp, drill instructors would hold the "Indy 500" and recruits would have deck towel races around the rows of racks.

The deck towelers could not get beneath the racks, since they were only about eighteen inches above the floor. To cover that space, you needed scuba divers. Scuba divers used the same technique with a folded wet towel, but instead of the push-up position, they laid on the floor with the towel out in front of them and used their elbows and legs to crawl along the floor, pushing the towel ahead of them. It was similar to the tactical movement called low crawling. You had to keep your head low and your body against the deck to prevent getting caught or cut by the springs on the bottom of the racks. It was a nasty job. Most of the filth of the squad bay ended up under the racks, and because you were following a wet towel, your cammies got soaked on the front. Any dirt, sand, etc. that you missed with the towel ended up on your cammies. Standing in the cold, dark line for chow for twenty minutes with soaked cammies was not terribly comfortable. However, an hour later, it didn't matter much because by then we would be soaking wet from sweat. Plus, chances were good that we would have already paid a visit to the sand pit for a "workout" because someone had screwed something up.

I became a pro scuba diver. No one wanted to do it, so by volunteering, I was assured of getting the job. I liked knowing exactly what I was going to do each day. That way I avoided the three-minute period of chaos while other recruits tried to figure out what needed to be done and who was going to do what (and then, because they always spent too long sorting it out, the DIs would start yelling at them). Meanwhile, I would be calmly scuba diving under the racks with no one messing with me. I found it worth the uncomfortable feeling of starting the day wet and filthy.

Slowly, I perfected my technique. For example, I would wring the towel out really well so it was only damp instead of dripping, which helped immensely. I also ended up with an extra blouse (not a shirt; it's a blouse). Scuba diving every morning wore holes in the front of my blouse where the fabric covers the buttons. It was unsatisfactory (unsat) looking so the DIs got me a new blouse. With the extra one, I could wear the unsat one while I scuba dived and then swap for a good one before we headed out from morning cleanup. My T-shirt would still be wet but it wasn't too bad. I had to be quick, though, and there were a few mornings where I didn't get it done fast enough and took heat all day for wearing an unsat blouse.

Boot camp was full of arcane little details that seemed to make no sense at the time. For example, we had to sit with our legs crossed left over right, which got extremely painful after about fifteen minutes. Often, a leg would go to sleep, which was hell when you jumped up and attempted to run somewhere. Although we didn't realize it at the time, the DIs were starting our physical conditioning. Sitting cross-legged like that stretched the ligaments and tendons that if tight would cause problems later on when we would run significant mileage. It also prepared us for the rifle range, where we had to shoot from that position. The more flexible we were, the more stable our shooting position, which of course resulted in higher scores. But at the time it appeared to be just another thing to harass recruits about. Some things, like sitting cross-legged, had a purpose that actually became clear during our time in boot camp. Other things would take years to understand. Against the backdrop of the constant movement, pain and chaos, the little things that we were powerless to affect were incredibly annoying.

We were rapidly indoctrinated into wearing our cammies correctly. Part of this was to press (iron) them so the creases were sharp and the pleated pockets lay flat. Since we were constantly sweating, a good press job wouldn't last very long, so we had to press our cammies every night.

There were pleated pockets on the blouse and cargo pockets on the trousers (not pants; they are trousers). And since we couldn't have anything in our hands when marching except our rifle, we had to put everything in our perfectly pressed and pleated pockets, which soon ballooned with stuff.

During the first week, we each were issued a small five- by seven-inch plastic three-ring binder. The plastic cover was camouflaged, and like most everything in boot camp, had an Eagle, Globe, and Anchor insignia in the middle, referred to as an EGA. The binder contained an inch-thick study guide that covered many of the things recruits had to memorize. It had sections on history, first aid, eleven general orders, tactics, rank insignia – all kinds of stuff. The DIs referred to it as "knowledge." We had to take our knowledge with us everywhere and study it whenever we were standing around waiting – in line before and after chow, in line before haircuts, or before a class started.

This binder almost fit in the cargo pocket of our cammie trousers. However, the binder was about an inch too tall, so it was impossible to close the top flap of the cargo pocket. The top plastic edge and the steel lever to open the rings were at knuckle level, so while marching our knuckles became raw dragging across them. To make matters worse, we had a canteen in the other cargo pocket and the cap to the canteen had a sharp edge that scraped our other knuckles. It didn't matter what I did; the canteen cap and the binder edge were always at knuckle level. How hard would it be to make those pockets one inch deeper or at least the binder one inch shorter?

Most evenings, as the day was winding down, the drill instructors would sound mail call. All the recruits would scramble to the front classroom and sit in the prescribed order, with legs crossed left over right. One of the DIs would bring a box of mail out of the duty hut and set it on the instructor's podium. Then he would pull a letter out of the box, give it a once-over to make sure no contraband was enclosed, call out the recipient, and throw it to the crowd. We would dutifully catch it and pass it to the correct recruit. Of course there were extra comments from the DI if the letter smelled good or had anything extra written on the exterior. On more than one occasion, a recruit paid in sweat if his mail had something written on the outside of the envelope.

Usually it would go something like, "Recruit Farley, you have a letter from a Peter Jones. Apparently, he thinks we are being too hard on you! After mail call, meet me in the back classroom."

"Sir yes Sir!"

After mail call, Farley and a few others would do some "exercises" in the back classroom until the DI was either bored, satisfied they had sweated enough, or had used up too much time from the next event.

Even so, mail call still made us giddy. Sometimes someone would get a package. The recruit would have to open it there on the podium under the watchful eye of the drill instructor. Lots of funny stories come out of receiving a box in boot camp, like the blow-up doll that recruit Johns got one time. Johns had to do push-ups on that blow-up doll every night before we went to bed for at least two weeks. Another recruit received a couple of candy bars. Since we'd had a pretty good day, the drill instructor allowed him to keep them. However, he had to share equally with everyone and we wasted twenty minutes trying to cut two candy bars into forty or so equal pieces. When the DI was satisfied they were all equal, everyone got one of the tiny slivers.

I got several boxes over the course of boot camp. I had written all my friends requesting various items, and my buddies all hooked me up. Of course the main thing I always asked for was dip, though this was quite risky. One buddy sent me some allowable hygiene items such as soap, toothpaste, and a bottle of vitamin C. Still, I was surprised that the DI let me keep it. Later that night, I realized that the tablets had been dumped out, the bottle filled with dip, and the seal super-glued back on. Nice!

The best package was from an old girlfriend who filled a huge two-foot-square box with cookies she had baked. Must have been two hundred cookies. On top of the cookies was a can of Skoal, but underneath them were two more cans disguised in soap boxes! I opened the box in front of the drill instructor and he immediately snatched the can on top.

"Give me that! I'm out of dip!"

"Sir yes Sir!"

He rifled through the cookies a little bit, which was difficult because the box was so full, then told me to start passing them out. I ran up and down the rows handing each recruit a cookie until they were all gone. I think we all got four cookies out of it. As I crushed up the box to fit in the trash, I palmed the two soap boxes filled with Skoal into my cargo pocket.

Another attempt didn't work out so well. We were all sitting in the classroom for mail call when the DI walked out of the duty hut with the box of mail. I could smell dip already. Shit! I had a feeling I knew where this was going.

Sure enough, when he got to the packages, Drill Instructor Sgt Barksdale held up a yellow padded envelope with my name on it.

"Hesterman," he said, in a singsong manner. "Come heeerrreee!"

"Sir yes Sir!"

I could smell the Skoal Wintergreen as I ran to the front. I could hear the rest of the recruits giggling as I opened the envelope. Inside was a toothpaste box dutifully glued back closed. I held it up to show the DI, praying for a miracle. No such luck.

"OPEN IT!"

"Sir yes Sir!"

Inside the box was a full can of Skoal dumped into a piece of aluminum foil and then rolled up like some kind of weird joint.

"UNROLL IT!"

"Sir yes Sir!"

"Give me that! Now give me a diamond!"

"Sir?"

"GET ON THE FLOOR AND GIVE ME A DIAMOND!"

Now I understood: diamond pushups. I dropped to the deck with my thumbs and forefingers touching, making a diamond shape. Executing diamond push-ups involved touching your nose to the deck inside that diamond.

Sgt Barksdale dumped the contents of the foil in my diamond. "BEGIN!"

I began doing the four-count push-ups, calling out the cadence and repetitions: "One two three, ONE!"

"SNORT!"

"Sir?"

"SNORT IN THE DOWN POSITION"

Snuff is just a euphemism. Skoal Wintergreen is not really snuff even though it says so on the can. I swear my sinuses and eyes burned for a week.

A week later I received another package (just as my sinuses had recovered). This one had a can of tobacco that wasn't even hidden.

Drill Instructor Sgt King was on duty that night. He looked disappointed and gave a sigh. Then he said, "Eat it!"

"Sir?"

"Open that can and EAT IT! You are a repeat offender and we are going to fix that!"

So like a five-year-old trying to avoid vegetables at the dinner table, I opened the can and started eating it pinch by pinch. It wasn't that bad at first but I knew it would get worse. A quarter of the way into the can, I got the hiccups from the burn developing in my esophagus. The rest of the platoon was either trying not to laugh or had that "oh shit" empathetic look. I kept plugging away, probably dropping as much as I was getting in my mouth.

When I started to gag, Sgt King said, "All right, recruit, go to the head, then come back and clean this crap up! Write to everyone you know and tell them to stop sending you tobacco! GO!"

I ran to the head and put my finger down my throat. Yeah, it was a little spicy coming back up, but honestly, it wasn't as bad as I would have expected. I immediately wrote to everyone and told them to stop sending my tobacco unless it was VERY well disguised and sealed.

After mail call, just before lights out, we got about an hour of "free time." This was when we shit, showered, and shaved, polished our boots and belt buckles, maybe wrote a really quick letter, studied a little bit, and cleaned our rifles and gear. We had learned that we would get maybe thirty seconds at most to use the head throughout the day, so most everybody got on an evening schedule. Most of us were still pretty light-haired so we could get away with shaving the night before. So we would get all set for the next day during that hour. And what we didn't get done, we had to do in the middle of the night.

The tired fog of getting only four to five hours of sleep made it really hard to get up at night, but I think everyone did at some point or another. It was common to see eight or ten recruits up studying, writing letters, polishing boots, etc., at any given time. It was strictly forbidden by the drill instructors but we never had any issues. As long as you hit the rack at lights out and were in the rack thirty minutes or so before reveille, there weren't any issues.

From lights out at night until lights on at about 4:30 in the morning, there were two recruits watching the squad bay. This was firewatch. One covered the front door and one covered the back door. The duty rotated every hour. Your predecessor woke you up five minutes before your duty, then you woke up your relief five minutes before he was supposed to replace you.

The last firewatch of the day would wake up the duty drill instructor at the requested time. Firewatch was supposed to make sure none of the recruits got up after lights out, prevent any recruits from rat-fucking (stealing) each other's gear, and prevent any blanket parties. (If you have seen the movie *Full Metal Jacket*, which hit theaters just a few months after we finished boot camp, you will be familiar with this practice; basically you use a blanket to pin down the recruit in his bed, then pummel the crap out of him.) So, if any of these activities were to occur, the firewatch had to be all over it. I don't remember any issues of recruits rat-fucking each other's gear at night. There were several blanket parties, but I wasn't involved so I was happy not to know anything about it.

Rule number one of boot camp is do not stand out. Don't be first, don't be last – just stay in the middle of the pack. I messed that up a few times. The first time was during the initial physical fitness test when I ran faster than anyone in our company (six platoons). After that I was always chosen whenever something needed running somewhere. Of course no matter how fast I ran, it was never fast enough and I took extra flack.

The other place I messed up was academically. I got 100 percent on the first academic tests. That really isn't a big achievement because the academics of boot camp are simple memorization. Still, the drill instructors assigned me to help some of the academic problem children. The only way I could think of to do that was to hold study groups. I held them for forty-five minutes in the middle of the night in the bathroom. The other guys were very receptive and wanted the help. We would work on mnemonic devices and other techniques for memorizing the large volume of material.

This was the only time in the barracks setting that I felt bold enough to have tobacco in my mouth. The other guys didn't complain or turn me in because they were happy for the help. Sitting on the benches in the head, having a dip, and whispering stories about cars, girls, or other things from our lives back in the real world is one of my fondest memories from boot camp.

In the fourth week of boot camp a rumor went around that there had been a suicide attempt. The Marine Corps has always had a high rate of suicide – higher than the other services and much higher than the civilian rate. When you work hard, get pushed hard, and are conditioned that your job is the only thing that matters in life, you are going to have issues with depression. Obviously, someone prone to suicide is not going to fit well into military service so the Marine Corps has always worked hard to weed those types out.

A few days after the rumor started, Drill Instructor Sergeant Moore took us all into the back classroom. We sat cross-legged on the industrial tiled floor and waited for the class to begin.

Sergeant Moore was bigger than our other drill instructors, who for the most part fit into the category of lean, mean fighting machines. Moore was more like a lineman. He had a hint of a southern drawl, and the little bit of hair he had was reddish blond. We didn't know all the cues for seniority but suspected he was the most junior. Not that it made any difference to us. We were all just pond scum.

Sergeant Moore started off the class with "Marines don't do anything half-assed and that includes suicide." He told us that if we wanted to kill ourselves, we needed to do it properly. But he acknowledged that there were limited options available to us at boot camp. We didn't have access to ammunition yet and except for Motrin, medications were pretty much non-existent on the base. That left hanging and slitting your wrists as the most readily available methods for ending your life.

For hanging, the sergeant recommended that we use a twisted-up bed sheet with a slip knot snugged up around our neck and a lock knot around the rifle racks under the windows on the second or third floors. Jumping out the window raised your potential success rate because it was more difficult to stop, you had a good chance of snapping your neck, and there was nothing to climb up on if you survived the initial jolt.

The wrist-slitting lesson started with a description of how to get the blade out of a safety razor. We were told to cut a vein lengthwise, not crosswise, and to use warm water to prevent the blood from clotting. He advised that we do this in the shower, because that would make cleanup easier on the rest of the platoon.

Completely bewildered and not knowing how to take this information, we filed it away in our "brain housing groups" and moved on to our evening routines.

A few hours after lights out, Sergeant Moore rousted recruit Liver. Liver was a tall, thin Southerner. I don't know where he was from but his drawl was so thick, I had trouble understanding him at times. I don't think I ever saw Liver with any expression other than a furrowed brow and pursed lips. And while even the whitest of us had begun to tan on our arms, necks, and sides of our heads, Liver had a slightly yellow, jaundiced tint to his skin.

Evidently Sergeant Moore suspected Liver of having suicidal thoughts and had decided to teach him a lesson. Sergeant Moore escorted Liver to the window looking out at the ground three stories below. Most of the other recruits were deep asleep and the firewatch recruits were properly stationed at the front and back doors, out of earshot. I was awake in my rack, just one rack over from where they looked out the window.

"Think you could jump out this window tonight recruit?"

"Sir no Sir."

"Scared? I doubt that would even hurt. I could jump out this window, run back up the ladderwell, and jump again."

Silence.

"If you did, you better dive out this window and try to smash your brain housing group on the concrete. If you landed any other way, I bet you wouldn't die and then we'd all have to come down and drag you off to Medical. That would be a failure recruit. Marines don't fail, so you'd better do it right."

More silence. Liver was shaking slightly.

The drill instructor finished with, "Get your ass in the rack. Don't let me frickin' hear about any of this."

Over in my rack, I didn't process it as anything other than fairly typical harassment and was mostly relieved that I hadn't drawn the DI's attention.

The next morning, the rest of the drill instructor staff showed up as we were going through the typical "dress by the numbers." After the platoon was turned over to the next DI, we never saw Sergeant Moore again. Nothing was ever said or explained. A new drill instructor joined us a few days later and that was that.

The rivalry between East Coast Marines and West Coast Marines starts with boot camp. Parris Island is the oldest Marine Corps Recruit Depot (MCRD) and claims to be the "real" boot camp, although the difference is about six years (1915 vs. 1921). MCRD San Diego Marines are often referred to as "Hollywood" Marines and are rumored to get issued silk running shorts and sunglasses. Male recruits living east of the Mississippi River and female recruits from all over the United States report to Parris Island to receive their initial training. Male recruits living west of the Mississippi River, Illinois, Wisconsin, and some parts of Michigan receive their training at Marine Corps Recruit Depot San Diego, California.

Each MCRD has its own unique challenges. Parris Island is basically a swamp and has the weather challenges of the Southeast. The no-see-ums (biting gnats and flies) are brutal particularly while locked in the position of attention while standing in formation. A Hollywood Marine's response is usually, "But we have Mount Mother Fucker!"

Hollywood Marines do their field training portion at Camp Pendleton instead of on MCRD. While the weather is generally mild, the terrain is the steep coastal hills of California. There are several peaks and ridges that recruits hump that go from just about sea level to 1,700 or 1,800 feet. Mount Mother, Recon Ridge, and the Reaper are a few of the peaks that recruits get to experience. There are trails that have switchbacks and lessen the grade but many go straight up the incline to the peak. The trails are usually severely rutted and extremely dusty. They are steep enough in places that our hands would drag the dust as we leaned into the incline and clawed our way to the top.

In a hump or forced march, Marines are supposed to maintain an interval of forty inches. In boot camp, we frequently heard (at high volume), "AT&T, reach out and touch someone," which got abbreviated to "AT&T!" That meant each recruit was supposed to reach out and hold onto the pack in front of them. If the interval was too big, we had to sprint quickly to reach that pack. Of course, the accordion effect left the recruits in the back of the formation running as the relatively small gaps of recruits towards the front accumulated into large distances toward the back.

"AT&T" became a hated command because it meant we were sprinting and getting yelled at and our already miserable state was amplified. Being at the back of a hump sucked! Having to sprint and then immediately stop and have the recruit behind you bump into you produced some comical domino scenarios. Picture unbalanced recruits carrying heavy packs falling down and taking several others with them, then scrambling to get back into formation. Of course, it was often dark and the recruits would swear at each other under their breaths.

Climbing up Mount Mother was a bitch. Coming down the other side was downright dangerous. On my first descent of Mount Mother I honestly thought I was going to die. Sleep deprived, exhausted, and generally only half-aware of my environment, I found myself one recruit back from the drill instructor leading the hump as we started down the steep descent. The footing was treacherous from the rutted trail; our legs were numb and used to the short stride of climbing steps. Moments later the recruit behind me stumbled and fell against my pack, pushing my center of gravity forward farther than my legs could catch. I ended up doing the same to the recruit in front of me. He crumpled and we both slammed into the back of the drill Instructor in front of him.

The drill instructor seemed to fly forward. His revered smokey bear hat (or "cover" in Marine speak) was launched into the darkness. I swear I could see the stars twinkling off the patent leather band as the cover disappeared into the void in front of us. Maybe it was the stars from my helmet impacting the ground and transferring that impact to my brain housing group.

It seemed like an eternity before we were able to untangle ourselves and get back upright. The two recruits I was entangled with were cussing and fussing: "What the fuck, man?" and "Asshole, what is wrong with you?" and "Get off me, motherfucker!"

Drill Instructor Sgt Daniel seemed to lithely roll and spring back to his feet. Possibly the worst offense a recruit could commit was to cause damage to a drill instructor's cover. It was the DI's badge, their source of power, and it signified everything about their god-like status. So right then I was focused on the man who was about to send our souls to hell. Instead, he simply stood with his hands on his hips and said, "Find my cover."

The rest of the platoon halted as three of us slid, rolled, clawed, and scrambled down the trail and into the bushes, trying to find the DI's cover. We eventually found it, and took turns attempting to brush off the dust, dirt, and dry weeds as we clambered back up the hill. I was sure that once the cover was returned, the fire would erupt from the drill instructor's eyes and incinerate us to smoldering piles of ash. And so it seemed like a dream when he quietly said (enunciating each word forcefully), "Never…breathe…a word…of this. Don't…ever…touch…me…again." Then in classic drill instructor growl: "NOW GET THE HELL BACK IN THE DOGGONE FORMATION!"

So we continued our hump down Mount Mother, never to speak of the incident again.

A night or two later on those same hills and trails, we received the hand and arm signal to stop and get down into a defensive position. The road we were on was perpendicular to the steep slope, and I was on the uphill side of the road. There were waist-high weeds on either side and we were supposed to get off the road, conceal ourselves by lying down in the weeds, and turn our focus outward to any potential (but imaginary) threat.

I knew there was a ditch on the uphill side but couldn't tell in the dark how deep it was. If I got off the road in the ditch, I envisioned myself laying against the steep slope in an almost vertical position, unable to see anything above me and therefore in a very absurd tactical position. Instead, I crouched in the weeds at the immediate edge of the dirt road and pointed my rifle and attention up the slope.

The drill instructor who had been bringing up the rear came striding up the road, correcting recruits as he went. As he passed me, he said, "Recruit, get OFF the friggin' road!" I stood up to a low crouch and took one small step into the void. The ditch was much deeper than I expected and I tumbled violently down into the deep chasm. I managed to perform a partial rotation in the air, and after what seemed an eternity of falling, landed on my pack in the V-shaped bottom of the ditch. My pack padded my fall but the back edge of my helmet slammed into the back of my neck as my head snapped back.

I was a bit stunned and just lay there for a moment before I realized that because of the V shape of the ditch and the weight of my pack, I was stuck like an overturned turtle, unable to right myself. I may have grunted or swore, or maybe it was the sound of the impact that brought the drill instructor back. He stood at the edge of the road above me, calling into the darkness, "Hey, recruit!" Then, "Recruit? What the hell? Are you okay?"

I couldn't quite find my voice and didn't really know what to say. I squeaked out, "Assistance?"

The drill instructor growled to the other recruits to "find that recruit and get him out of the friggin' ditch." They dutifully scrambled down and extracted me from the clutches of that damn ditch.

In the light of day the next morning, recruit Silvera, a friend of mine, remarked at how nasty the very tender spot on the back of my neck looked. The painful bruise had turned a deep purple. Of course a week or so later it turned a disgusting yellowish black, and I continually took heat from the drill instructors that my brain was diseased and dying and leaking down my spinal column. "That don't matter, though, recruit! All you have to do is follow doggone orders! You don't get paid to friggin' think!"

After field training, we went to Edson Range on Camp Pendleton for marksmanship training. By this time, we were starting to shape up pretty well. We had been in boot camp for seven weeks and had started to figure out the systems and games. This isn't to say that the stress or the constant yelling wasn't still there, but we started to believe that we might just survive boot camp. Instead of just making it to the next mealtime, we started looking a day or two down the road. Also, the significance of making good marksmen out of the recruits and the seriousness of proximity to live ammunition meant that the games were somewhat reduced.

Every Marine is a rifleman so it is probably self-evident that marksmanship is important to the recruits and to the staff. A recruit doesn't graduate boot camp if he doesn't at least qualify as a marksman with his service rifle. Sharpshooter is the next level and expert is the top qualification. Everyone wants to wear an expert shooting badge on their uniform. I had a little shooting experience and fell into the training fairly easily. I didn't have many bad habits to unlearn, and the training was broken down into pretty simple pieces.

Several of the seemingly useless things we had done before now made sense. Sitting cross-legged for hours in classes until our legs went to sleep now paid off as we shot from that position at both the 200- and the 300-yard line. We learned about the muscle to bone and bone to muscle contact to form a stable shooting platform. We learned sight alignment and sight picture, natural point of aim, focusing on the front sight instead of the target, and a myriad of other things.

The M-16, now in the A-2 version, is a pretty nice weapon and a Marine Corps mainstay. If kept clean and taken care of, it is reliable and accurate. Even the abused and beaten recruit issue rifles worked pretty well. Many of them were almost silver from being scrubbed so often. The black coating, called parkerization, had worn off from being scrubbed, dropped, dragged and mishandled by so many recruits. At the command of the drill instructors, we all named our rifles and memorized the serial number just like they show in the movies. We totally bought into the rifleman's creed that we had memorized. Without a rifle, a rifleman is useless. And without a rifleman, the rifle is useless.

The rifle range training was two weeks. The first week was called "snapping in." We were getting up earlier, about 0300 (zero three). Dressed, morning clean-up, chow hall, and then off to the rifle range to be in the outdoor classroom area before the sun came up. Most of each morning was taken up by classes on different aspects of marksmanship. We would have a short break for an MRE and then we were at the firing positions practicing sighting in, firing positions, squeezing the trigger, etc., all with no ammunition.

It sounds silly, but all that practice without ammo seemed to work because everyone in my platoon eventually qualified. While we were standing, sitting, kneeling, or laying on the four-foot berm that is the firing points on the range, the drill instructors would walk behind us, correcting errors and suggesting improvements. "Get that elbow tight to your ribs" or "Keep that magazine off the deck" or "Tighten that sling." Occasionally someone would do something wrong and would be pulled off the firing line and thrashed at the bottom of the berm, but for the most part, that didn't happen on the rifle range.

We had already memorized the four basic rules of weapons handling:

1. Treat every weapon as if it were loaded.
2. Keep your finger straight and off the trigger until you intend to fire.
3. Never point your weapon at anything you don't intend to shoot.
4. Keep your weapon on safe until you intend to fire.

But now these rules were practiced with vigor. The fastest way to get a thrashing was to not pay attention to where our weapon was pointed. Carrying a rifle around all day in a large group and never pointing it at someone is difficult. But we learned to do it and soon it became second nature. Most of the time we simply kept the weapon pointed at the dirt near (but not at!) our feet or elevated, pointed to the sky. The main point is that we ALWAYS had to pay attention to where our weapon was pointed.

At the range we would sight in on our target with our trigger finger along the side of the rifle. And when ready to shoot, we would slide our finger into the trigger housing and squeeze the trigger – almost all in one motion. If you see a picture of a Marine in combat, look closely and you will probably see that his finger is not on the trigger unless he is actually sending a round "downrange."

Before we were ever handed a round we had the five stages of the qualification course memorized – in both our minds and muscles. Stage one: from the 200-yard line fire five rounds from sitting position, five rounds from kneeling position, and five rounds from standing position in twenty minutes. Stage two: from the 200-yard line, fire five rounds, change magazines, fire another five rounds from the kneeling position in seventy seconds. Stage three: from the 300-yard line fire five rounds from the kneeling position in five minutes. Stage four: from the 300-yard line fire five rounds, change magazines, fire another five rounds from the kneeling position in seventy seconds. Stage five (my favorite): from the 500-yard line fire ten rounds in the prone position in ten minutes.

The next week was much the same except now we actually got to fire! We spent a little less time in the bleachers of the outside classroom and a little more time on the actual firing position. The process went a little slower because only one recruit could fire on a target at a time as opposed to the previous week, when two or three were "dry" firing at each target.

Slowly and methodically we would shoot. We were finally using the adjustments on the rifle sights, looking at the impacts on the targets, adjusting for winds, relaxing our breathing, pause, squeeze, BANG! I liked the feeling of the recoil in my shoulder and felt a sense of accomplishment when my rifle settled back down from the recoil and was still centered on the target. I felt slight elation when the impact was in the bullseye. It was methodical and technical. There were no thoughts of shooting the enemy or killing; it was simply punching holes in paper at the right place. A weapon is a powerful tool, and I felt the power of using it correctly.

My favorite stage was firing in the prone position from the 500-yard line. Because of the distance, it is more technical and mistakes tend to cause greater error. Reaching out half a kilometer away and putting a 5.56 mm hole exactly where I wanted in a piece of paper was the greatest sense of power.

I never mastered the standing position at the 200-yard line and that kept me from platoon high shooter score. I did qualify as an expert, though, and consoled myself with the thought that I would never shoot from a standing position in a real combat environment. Years later, with several combat shooting schools and a couple of tours in combat zones under my belt, I realized that LOTS of combat shooting is from the standing position.

The Edson Range barracks area was about four hundred meters from Interstate 5, the major connection between the Los Angeles basin and San Diego. The interstate is four or five lanes each way, and even in 1987 had a lot of traffic, twenty-four hours a day.

There was a reststop about half a mile north, within view of the barracks. Plenty of times we got busted for staring at the traffic hustling by. Oh, how we envied the civilians and their ability to go where they wanted, when they wanted.

One night I got up to do a little uniform prep and noticed that no one else was awake except the firewatch. Generally, at least one or two other recruits would be awake at different times through the night, studying, working on drill maneuvers, or preparing uniforms. The lack of other recruits awake at that hour made me decide to risk acting on an idea I'd been toying with recently. I knew there had to be vending machines at the rest stop. There even might be chewing tobacco.

I dressed in my least smelly cammies, grabbed my camouflage duffle bag, and went to make a deal with recruit Raynes, who was on firewatch by the back door. I promised him a large-sized candy bar if he didn't report that I was leaving the squad bay. His eyes lit up when I said the words "candy bar." We hadn't seen candy in at least seven weeks. I could almost see the wheels churning in his mind. Then he said, "What are you going to do?"

"It's probably better that you don't know. I'll be back in a little while and I'll bring you a Snickers or something."

"Okay. But if you get caught, I didn't see you leave."

"Fair enough."

I slipped out the back door and headed toward I-5. Using all the stealth I had learned through field training, I crossed the two-lane road, slipped low across the grass field, and then jumped and rolled over the six-foot chain-link fence.

I was surprised to find a railroad track between the fence and the freeway, but it provided an easy place to jog the half-mile to the rest stop without exposing myself on the freeway shoulder. The railroad bed dipped down a little lower than the freeway and the rest stop was a little higher, so it was easy to slip up the incline behind the restroom building, straighten myself out, then walk around casually, like I was just another Marine headed home on I-5.

Just as I had predicted, there was a small kiosk with a couple of vending machines. Better still, there was a shiny silver vending truck. For a moment I stood in awe of all the sodas, candy bars, Pop Tarts, and frozen burritos.

The driver/salesman hopped out of the truck and asked what I wanted. He had two cans of tobacco so I put those on the small stainless counter. Then I started stacking up candy bars and sodas. I only had about $25, but back then a can of dip was about 85 cents and candy bars were about 50 cents. While the frozen burritos really tempted me, I figured they would be of no use since I couldn't think of how I would heat them up.

On a whim, I asked the guy if he had any cigarettes, since there weren't any displayed. He didn't, but he immediately offered to sell me two of his personal packs he had in the cab of the truck. I was nervous and trying to steady my shaking knees, but he didn't seem to notice. In retrospect, I think he knew exactly what was going on. But a sale is a sale. He took my $25 and I strode off with a duffle bag full of goodies.

With a quick glance to ensure no one was watching, I ditched down the hill to the railroad tracks and retraced my steps back toward the squad bay, enjoying a fresh dip along the way. I had to get back before Raynes was relieved on firewatch or there would be someone else to deal with.

It seemed to take forever as I lay in the grass next to the road, waiting for one lone car to pass. Then I jumped up and crossed to the barracks building. Slowly, I peeked through the small window with the diamond-shaped reinforcements on the back door. I half expected the lights to be on and to see recruits getting thrashed by the drill instructors. But all was quiet, with recruits in their racks, so I slipped back in.

Raynes was waiting for me. It seemed like he had been holding his breath the entire time I had been gone.

"So? Did you get it?"

"Even better!" I slipped out a cigarette and handed it to him. I knew Raynes was a smoker.

"Ooooh." He held it with absolute reverence. "Do you have any more?"

"Yup."

"How much? I'll buy them from you."

"How about $1 each?"

"I'll take the whole pack!"

Raynes gave me $20 – I had almost broken even already! I gave him a pack of cigarettes and a candy bar and stowed the rest of my booty in a laundry sack in the air vent in the head. Then I played firewatch while Raynes huddled just out the back door, having his first cigarette in several weeks. He was obviously wired when he came back in. I was still shaking from the adrenaline of my adventure, too.

It was time for Raynes to wake up the next firewatch. He woke up recruit Grimes, and while Grimes was getting dressed by red lens flashlight, Raynes and I stood by the back hatch talking about the real world in hushed tones. When Grimes came over to replace Raynes he could tell something was up. We were a bit giddy and I just couldn't keep things to myself.

"Hey, Grimes, if I give you a candy bar, can you keep to yourself and promise not to tell anyone?"

"Where did you get a candy bar? Hidden in one of your mail packages?"

"Something like that, but you gotta make sure you get rid of the wrapper! Flush it down the toilet or something. Don't just throw it in the trash."

"Okay!"

So I went back to the head and grabbed a Snickers bar for Grimes. Again, I got to see that look of admiration as he held it in his hands. Oh, how the simple things seem so significant when you are without them for so long.

After field training and rifle range training at Camp Pendleton, we returned to MCRD San Diego for the third phase of boot camp. I've heard horror stories about the cattle car ride from Pendleton to San Diego – basically a large box truck with no seats – but we got lucky and had white school buses.

We made the trip in the middle of the night. Everyone sat locked into position, eyes straight ahead, left hand left knee, right-hand right knee for the entire hour drive south. But in our peripheral vision, we gazed in amazement at the outside world that had continued on without us. The buses were pretty loud so the recruits sitting toward the back were able to get away with talking in low whispers.

Most of the recruits had never been to California before, and they were in awe of what flashed by outside the bus windows. By then it was June so occasionally we would get a glimpse of summertime attire on the girls. It was amazing how observant we had become and how much you could see out of the corner of your eye!

"Did you see the chick in that last car?"

"Damn, she was hot!"

"Oh man, I can't wait to go home on leave!"

"Yeah, my girl ain't gonna wear nothing but shorts and bikinis the whole time I'm home."

"Mine ain't going to wear anything!"

"Man, I miss driving my car!"

"I'm gonna just drive around listening to music full blast for the first couple days."

"Music, what's music? Ha ha."

It was back to business at MCRD San Diego. However, we now had a sense of accomplishment because we had made it through the first two phases of boot camp and were starting to look like Marines. We had earned the right to wear our cammies like Marines, which means we got to unbutton the top button of our blouses and roll the bottom of our trouser legs into an elastic band called a boot band. This is called "blousing" your trousers. It keeps critters from crawling up your legs in the field, but more importantly, it is how true Marines wear their trousers.

Our hair had been growing out although we shaved the sides weekly. Instead of the fuzzy, bald recruit look, we were now wearing the iconic Marine high and tight. The platoon marched liked a well-oiled machine and we knew our way through the day. We were all in much better shape and looking like lean, mean, fighting machines instead of doughy recruits. And of course, graduation was only four weeks away.

By now the drill instructors had decided that most of the recruits would make it. I suppose there were still a few in question, but for the most part, the DIs were throttling back on the abuse.

The platoon had become a team, and even though we didn't necessarily like each other, we supported each other and took care of each other to the best of our ability. Now when someone got singled to go to the pit and exercise, the entire platoon would join in without hesitation. The drill instructors were pleasantly surprised, but of course tried to hide it.

This is not to suggest that the rest of boot camp was all happy and fun. We still got yelled at, still worked hard every day, still were exhausted all the time, and were still nervous and stressed. And we did have more to lose now, which the drill instructors reminded us of daily.

"You haven't graduated yet! I still own you! MOVE WITH A SENSE OF PURPOSE!"

I had firewatch the night of Independence Day. It was about 2300 (11 p.m.) and everyone else was in the rack snoring. Dates and holidays don't exist in boot camp, so although I probably knew it was July 4th, I was surprised when the fireworks started at SeaWorld across the bay.

It was a strange moment. It was a beautiful show and I have always enjoyed fireworks and 4th of July celebrations. But boot camp had changed the way I felt about it. The history and customs classes had affected me. Somehow the day felt more somber. And although graduation was two weeks away, I was still in the purgatory of boot camp and missed being with friends and family.

So I just leaned on the windowsill and watched from a distance as the outside world celebrated our great nation's birthday. I've had that same lonely feeling in Kuwait, Bosnia, Iraq, Afghanistan, and a few other places.

It never rains in the summer in San Diego, but it rained on July 17, 1987. We had made it through boot camp and were about to be declared United States Marines. It was our big day, but now it was raining.

The ceremony was held in the large theater. I got to sit on the stage with a few other honored recruits because I had the top score on the physical fitness test. The rest of the company sat in the first few rows of the audience seats. I don't remember a word of any of the speeches. I don't remember who spoke. I knew that my family was somewhere out there in the darkness of the theater and I was one parade away from being free.

After the theater ceremony, we exited and formed into our platoons on the edge of the drill field. We were locked at attention, ramrod straight and not moving, but searching out of the corners of our eyes for a glimpse of our loved ones. The families respectfully walked by the platoon, searching, trying to pick their son, brother, or boyfriend out of the identical-looking almost Marines. Some were whispering; some even shouted and waved. My sisters figured out which platoon I was in and walked slowly along one side. When they saw me they started giggling and whispering, though I had no idea what they were saying. King, standing next to me, whispered out of the corner of his mouth, "Hey, man, are these your girls?"

"No, those are my sisters."

"They are cute, man!"

"Shut up, dude!"

Soon came the call for the guests to take their seats. Our wool shirts smelled like wet dogs in the light rain. The creases had flattened out and the mottled color on the tan between wet and dry spots made us look ratty. We wanted so badly to be squared away and look like stunning Marines, but our big moment had literally been dampened.

All thoughts faded out as the band started playing. We marched the best we had ever marched in our lives. Since we would be released as soon as the parade was over, we had turned in our rifles. It was strange marching without our rifles, but a bit freeing at the same time.

The parade concluded and the platoons all stood in a line facing the bleachers. The command was given: "Dismissed!" In unison, 240 brand new Marines shouted, "Dismissed, Aye Aye Sir!" We then took two steps back and executed a perfect about-face.

Some guys whooped or hollered. Others jumped for joy. But I just stood there. I didn't know what to do next. The band had stopped and the pomp and circumstance was over. No one was shouting orders at me. We hadn't rehearsed past this point, and I was a bit overwhelmed. It was a strange moment. I felt like I was alone.

Slowly the dimness faded from my vision, the sound came back up to full volume in my ears, and I felt I had control of my faculties again. I spun around and went to find my family.

Chapter 3

Comm School

Uncle Sam flew me home after graduation, so I arrived at my parents' house well before the rest of my family, who were still working their way up the California coast in my brother's RV. I immediately changed out of my uniform and into shorts and a T-shirt, then went to the kitchen and wolfed down half a gallon of ice cream and two bottles of my dad's beer. Then I went and crashed on the bunk bed in my old room and slept for sixteen hours straight.

I was still asleep when my parents got home. For some reason my mom thought it would be funny to wake me like they did in boot camp. She switched on the lights and started yelling for me to get up. I jumped up and smashed my face on the bottom of the top bunk. I didn't think it was very funny.

I had ten days' leave before I started Comm School. I was bummed that I didn't have a girlfriend, so I just ended up hanging out with some of my guy friends and went to the beach and went windsurfing. I bought my friend's 1982 Yamaha Vision 550 with my boot camp paycheck (about $1,500) and rode it around a lot, wearing my cheap leather flight jacket with the "Semper Fi" sticker on the back.

It was a bit of a shock to go from having my day planned out 24/7 to having total free rein. My mom had arranged a bunch of things for me to do (mostly people to see) and I resented that a bit. I often stayed out late and slept in late. But I was starting to feel distanced from the Palo Alto scene. Most of my friends had left the area. I found myself missing some of my buds from boot camp.

So I was okay with going back to the Marine Corps ten days later. I looked forward to seeing some of my boot camp friends who would be with me at Comm School – guys like Silvera, Gomez, and Moore. I was a bit nervous about heading back into the rigidity of Marine Corps life, but I was no longer a recruit and had been assured that Comm School would be different than boot camp.

I had been getting pretty shaggy, so I got a fresh haircut at the local barber, who managed to get pretty close to a regulation high and tight. I really liked the hot cream and straight razor instead of the rushed clipper job we had had in boot camp. I dressed in my freshly pressed Alpha uniform – dark green trousers and coat over a tan shirt and tie. My dad dropped me off at the airport with my sea bag, which contained everything I would have with me for the next few months.

Waiting at the gate, I was happy to see my buddy Silvera from boot camp. That was a relief. Now at least if I was wrong, I wouldn't be wrong alone! We shook hands formally (displays of affection are not allowed in uniform) and talked a bit about leave while we waited for the flight.

It was a short flight. Soon, we landed in Palm Springs and were hit by a blast of hot air as we exited the plane. I couldn't believe how hot it was! Welcome to July in the Mojave Desert. We hurried into the terminal, thankful for the air conditioning and worrying that we had sweated all the creases out of our uniforms.

The Marine Corps Air Ground Combat Center is in Twentynine Palms, California. The base is often referred to as Twentynine Stumps or simply The Stumps. As I would find out, there were no longer twenty-nine palms in Twentynine Palms. (In 2005, to correct this problem, the Commanding General of the base had twenty-nine palms planted along the road just inside the main gate. Everyone still refers to it as "The Stumps," though.)

The terrain around Twentynine Palms is mostly mountain ridges with lots of dry lakebeds in between. The most common plant is a creosote bush – not much else survives out there. Base elevation is 1,800 feet with mountain peaks reaching 4,500 feet. It is hot in the summer and cold in the winter. Average high in the summer is one hundred degrees Fahrenheit with 115 common. Average low in the winter is forty with twenties being common. It snows occasionally in the winter but otherwise there is not much precipitation, so it is usually hot and dry. But when it does rain, it rains hard and floods are common.

Twentynine Palms is the largest USMC base and the only place that Marines can test every weapon in the arsenal (including aircraft-delivered ordnance). The entire base is over nine hundred square miles and covers almost the entire distance between I-40 and I-10. The vast majority of the base is unoccupied desert. It's basically one giant open range.

The cantonment area (or what we call mainside) is about 1.5 square miles, and is like a small town. There were about eight thousand Marines in Twentynine Palms, so in that respect Camp Pendleton and Camp Lejeune are far bigger (with about 35,000 to 40,000 Marines each). There is an exchange, which is very similar to a small Walmart, plus a separate commissary (grocery store), gas station, movie theater, eighteen-hole golf course, auto repair shop, pizza place, Burger King, and one other restaurant. There was also an officers club, an enlisted club, and one more bar. You could get around fine walking except that you sweat to death in the summer. There was a huge pool where all the enlisted guys hung out. Very few of the buildings had A/C – they mostly used swamp coolers (evaporative coolers). The movie theater was always nice and cool, and sometimes we would go watch movies just to hang out in the cool (plus it was free). Before the movies, they always played the national anthem and the Marine Corps hymn and everyone would stand up and sing along. I remember one time they had a glitch in the sound system and the national anthem stopped in the middle and started again at the beginning a couple of times. The third or fourth time, they just left it off, but everyone kept singing and finished the national anthem.

The mainside area is on a west-facing slope, and at the bottom of the slope is Lake Bandini. It's really just a series of sewage ponds. In the afternoon, the winds come from the west and the whole place stinks. They also use recycled water on the lawn, so when the sprinklers are running it stinks, too. When I first got there, I didn't know what Lake Bandini was and asked someone about going fishing. They told me all I'd catch was brown trout. I was amazed to hear there was brown trout in the desert – until I figured out what they really meant.

There is also the civilian town of Twentynine Palms, which is small and kind of dumpy. There are quite a few desert dwellers that just live out there. In 1987, I think the population was about 12,000, and half of that was probably related to the base. There were a few tattoo places, a couple of used car places and bars (typical of towns next to a base). The closest Walmart was two towns over in Yucca Valley.

After we checked in, we were sent to the Bravo Company office, which would be our company. Everyone we had talked to so far had been lance corporals or corporals with just slightly more rank than us. When we got to the Bravo Company office, we met Staff Sergeant Mack, who was five-foot-eight, 130 pounds and mean. He was the company first sergeant, which meant he was responsible for all things administrative. He processed our paperwork while we stood at parade rest, patiently waiting.

In boot camp, we had been taught that our first name was our rank, which at that time was "recruit." Now we were privates and PFCs. As a PFC, I had a red chevron sewn on the sleeve of my jacket at the shoulder.

SSgt Mack growled, "Hesterman, what's your first name?"

He could obviously see I was a PFC, so I assumed he meant my real first name. So I said, "Andrew, SSgt."

"Oh, oh! Hey Corporal Smith! Meet Andrew! Lance Corporal Peters! Come over here, meet Andrew! Hey Lance Corporal Jones, this is Andrew!"

Smith, Peters, and Jones barely looked up from their paperwork.

With an icy stare, SSgt Mack said, "No, dumbass! What is your rank? Where did you go to boot camp? Did you even go to boot camp? Did you buy that uniform at the surplus store? When someone asks your first name they want to know your rank, idiot! What the fuck is your rank?!"

I snapped into boot camp mode. "Sir PFC, Sir!"

"You see all these chevrons on my collar? See how there are three on top and one rocker on the bottom?" He was pointing at his rank insignia on his cammie collar. "That makes me a STAFF SERGEANT! I swear you act like you don't know nuthin'! I work for a living – I'm not a damn officer! You will address me as Staff Sergeant Mack or Staff Sergeant. Don't call me Sir or anything else!"

"Yes, Staff Sergeant!"

I felt like a turd. Later I realized he used this routine on all the boot camp fodder that came to his desk each week.

We finally got out of SSgt Mack's office and six of us headed over to the receiving squad bay, which is where they house Marines who haven't yet been assigned to permanent quarters. It was dark now but I swear it was even hotter.

A Lance Corporal was sitting at the small duty desk in the front of the squad bay. He had a small lamp on the desk that provided a circle of white light. The rest of the squad bay was bathed in dim red light.

The Lance Corporal (LCpl) was helpful and very casual with us. He laughed when we told him about SSgt Mack and said that everyone on base knew him. He said, "He just wishes he was still a drill instructor." Then he said, "Don't worry, this is not going to be more boot camp."

He wrote our names down in his logbook (the universal 9x12 hardbound book covered in light green canvas-type cloth). He gave us each a set of linens, two white flat sheets, one pillowcase, and an olive drab wool blanket just like we had in boot camp. We each signed for them in another logbook and then he told us to just go pick a rack that wasn't occupied.

The room was set up just like the squad bay in boot camp, except that the front classroom was a TV lounge with couches facing a TV and VCR mounted on the wall. Three Marines were watching a movie turned down low. The back classroom had two round tables with chairs and a bookshelf full of tattered paperbacks and old magazines. Two Marines sat at the tables writing, using their issued angle flashlights for more light. Ten or twelve other Marines were in the squad bay, either sleeping or preparing for rack out. Everyone was wearing shorts with either a T-shirt or no shirt.

Silvera and I found two adjacent unoccupied racks in the middle of the room. We made our racks up and stowed our gear. Then we headed over to the convenience store.

Marines usually refer to the convenience store as the "seven-day store," as it is the only store open seven days a week on base. I got a fresh can of dip and a soda called Cactus Cooler, which I hadn't seen before. I ended up drinking a lot of that over the next few months. Silvera got a soda and a candy bar and we headed back to the squad bay. We walked in step with each other as we had been taught in boot camp and had a good laugh about it when Silvera pointed it out. I still tend to walk in step with whomever I happen to be walking with. We hit the rack uncertain what the next day would hold for us.

Comm School is short for Marine Corps Communications and Electronics School (MCCES pronounced mick-ses). The school has many courses ranging from electronics technician to wireman. The radioman course was called Field Radio Operators Course (FROC) and it taught the basics of being a field radio operator, using HF, VHF, and UHF radios, along with tactical field phones and the associated gear. There were tech and maintenance courses, courses on running data systems, a wireman course about laying wire (including telephone pole type stuff), and a whole lot more.

The school environment in Twentynine Palms worked pretty well for me. I was making more money than I ever had in my life, about $700 per month, with free housing and food. Of course, I was working more than I ever had in my life, too. This included physical training at 5:30 and then school until 4:30 in the afternoon. Plus guard duty once a week at night. I made a little extra money by ironing uniforms for other guys who were too lazy to do it themselves. I guess I had a knack for it. I could knock out military creases on a "Charlie" dress shirt pretty quickly. Seemed like I was always getting free pizza because someone owed me.

Living in the squad bay with so many other guys was kind of a drag but I'd grown up sharing a room, so the lack of privacy didn't bother me. It kind of sucked at night, trying to go to sleep when there was always someone talking or had their headphones cranked up so loudly that everyone could hear it. At 2200 (10 p.m.), the lights turned to red and it was quiet time, but there were always people up making noise and the red lights weren't all that dim. The upside was that the entire squad bay got up at 0430 so I was never late. I've always had trouble getting going in the morning, but you can't sleep in when there are forty guys getting ready in the same room.

My biggest complaint was probably the lack of storage space. We each had a wall locker and a footlocker and you just can't fit that much stuff in there. I've always had a few toys like bikes, skateboards, surfboards, etc., and I didn't have any place to keep tools. I didn't like being without tools.

The schoolwork itself was pretty easy, mostly rote memorization. We had to memorize a lot of different pieces of gear and they all had goofy alpha-numeric identifiers like MX-185 (a two-pound sledge) or BA-4386 (a type of battery). We had to know which pieces of gear worked with each other along with all the specifications, frequencies, ranges, battery types, expected lifecycles, etc. Once a week we would spend the entire day outside playing with the equipment. That was what I liked. Seeing how fast I could set stuff up and troubleshoot it when it didn't work.

I really enjoyed messing with antennas. We got some antenna theory in class, but I took it upon myself to study more on my own. Wavelengths and wave propagation was magical. When it comes down to it, it doesn't matter how good your radio is if you don't have an appropriate antenna. The two secrets to being a good radioman in the Marine Corps are take care of your gear and be good with antennas. I had it covered.

We also used an antenna that was hooked to a high-frequency (HF) radio that put out four hundred watts with conducting elements from the top of the antenna to the ground. We got tons of warnings about the danger of this setup. The class instructors told us that a Marine from a previous class had been killed by one of these powerful antennas.

We had one week of field-expedient antennas, where we learned how to make antennas out of various random parts that we could scavenge. During practical application, I laid out a massive HF antenna hooked to the gutter of the building and to our measly four-watt HF radio. When I broadcasted, I had an echo of myself after a few seconds. I couldn't understand what was going on! When Sgt Inglewood came to check on my progress, he laughed and explained that I was bouncing the signal off the ionosphere and hearing my own broadcast as it circled the globe.

Before radios, Marine Corps communication was done with flags and signals. They used flags to communicate from the shore to Navy ships or ship to ship. Sometimes they used flags unit to unit on the battlefield. Other times they would use lights to flash codes. Radios became the primary means of military communication after World War I, first in the Navy and Coast Guard, then in the other services.

The official description of a radioman is as follows: "Field radio operators employ radio to send and receive messages. Typical duties include the setup and tuning of radio equipment, including antennas and power sources; establishing contact with distant stations; processing and logging of messages; making changes to frequencies or cryptographic codes; and maintaining equipment at the first echelon."

At the most basic level, a radioman is responsible for establishing and maintaining communications with other units. Duties vary based on the unit. In an infantry platoon, the radioman talks to company headquarters. At the company level, though, the radioman talks to the platoon but also communicates with the higher headquarters at battalion (up and down in the chain of command). Sometimes a radioman needs to communicate with adjacent units such as other platoons or companies in the battalion. Or they may need to talk to supporting units, such as mortars, artillery, or aviation.

The radioman is also responsible for the use and maintenance of the equipment. Obviously, he must know how to make it function, but he also has to know how to maximize its potential because units almost always find themselves in places that challenge radio functions. That's where the bit about antennas comes in. Most good radiomen know how to make homemade antennas with wire that work better than the official antennas. There is also an art to talking on the radio and ways to encrypt messages if you do not have frequency encryption. A great radioman will know the frequencies for everyone from two headquarters higher to the squadrons that are flying in the vicinity to the MedEvac aircraft to the closest artillery units to the units on either side on the battlefield. A great radioman is always cleaning and maintaining his equipment, knows how much time he has left on each battery, and makes sure that he has an extra battery ready to go. Most importantly, he is always able to anticipate his commanding officer's needs.

At a platoon level the radioman basically runs around with the CO, so when he shouts that he wants to talk to someone, the radioman hands him the handset. Higher than battalion, it becomes a vehicle or desk job, based on the mobility of the unit.

In 1987 we mostly used VHF FM radios. We also used some HF and some UHF radios, including vehicle-mounted and man-portable radios. If you understood the three basic radios, you could figure out the other versions. Each of the three had a different encryption device, and of course they used different antennas and batteries, too.

Nowadays, field radio operators are being replaced with data guys. Satellite communications, portable dishes to establish computer networks, cell phones, etc., are all replacing radio. Instead of troubleshooting, you now hook the gear up to a computer to find out what is wrong with it. There are still radiomen, and there are still radios, but they tend to be only at the small unit level. The radios today are smaller and lighter, but they are also more complicated. They are all programmable so instead of carrying a waterproofed book with all your codes and frequencies, you just program it all into your radio. Now there is one radio that replaces the UHF, VHF, and HF versions I used back at that time. You can also monitor multiple frequencies at one time on one radio so you don't have to carry three radios to listen to three networks.

Most of the radios we used back then were Vietnam era stuff: PRC-77, PRC-104, and PRC-113. Just about any Marine older than thirty will know what a PRC-77 (pronounced prick seventy-seven) is. Everything was painted olive green. The PRC-77 (VHF) was about the size of two cereal boxes and weighed fifteen pounds. Each battery was the size of a small brick and weighed a few pounds. PRC 113 (UHF) was about the same size but actually had a digital readout. The PRC 104 (HF) was a little bigger and heavier. There were no chips in them but they were "solid state" technology.

We joked that the connectors were "Marine proof." They were all different so you couldn't screw anything up by hooking the wrong cable to the wrong place. If it fit, it was supposed to go there. (Although one time I did see some knuckleheads break stuff by trying to make it fit – I guess it wasn't really Marine proof.)

Everything was overbuilt, so a cable that had two wires was as big as a civilian cable with six wires. But that helped keep stuff reliable. But there were some crazy things, too, like the battery that off gassed hydrogen. Don't smoke while using that radio! And you had to be careful with the battery tray – sometime the vent would clog and when you unclipped the latches, the tray would fly off from the pressure!

Many times troubleshooting in the Marine Corps involved the "drop test," which simply meant dropping a piece of gear from a foot or two off the ground. I guess sometimes the contacts inside corroded and the jolt would jiggle them just enough to make contact again. But most of the gear was so rugged, you could literally drive a Hummvee over it and it wouldn't get hurt. I wouldn't try that with any of the new radios today.

Anything fabric was olive drab heavy canvas, which is a little bit heavier than denim. Each radio came with an accessory bag that was triangle shaped, eighteen inches long and four inches wide on the wider end. The small antennas folded up and fit in the bag along with the handset. The big antennas like the RC-292 and AS 2259 came in a big canvas wrap about 3.5 feet long and roundish, maybe sixteen inches in diameter. All the pole sections, cable, different fittings, stakes, etc., fit in this canvas wrap, which laid out flat with little straps to hold the different parts in place. You folded in the two ends, rolled it up, and secured with the straps that were sewn on the outside.

I liked living in the desert. The convenience store on base kept the chewing tobacco in the coolers, and after dismissal my buddy and I would race to the store to get a fresh can. They had the freshest Copenhagen

I've ever seen. Nothing like a fresh dip and a cold beer after a hot, sweaty day in the desert. Hanging out on the picnic table in the warm evenings, having an icy cold beer with a couple of buds was a really good way to end the day.

We had a lot of fun on weekends. A good friend had a VW Westfalia bus and took us on several camping trips out to Havasu, which was always a blast. We spent a few weekends in LA, too, bodyboarding and bikini watching at the beach. Joshua Tree National Park was fifteen minutes away, and at least once a week we'd go bouldering or hiking. My buddy Cunningham and I got to be pretty good climbers.

I had my Yamaha Vision 550 and I loved riding the curvy outback roads of the desert. I wasn't allowed to bring it on base because I hadn't taken the required safety course, so I'd left the bike in a convenient parking lot by the front gate and walked the mile to the barracks. More than a few nights, we partied it up at a large club in Riverside. We even got kicked out one time. We didn't start the fight but we definitely finished it.

Young Marines are already convinced that they are bulletproof. And they are known to be somewhat wild. But I think there is something about the desert that amplifies this and makes Marines more cocky – and more reckless. During my first three months in Twentynine Palms I know of four Marines who died.

The first guy managed to get killed before classes had even started. He was another young Marine from Los Angeles. He had driven his dune buggy to the base, and on weekends he would go driving the dunes out in the desert. One Monday morning he didn't show up for formation. Later that week, I heard that he and a friend had rolled the dune buggy out in the desert and were killed. Shortly after that his bashed-up dune buggy appeared in the impound lot by the front gate. It had a single roll bar but the windshield was crushed flat.

When my class finally formed we had forty-two Marines. Seven disappeared at some point during the three-month course. A few of them were simply guys who failed and were too embarrassed to be seen by former platoon mates – you'd see them remove their stuff and say goodbye to friends, and maybe later you'd see them around the base or you'd run into someone who knew them and knew where they had gone. But three Marines from my class of forty-two Marines died.

I knew PFC Raynes fairly well. He was a bit older than most of us and had done a stint in the Army. I never did get the story from him why he got out of the Army and joined the Marines. He was a drinker. He spent most of his evenings and weekends at the enlisted club on base. Raynes was usually on time, did what he was supposed to do, and was passing the course. He was a likable fellow so there really weren't any problems. That is until he didn't show up for Monday morning formation one week. No one had any idea where he was. We went about our business as usual and then later that evening a corporal from the Provost Marshals' Office came into our squad bay with a letter and a bolt cutter. The letter had orders for him to collect Raynes' gear. He cut the locks and we helped him pack it all into a couple of seabags labeled "Raynes: personal effects."

The corporal told us what he knew. Apparently, Raynes had been out at the enlisted club. Later, when he was stumbling back to the squad bay, he fell into one of the many ditches around the base. He passed out and rolled onto a rattlesnake, which were common at Twentynine Palms. Because he was drunk and unconscious, the venom of the snake killed him.

I didn't know PFC Lindsey well. But one day he didn't show up for formation, and again that evening, the PMO showed up to collect his personal effects. Lindsey had been driving drunk in his Camaro and misjudged a particularly bad turn on the long road from town to the base. He was killed when he hit a telephone pole. Everyone called that turn "Deadman's Curve" because similar accidents had happened there in the past. (The front entrance to the base and the road leading to it were rebuilt in the early '90s and Deadman's Curve no longer exists.)

The last death was a lot closer to home. PFC Scott Cunningham was a good friend of mine. He was the guy you pictured when someone says "all-American guy." He looked like he spent a fair amount of time in the gym, always had an infectious, bright smile, and was positive about everything. He knew a lot but never came off as conceited. He was a legacy Marine in that his father and grandfather were both Marines, and you could tell he was really proud of it.

Typically we spent Monday through Thursday in the classroom learning principles of radio communication and specific radios, antennas, and other gear. Friday was usually Practical Application or PracApp and would be spent out in the large, empty lot behind the school building, where we practiced setting up and using the gear. At the end of each month, we would hike out to the field for four or five days and have a larger exercise using the gear we had learned about that month. Often we worked in two-man teams, and when we did I would pair up with PFC Cunningham.

One of the antennas we used was thirty feet tall and made up of three-foot sections. The top section looked a bit like a giant asterisk with twenty- to sixty-inch elements sticking out in different directions. The antenna had two sets of three guy ropes at different heights to keep it stable. If the guy ropes didn't have the correct tension on them, the antenna would start to curve (not a good thing). By the book, two Marines should be able to set the antenna up in fifteen minutes. We got tested to that standard and actually had fun, racing to see what teams could set it up the fastest. There was some math to it, as the conductive elements at the top were made of twenty-inch sections that screwed together and then screwed into the antenna base. This in turn sat on top of thirty-foot poles and formed the nucleus of the asterisk. The number of elements you used was determined by the frequency you were going to be transmitting and receiving.

To set up the antenna, one team member figured out which elements to use and assembled the asterisk while the other team member fit together the main pole, attached the guy ropes, estimated the correct lengths, and staked off two of the three from each set of guy ropes. The first team member would then pick up the completed asterisk and fasten it to the top of the pole. As one team member pulled backward on the unstaked guy ropes, the other would push up on the top end of the main pole and work his way down as the antenna leaned into an upright position. Then all that remained to do was to stake off the final two guy ropes and hook up the radio.

There were plenty of times we dropped antennas. Sometimes a stake would come out of the sand, or the ropes weren't properly tied off to the stake. One time the entire asterisk at the top wasn't fastened correctly and came tumbling down.

A falling antenna was dangerous. The elements of the asterisk were pointy and slightly larger than a pencil diameter. They were also expensive and would break when they smacked the hard sand, so we learned ways to catch a falling antenna. If you tried to catch the main pole in the middle, it would flex and the asterisk would still smack the ground. Obviously, you couldn't catch the asterisk. So the ideal place to catch the antenna was about six feet down the mast. But as you caught it you had to turn your face away in case an element snapped or flicked sand and rocks.

PFC Cunningham and I were pros at putting up these antennas. One day we had a challenge to test our speed against the other teams in the field – so the race was on! I pushed the antenna up while Cunningham pulled the guy ropes. Cunningham had a technique for staking the ropes while holding them. I was on my knees, bent over the radio, hooking it up and tuning it while he finished staking off the ropes behind me. Suddenly I heard a yell and looked up to see Cunningham running past me. One of the stakes had popped and the antenna was falling toward me. Cunningham caught it just a few feet below the top. But he was too close, and as the mast flexed, one of the elements pierced him in the back of the knee. Holy crap! Talk about pain! Imagine having someone jam a pencil into the back of your knee.

It wasn't a life-threatening injury, but an off-road ambulance came to get Cunningham because he wasn't able to hike back with us. He ended up needing surgery to repair some damaged ligaments in his knee and was dropped from our class. I still saw him occasionally after that. He was on crutches for what seemed like an eternity.

But here's the thing: A few months later Cunningham committed suicide. I don't know all the things he had going on in his life, but I think having knee trouble and being sidelined from the Marine Corps made him feel like a failure.

To this day I still feel a bit culpable in his death. We could have been safer or done something different when setting up that antenna. But more importantly, I lost touch with him after he left our class. I should have been there for him when he was having trouble.

On the last day we had a cheesy little graduation ceremony in our classroom. We were all privates and PFCs so we didn't know any of the school staff besides our three instructors. So when a captain came in the classroom, we were all surprised – we had no idea who he was. Our senior instructor, Sergeant Brown, called the room to attention. Then the captain called me up front. I was baffled. In proper military fashion, I executed facing movements and marched up to face him, stopping two paces away.

The captain said, "Congratulations, PFC Hesterman, nice job!'

"Thank you, Sir!"

"You did outstanding in this course."

"Thank you, Sir!"

"What was your score?"

"Uhhh…" I had no idea, honestly. So I made something up. "Uhh, 95, Sir?" That sounded like a high score to me.

"Ninety-five? Must have been 95 and some change."

"Uh, yes, Sir!"

He was chuckling. "Okay, 95. Congratulations. Keep up the hard work!"

He handed me a plaque with my name that said "honor graduate." He shook my hand and I returned to my desk.

Sergeant Brown called, "Seats!" and we all sat down. Sgt Brown then read each class member's name and score and they each walked up to get a certificate and handshake from the captain. There were plenty of scores over 95, so I had obviously underestimated. I had scored the highest physical fitness score in my boot camp company, and now I was an honor graduate from Comm School (for this week's class). I was thinking the whole Marine Corps thing wasn't so hard.

Chapter 4

The Reserves

Back in the '80s, billboards and TV ads for the reserves touted "one weekend a month and two weeks in the summer." And that was pretty much true. However, it didn't include the days spent studying, preparing for drill, and maintaining uniforms. Fortunately, the physical training required was something I was doing anyway – running three or four days a week and lifting weights the other days.

I was always excited to go to drill. I was assigned to 23rd Marines, a regimental headquarters, in Alameda California. I usually spent the Thursday evening prior getting ready and Sunday night cleaning up. I'd get a fresh haircut, iron two sets of cammies, and have two sets of boots polished and ready. If we were going to the field, I'd have my field gear all prepared and in my pack. It made for a long weekend and long weeks because I had to take off early from work on Fridays to make it to Alameda in time for the 1800 formation.

We got to do a lot of training that was not typical of regimental headquarters companies. We did a lot of MILES gear training, which is like advanced laser tag. You put an adapter on your M-16 that shot an invisible laser beam every time you fired a blank. Everyone wore a sensor ring on their helmet, plus a sensor vest over their gear, and when you were hit the sensor vest emitted an ear-splitting squeal so there was no question you were "dead." Sometimes MILES training emphasized small unit tactics and sometimes it was more like capture the flag. Either way, I enjoyed it immensely, from putting camo paint on my face and sticking grass and branches in my helmet to low-crawling through the brush and setting up ambush zones. Other training we did included small boat raids on Coast Guard Island in the Bay to a weekend of rappelling.

We also spent plenty of time practicing setting up command posts. We were responsible for setting up two types of command posts: a Main CP and a Jump CP. Each had eight to twelve radios and a couple of tables and map boards. The Main CP consisted of a large 20 x 30 canvas tent, two high-back Humvees, and the antenna Humvee with a trailer. In the trailer were twelve radios with remote receivers, cryptological gear, a whole mess of antennas, and a spool of giant cable that was almost as big around as my wrist. The jump CP was the mobile CP and could be set up or torn down much faster. It consisted of three Humvees with the gear already mounted in them.

Sometimes we set up CPs in the parking lot or the large dirt field behind the unit, and sometimes we set up at one of the bases that were a few hours drive' away. Oftentimes, we would set up one of the CPs, make a quick call on each radio to ensure they were set up right, then tear it down, drive five minutes, and do it again. We got pretty proficient.

So these were long, intense weekends, and by the time I got home on Sunday night I was pretty tired. I was back living with my parents, back in my old bunk bed. At twenty, that felt pretty lame, but I was broke, and like many of my peers in my Marine unit, I was trying to continue my education.

I had started back at Foothill Junior College and soon had a year's worth of college credits. Something had clicked for me at school. I was taking things a lot more seriously and rarely missed a class or failed to turn in a paper. I started getting decent grades. I still floundered a bit when it came to deciding what course of study to follow – I changed my major from English to journalism to business administration all within a year. Fortunately, community college is a forgiving and inexpensive place to explore different majors.

That is not to say I was fitting in. In fact, one time my psychology professor singled me out during one of his rants. He was talking about conformity and survival in the pack when he pointed at me and said, "You are a black pigeon in amongst a bunch of white ones. You are not going to survive." I wasn't sure how to take that.

The counseling office at school helped me find some job openings and I got a part-time job at Information Express, a small company in Palo Alto delivering documents to local tech companies like Hewlett Packard, Syntex, and Adobe Systems. I enjoyed running stuff around on my motorcycle.

All in all, I was staying pretty busy, which minimized my tendency to find trouble. I had made a few new friends at school who had similar interests and we occasionally went surfing or worked on cars together. A typical Saturday night was a couple of twelve-packs and a new set of shocks or brakes on someone's car.

Meanwhile, I dated a couple of girls from Foothill but nothing serious. I ran into a girl from my high school class and we went on several dates. In high school I had thought she was incredible and out of my league, and I was surprised that she wanted to go out with me now. But that didn't really work out, either.

Summer of 1988 was approaching fast. The last year had gone well for me at 23rd Marines. I had established myself in the communications platoon, the largest of four platoons in the unit. I was now one of the go-to guys when it came to comm gear. I was meritoriously promoted to lance corporal (LCpl), which spoke well of the leadership's confidence in my abilities.

Summer meant we had our two-week Annual Training Duty (ATD). This would be my first duty and I was excited. I'd joined the Marine Corps to see the world, but after a year the farthest I'd gotten was Southern California. So when I learned that my first ATD would be to Oregon, I felt a bit let down. I knew that Astoria and the Columbia River would be beautiful, but it wasn't quite what I had been hoping for.

We had nice buses for the trip instead of the standard white school buses, so that was a plus. It was a long drive and the bus got stinky pretty quickly. It never failed – you'd get all cleaned up, with a fresh haircut, fresh-pressed cammies and spit-shined boots, then immediately after roll call, you'd get called to the work party to load all the sea bags and gear onto the bus. We were sweaty within minutes, and then piled into a bus packed to capacity.

We arrived at the base and set up in an old wooden squad bay. It was the typical West Coast terrain – rolling hills dotted with green trees that in some places were clumped together thick enough to cover an entire hill. The Oregon grass was still green, though, which is different from California, where the grass turns to gold in early June. The main area of the base was fairly small, about five blocks square. The buildings were all nondescript, low, wood structures with peeling white paint and gray asphalt shingles.

We got to meet a lot of Marines from the battalions (Bns) that belong to 23rd Marines. I specifically remember Charlie Company, 1st Bn, based out of Corpus Christi, Texas. Because they were 70 percent Hispanic, they referred to themselves as Carlos Company. By the end of the first week, everyone called them that.

During the day, we would go set up the CPs and the regimental staff would exercise the battalions, giving directions for a big wargame exercise. Based on our role, we had no idea what was going on, but we didn't need to, either. We just kept the officers in touch with whoever they needed to talk to, then tore down and set up the CPs as needed. Usually around 6 p.m., they'd call "Op Pause" and we'd clean up, put fresh batteries in the gear, make sure everything was secure, and then head to the chow hall. The next morning, we'd set up and it would be "game on" again.

There were several nights that we operated all through the night. We took shifts so everyone could get a little rest. I never had trouble sleeping in strange places. I loved sleeping on top of a Humvee's canvas cover – it's kind of like a hammock and it keeps down on the creepy crawlies that get into your gear. There was duty, too, but I didn't get assigned any that first week.

On Friday they announced that we would have liberty Saturday and Sunday and could go into Astoria or wherever we wanted. I had read a lot about windsurfing on the Columbia River and was excited. The local evening paper came out with the headline: "The Marines are invading, lock up your women and daughters!" We all got a pretty good chuckle out of that. But then the communications chief called me over to his area. Since I hadn't had any duty, Sgt Brands had assigned me guard duty over the weekend. So I'd be stuck on base while everyone else was out having fun. What a shit deal!

On Friday night everyone but four of us got in buses and taxis and headed into town. The other unlucky fellows and I reported to the MPs for the description of our duties. We were going to work eight hours on, eight hours off and would be watching several posts. I was assigned to the armory and motor pool and had that watch from midnight to 0800.

Obviously, the armory was pretty well secured, since that is where all the weapons and ammo were stored. But when I walked over to the motor pool I found that the front gate didn't lock. I walked around all the vehicles and checked them out. There were lots of Marine vehicles and there were some National Guard vehicles, too. Most tactical vehicles don't require a key – there is just a big paddle switch you flip to the "on" position, wait until the glow plug light goes out, then flip the paddle to start. A cable lock kit is often issued to go around the seat and the steering wheel so a vehicle can't be driven, but they were a pain and no one used them. I looked at the controls of a Humvee and knew it would be easy to drive.

I walked back over to the armory to make sure nothing was amiss. Of course, I had no idea what I would have done if I'd found someone. I had an M-16 but no ammunition. I guess I could scream and yell and butt-stroke them with the M-16 if I managed to get close enough. I had done pretty well in pugil stick training, which was supposed to represent bayoneting and butt-stroking an opponent.

The night was quiet and all I could think about was how everyone else was in town having fun. At 0800 my relief showed up as planned and we swapped. I went back to the guard shack, locked in my rifle, and then ran over to catch breakfast before they closed. After breakfast I headed back to the squad bay. There were a few guys there who hadn't spent the night in town but were fixing to go back out. It sounded like a nice resort-type town with shopping and some good bars.

I lay down in my rack but couldn't sleep. So I got up and started walking around the base. I had six hours before going back on duty. What fun could I find? Hmmm.

I walked back down to the motor pool. The guard was not there, which made sense – I expected he would spend most of his time over at the armory. So I walked in. I thought that if someone showed up I could always say I'd left my flashlight and was retracing my steps, trying to find it.

I ended up back at the Humvees. Somehow it just seemed less bad to take a National Guard Humvee instead of one of ours. I figured if I could just get it out the gate, I'd be home free. As long as I didn't do anything stupid, no one would stop to question me.

I got in and looked at the controls. Yep, total piece of cake. I looked one more time to see if anyone was around, then I cranked it up. The big diesel roared to life. I checked to see that it was topped off on fuel, put it in gear, and headed out the gate.

Humvees are a little tricky to drive because of how wide they are, plus they have horrible visibility. At first I kept hanging a wheel up the curb but I figured it out pretty quickly. I made a few uneventful laps around the quiet streets of the main base area and then decided to be more adventurous. Humvees were supposed to be able to go anywhere and do anything, so why not find some trails? Or…the beach!

The beaches in this part of Oregon have sand that is hard-packed and flat – not like the steeper beaches of Southern California – so I headed out into the wet sand. I was already getting more confident controlling the vehicle. I tried a couple 360s, gassing it pretty hard to get a nice rooster tail. That was fun. I drove down to where the water was four or five inches deep and that was pretty fun, too.

I noticed some small sand dunes up closer to the treeline and wondered if I could jump the thing. I found one dune that had just the right shape with plenty of room on either side. So I circled back around and took progressively faster and faster runs. I thought I was getting it off the ground but it was hard to tell. I was definitely getting that nice weightless feeling. I decided to try a slightly bigger dune a little farther down the beach. I circled back again and then made a high speed run at it.

I swear I was mid-jump when I saw the MP car. It was parked where one of the dirt roads from the base ended at the sand. I think they were eating McDonald's and enjoying the ocean view when all of a sudden I came flying over the dunes in a government Humvee. Although not entirely accurate, the picture in my mind is of the Humvee completely airborne with sand and water streaming off the bottom, and me singing the theme from *Dukes of Hazzard* at the top of my lungs. Well, their burgers, drinks, and fries must have gone flying because the lights and siren came on and they were behind me in a flash.

I braked to a stop and waited for them. Where was I gonna go? If I tried to get away, I knew they could close the base and find me pretty easily. So I figured I'd better just cooperate.

They approached with guns drawn, one on each side of the Humvee just like in the movies. I put my hands out the zip down window, then got out and lay on the ground. They cuffed me and stuffed me into the back of the cruiser.

They really didn't know what to do with me. I don't think they had ever arrested anyone before. They stuttered and stammered, asking me questions. I just told them the truth and that calmed them down a little. I guess they realized they were dealing with an adrenaline junkie and not a terrorist.

They took me back to the brig. Only they didn't have a real brig, so they handcuffed me to the footboard of a cot in the corner of their office. I gave them my whole chain of command but everyone was out in town for the weekend (this was before cell phones, and pagers weren't widely used). So they resigned themselves to holding me until Monday morning.

I mostly just sat on the cot and watched the TV hanging from the wall in the corner. The office wasn't very big, and the MPs whispered their conversations like I was some kind of spy trying to figure out their operations. Occasionally I had to ask to be uncuffed to go use the head. They were always cordial and I always used their proper rank and addressed them correctly. One guy would go into the head and check it, then the other one would uncuff me and wait outside the door for me. I'm not sure what they were checking for in the head. They were the only ones there and they would have seen anyone going into or out of the head, but I guess they had a procedure to follow (although I think they were making it up based on stuff they had seen on TV). They did bring me a styrofoam tray of chow from the chow hall for dinner and breakfast. They even uncuffed me to let me eat. I considered asking them to let me sit there without the cuffs, but I was too nervous and ashamed.

I really didn't know what was going to happen to me but I envisioned the worst. I couldn't even fathom trying to explain to my parents that I had gotten kicked out of the Marine Corps for stealing a Humvee. I imagined that I would be detained on base after my unit returned home. I was feeling pretty low.

First Sgt Bricca came storming in on Sunday afternoon. I should have known he would be the first one back to make sure the Marines had returned on time and that there weren't any problems.

First Sgt Bricca was a tall, thin man and wore glasses that were just a bit too big for his face. He wore his hair a little longer but it was still well within regulations. Most of the time he was just on the business side of jovial – the kind of Marine leader who exercises "leadership by walking around," meaning he would get out of the office to see what everyone was up to. Starting back at Alameda, there were six or seven of us that were considered First Sgt Bricca's "boys." When he needed something done he tasked one of us, but he always worked to add perks like getting off early or getting cut some slack somewhere. We did everything he asked and he looked out for us.

A Marine first sergeant outranks a National Guard sergeant by a significant amount. First Sgt Bricca immediately started telling the MPs how Marines have non-judicial punishment (NJP), and he basically bullied them into turning me over to him so he could "take care" of the situation. He told them about how the CO was a major so the punishments could be pretty significant. The CO could take half of my pay for two months, demote me to private first class, put me in the brig for up to thirty days, and put me on restriction for up to sixty days and give me up to forty-five days extra duties, or any combination of the above. At first, I had been happy to see First Sgt Bricca, but now I wasn't so sure!

The MPs uncuffed me and handed me over to First Sgt Bricca, who then turned to escort me out of the building. When I was the appropriate six paces away, I uttered a low but proper, "Good afternoon, First Sergeant."

"Hesty! What in the sam hell! I can't freaking believe you."

"Sir."

"What the hell were you thinking? Wait – no, I know exactly. You weren't thinking, you moron!"

"Sir."

"I'm gonna set up NJP tomorrow morning and Major Kent is going to hang you!"

"Sir."

The MPs were ooh-ing and ahh-ing in the background. They were pretty sure I was done and I was starting to believe it, too.

We got in First Sgt Bricca's white four-door government sedan. I sat down in the back, buckled up, and waited for the barrage to begin again. First Sgt Bricca walked around to the driver's door and then slid in with a huge sigh.

"Thank God I got back first!"

"Sir?"

"Do you know the position you put me in? I am really disappointed in you, Andy."

I was surprised to hear him use my first name instead of my nickname.

"We are never going to mention this again. We all make mistakes. But if you make another one like this, you will go directly to Regimental COs NJP. Learn from this, get back to who you normally are, and this will never bother you. But I own you now."

And that was it. I owe First Sgt Bricca a lot. And for more than just this incident. He was my first significant command role model and mentor.

The Marine Corps hands out ribbons and awards much less often than the other services. But they have a good conduct ribbon (nicknamed "good cookie"), which you get after a number of years if you managed to get by without getting into trouble. First Sgt never entered anything into my record book about the Humvee incident, but when my time came up to be awarded the good conduct ribbon, I was passed over. I think it was his doing and I consider it fair in all regards.

This actually worked in my favor many years later. When you are an officer who has done time as an enlisted man, the other enlisted men tend to gravitate to you because they assume that you will understand their position better than someone who became an officer by going to college. When I became an officer, the enlisted Marines liked to work for me and be in my department or shop. It was usual for them to scrutinize all my ribbons, and several times one of them mentioned, "Sir, I see you don't have a good cookie?" But it was always more of a statement than a question: They were telling me that they understood I had been into trouble somewhere along the line and that I wasn't as straight-laced as I attempted to appear. And most of the time, it implied an extra degree of respect.

Chapter 5

Corporal

I'm not sure how 1st Sgt Bricca felt about it, but he had to approve my request to attend military driving school. He had treated me the same since the Humvee incident in Oregon, though, so I thought all was good.

So in March, I took a week off from school to earn my license to drive the Humvee, CUC V (¾ ton Chevy truck) and the famous 2½ ton M-35, affectionately known as the "Deuce and a Half." The first two days were split between the classroom and the shop, reviewing servicing and maintenance. The next three days were spent driving the vehicles. We did some urban driving in Oakland and joked that we needed to mount the 50-cal machine guns for some of the neighborhoods. Driving on Interstate 880 was interesting, too. The vehicles were geared for field use, and winding them out to 55 mph was loud and uncomfortable. And they were almost as wide as the lanes, so it was tough to keep them between the lines.

My favorite was the field driving. The slopes that the Humvee can tackle are amazing. We got to play with the fording kit and drive the Deuce and a Half and the Humvees through four feet of water. That was a lot of fun, but later it took us several hours to get all the mud out of the floor pans.

On Friday we had a written test, a maintenance demo test, then a driving test. None of it was very hard. I loved playing with vehicles and driving vehicles so I passed easily. I couldn't believe I was getting paid for this stuff!

Now that I was a licensed Humvee driver, I got to drive a Humvee every time we went to the field. I was also responsible for the vehicle while we were there. That meant I could stash personal stuff in my Humvee, like snacks and a lawn chair. Plus at night I always got my favorite sleeping spot on the hammock-like canvas top of the Humvee.

When you are running the vehicle radios, you need to idle the vehicle for fifteen minutes every few hours to charge the battery. So when I got up at zero dark thirty, I'd put my aluminum field cup on the engine block while it idled. Presto, fifteen minutes later I had hot water to make coffee. I couldn't do that when I bivouacked with everyone else in the tent rows!

But there were disadvantages to being a driver, too. When we came back from the field, everyone cleaned weapons together. But then the drivers had to go back to the motor pool to clean and service the vehicles while everyone else turned in their gear and got released. That was kind of a bummer. The other drawback was you didn't get to sleep on long drives. When we met at 1800 on Friday afternoon and then loaded up for the three-hour drive to Fort Hunter-Liggett or Camp Roberts, everyone riding the bus got to sleep for a bit. Drivers obviously had to stay awake. All in all, though, I was happy to be a driver and thought it was a good deal.

Our Annual Training Duty for June 1989 was at Camp Pendleton. I still hadn't been anywhere besides the West Coast and was frustrated that we were going back to a place I'd already visited. Still, I was excited because it sounded like we had a lot of cool training ahead of us.

It was a long drive from Alameda to Camp Pendleton. At first it was fun driving in a convoy of ten military vehicles down 1-5, but after that the novelty wore off and it got boring and painful. The seats in a Humvee are plate aluminum with maybe an inch of crappy foam on top. There is no A/C and the heat from the engine really comes through the front panel after an hour of driving. With the high ratio power steering, it takes work to keep the vehicle in the lane, and you also have to pay a lot of attention to maintain your proper interval in the convoy. The tires and engine make a lot of noise at 55 mph so you can't really have a conversation with your assistant driver. We stopped every two hours to take a break. I bet I drank three liters of Mountain Dew on the trip. I was pretty frazzled nine hours later when we arrived in Camp Pendleton.

We stayed in Camp Talega, in the classic rows of Quonset huts where they filmed *Heartbreak Ridge* a few years earlier. The views from Camp Talega are amazing. To the northwest you look down the canyon of Cristianitos Creek all the way to the ocean. And on the other three sides you have the golden rolling hills of Camp Pendleton dotted with dark green oak trees.

We had a great week doing infantry-style training. We shot M-60s and M2 50-caliber machine guns at the machine gun range. We spent one afternoon doing hand grenade training. We did two days of patrolling and then a night of patrolling, too. We did a few humps and even got to visit Mount Mother again.

It wasn't all fun and games, though. We also had to visit the gas chamber, which sucked. There had been reports of the Soviets using gas in Afghanistan, so we did a fair amount of NBC training (Nuclear, Biological, Chemical). The gas chamber was an annual training event, with a refresher every year.

The gas chamber is a cinderblock building that can fit thirty Marines standing shoulder to shoulder in a circle. In the center is a small propane stove, which they fill with tear gas pellets. The procedures for the gas chamber have evolved over the years, but back then you would file into the building with your mask already on (donned and cleared) so the gas wouldn't bother you too much. But then after a minute or so it would start to burn and itch on any exposed skin. The gas got so thick you could hardly see the Marine directly across from you.

The instructors would circle around and make sure everyone was doing okay and had their masks secured correctly. You can tell pretty quickly if someone is having trouble because they either start hopping and dancing or bolt for the door. After everyone got checked, the instructors would have us pull out a canteen and drink a little bit through the drinking tube. Then we'd do some jumping jacks to get our heart rate up.

The next part was the crappy part. After we were all panting and breathing hard, the instructors would have us take a deep breath, remove our masks, and hold them above our heads. As soon as everyone was holding their mask up, they'd holler, "Don and clear!" That meant you put your mask on and clear it. Sometimes you could hold your breath that long and sometimes you couldn't. It was a lot more painful if you couldn't. If you had managed to hold your breath, you simply put your mask back on, put two fingers over the exhaust vent on the front of the mask, and exhaled forcibly. Your exhale flushed the contaminated air and gas out of your mask. Then you covered the inlet valve with your palm and tried to breathe in. The mask would collapse against your face if you had a good seal. Then you could inhale and open your eyes. You would still have some tear gas in your mask and your nose would immediately start running and your eyes would start stinging. But if you could stay calm it wasn't too bad. The other trick was to close your eyes but not crinkle them closed – seemed like you got more in your eyes the harder you tried to shut them.

Invariably there would be someone who couldn't get his mask to seal correctly, even though we had all practiced it fifty times before going into the chamber. Usually they started doing the funky chicken or just bolted for the door, which was always blocked by a large instructor. The rest of us would stand as still and calm as we could, sneezing in our masks with our eyes burning while the instructors sorted out whoever was having a problem.

Once everyone was sorted out, we would finally be able to file out into the nice cool, clean air and take off our masks. It was kind of gross but funny, too, as some guys would have snot hanging halfway to their knees. The temptation was always to rub your eyes and face but that only made it worse. So most everyone would just stand there, eyes tearing, neck and face burning, snot hanging, hands out to their sides, waiting for the pain to subside. It usually did after about twenty minutes.

On Friday we went to the pool for swim qualifications. We had the pool for the whole day so we started with the easiest qualification level and just kept going. As long as there was someone passing the level, we got to continue. It was all done in cammies, which was deceiving. They don't really drag you down, but it feels like it. Just like in the gas chamber, the secret to the pool (or water in general) is to stay calm. By the time we got to the top level, Water Survival Qualified (WSQ), we still had about twenty Marines passing. The hardest part was a mile swim in cammies and boots straight into treading water for thirty minutes. I was very happy to make WSQ but I was worn out.

That evening when we got back to the camp area, 1st Sgt Bricca called a formation in the parking lot. A rumor had spread that General Boomer was coming to talk to us. General Boomer was pretty well known by the Marines. He was a major general (two stars) and the commanding general of all Marine Reserves. We knew he was a Vietnam veteran and had won the Silver Star there. (The following year he became more famous by leading the Marines in Desert Shield and Desert Storm.)

We all stood in our platoons and helped each other straighten up our uniforms the best we could. Most everyone tried to quickly polish the toes of their boots by rubbing them on the calf of their other leg, then switching to polish the other shoe. It's one of those instinctive habits that Marines do without even thinking.

Staff Sergeant Rincon came up behind our platoon and hollered for LCpl Carr and LCpl Hesterman to come to the rear of the formation. Oh crap! What had I done wrong? I snapped my heels together, took a step back, then turned and jogged between the rows of the Marines to the end of the platoon to meet SSgt Rincon, just as LCpl Carr did the same.

The formation had four platoons of about thirty to forty Marines each. SSgt Rincon took us behind 2nd Platoon and had LCpl Carr stand on the right and me on the left. He asked me if I knew what to do.

"Uh, Staff Sergeant?" I didn't know what he was talking about.

"Since you are in the back, you call the facing movements, the cadence, and the salute."

I'd seen it done plenty of times before. It was finally dawning on me: LCpl Carr and I were getting meritoriously promoted to corporal and by General Boomer.

"Staff Sergeant, we are going up to see General Boomer?"

"Yes, dumbass! How else is he going to promote you?"

"Yes, Staff Sergeant!"

I was so nervous. I made sure my belt was on straight and lined up with the seam on my trousers, double-checked to make sure all my pocket flaps were buttoned down correctly, polished my boot toes on my calves again, and made sure my cover was on just right. I looked over at Carr. I had known him maybe a year. I don't remember him being particularly motivated, but he was smart and he must have done pretty well to have been selected for meritorious promotion. Carr's bright white smile was a sure sign that he was excited and nervous, too.

The CO is usually authorized to meritoriously promote a small percentage from each unit every year. In the Marine Corps, corporal is considered a non-commissioned officer (NCO) and that is a big deal. There is a lot more responsibility and more expected of you. Also, the competitive nature of the rank makes it more prestigious. PFC and LCpl are kind of "give me" ranks – basically it means you've done the six months or eighteen months. But if you are a corporal, you obviously have some trust from your command.

First Sgt Bricca called the company to attention and we snapped into position: shoulders back, chest out, chin tucked, heels together, and feet at a forty-five-degree angle, hands in a half fist with thumbs along the trouser seams. First Sgt Bricca was facing us, standing about twenty paces in front of the gap between the 2nd and 3rd Platoons. Each platoon reported all present or accounted for, then 1st Sgt Bricca turned the company over to the CO, Major Kent. As 1st Sgt Bricca walked to his position, he shot a grin over at Carr and me.

As soon as the movement ceased, Major Kent did an about-face so he was facing away from us. General Boomer walked up and stood about three paces in front of Major Kent. After exchanging salutes, Major Kent walked around General Boomer and stood on his left facing the platoons.

"Personnel to be promoted, front and center!"

I used a deep, low voice to call the facing movement and forward march. In unison Carr and I turned to the right, marched to the end of the first platoon, then executed a ninety-degree left turn. As Carr stepped out of the turn, I caught a glimpse of something white at the top of his boot. His trouser bands had crept up a little from the top of his boots and I could see that he was wearing white socks. I couldn't believe it. We were getting meritoriously promoted and by a Marine hero general, and Carr was wearing white socks! How hard would it be to wear proper uniform socks? I was embarrassed.

I have heard Marines complain about uniform socks and how white ones are more comfortable, but I always thought that was bullshit. First of all, back then, white socks were cotton and cotton is the worst fabric to have on your feet when you are hiking or walking a lot. Secondly, if you really needed cotton socks, you could buy green or black cotton socks – they had them at the exchange for $1.50 a pair! But to me, white socks just ruined the look of the uniform.

In high school I had done everything I could to look different – from goofy hats to earrings to artfully torn and patched clothing. But in the Marines I took my appearance and uniform very seriously and made a real effort to look "squared away." I even did things that were technically illegal, like using hem tape to iron down my pocket flaps, or cutting off buttons and sewing on velcro instead so I wouldn't get the circular rings on the flaps. I used fishing line in my creases – it melts when you iron it and makes a nice, sharp, permanent crease. I even cut a piece of plastic from an old binder cover and put that inside my hat so it would have that squared-away flat look on top.

We marched up to General Boomer and Major Kent, stopped, and saluted them. I had expected a general to be a bit pudgy, but Boomer was tall, thin, and almost youthful in appearance – he looked like he could still score a perfect 300 on the PFT.

Our promotion warrants were read aloud. General Boomer and Major Kent shook our hands and gave us a little advice about being non-commissioned officers (NCOs) and the responsibilities that come with it. We saluted and marched back behind the rest of the formation. General Boomer gave the order to fall out and form a circle around him.

As we all stepped out of formation and moved into a semicircle around the general, 1st Sgt Bricca came up behind me and whispered that I was out of uniform. What? Me? Then I understood he meant I didn't have corporal chevrons on my collar. He held out his hand and gave me a set of corporal chevrons to wear. That was a really cool way of congratulating me and a nice touch. I filed that one away in my mind for use later if I was ever in a position to give someone their first set of rank insignia.

After General Boomer talked to us for a little while, he and Major Kent left and 1st Sgt Bricca took over. Since it was Friday and we were about to be turned loose for the weekend, he gave us the mandatory safety brief about no drinking and driving, being careful out in town or at the beach, and the rest of the usual stuff, including a bit about safe sex. He also told us that an enlisted club had been set up in one of the Quonset huts, complete with pool tables, ping-pong tables, foosball, and loud music. Then he cut us all loose.

As we started back to the huts, SSgt Rincon hollered for me and Carr to come see him. He told us that since we were NCOs now, we had to move out of the non-rate Quonset hut (privates, PFCs, and LCpls) and move into the NCO hut.

I walked back to the hut and gathered up my stuff. I got a lot of congratulations from friends and peers, which was awesome. Then I headed back to the NCO hut with a seabag on my back, a rucksack on my front, and my linens and pillow stacked on top of my rucksack. As I walked up to the door, I saw two corporals quickly duck inside the hut. Something felt a little off but I thought it was probably just me being nervous.

I had a hard time opening the door with all that gear. When I stepped inside the hut it took me a second for my eyes to adjust and to realize what was happening. There were two rows of racks – one on each side – and standing in front of each rack was an NCO. They had formed a gauntlet and were waiting for me to walk down the center aisle.

When you reach the rank of corporal, you wear a red stripe down the seams of your trousers in your dress blues. This is called the blood stripe. Tradition says it represents the high casualty rate of NCOs and officers during the Battle of Chapultepec during the Mexican-American War. That's not true, but it is part of Marine Corps lore. The anti-hazing efforts of the last ten years have done away with this practice, but back then, when you got promoted to corporal, you got a punch in the shoulder and a knee to your thigh to congratulate you on getting your blood stripe. If you were tough you just took it and didn't flinch.

So I gritted my teeth and walked down the aisle, taking punches and knees on both sides. It was painful. A few of the NCOs didn't really lay into me, but I got more than enough purple bruising to "earn" my blood stripes and rank. And in some sick sense, it made me feel like I was welcome into their ranks.

I'm pretty sure Carr got the same treatment but I never saw it. I guess it's possible that he skated out of it. After it was done, I made up my rack, stowed my gear, and headed off to the temporary enlisted club with a few of my friends, feeling sore but happy.

Chapter 6

Transfer

I met Christy at Foothill College. I thought she was incredible. Tall and athletically thin with dark short hair and dark caramel eyes, she absolutely killed me. After some stuttering and looking at my shoes, I asked her out and she agreed. We became a tight couple pretty quickly.

Christy came from a wealthy family and I don't think her parents were impressed with me, but they were always cordial and nice. The only member of her family who was impressed by my Marine Corps status was her little brother. I had fun hanging with him and teaching him a little about the Marine Corps.

I admit I developed a bit of a hang-up about Christy's upbringing. Her family went on vacations and did things that I just couldn't afford to do. They often paid for me to join them and were always gracious about it. Her mother even got me a blazer and khaki trousers so I could go to dinner with them at the country club. It was generous of her and she meant it in the kindest way, but I felt like a charity project and worried that I wouldn't be considered good enough in the long run.

Christy and I went skiing at Lake Tahoe in the winter, went camping at some of the local parks in the spring and fall, and spent a lot of the summer water skiing or fishing or just sitting around. I was starting to think that maybe someday Christy and I would get married and that's what life would be like.

Christy and I were on similar schedules at Foothill so we were looking to transfer to four-year universities around the same time. I knew that if I moved away from the Bay Area, I would also have to transfer reserve units, so that was a big part of my decision process. I still wanted to be involved with a high-speed special unit, and so ultimately I was really only interested in two other reserve units: 4th Force Reconnaissance in Reno and 3rd ANGLICO in Long Beach.

So when Christy announced that she was planning to go to the University of Southern California (USC) I immediately called 3rd

ANGLICO. Fortunately, they needed radio operators and assured me that I would be able to get a transfer. Better still, I would get a slot for jump school within a year of joining them. I was excited about that. Not many Marines get to go to jump school.

I applied to several universities in the SoCal area. Soon we learned that Christy had been accepted to USC and that I had been accepted to Cal Poly Pomona. Big changes ahead!

The summer of 1990 was my last summer ATD with 23rd Marines, and we were going back to Twentynine Palms. I couldn't believe that I'd been in the Marine Corps three years and I still hadn't left the West Coast!

Every year, the Training Command at Twentynine Palms held sixteen three-week exercises called CAXs, an abbreviation for combined arms exercise. A CAX is a large-scale, live-fire exercise with all the elements of a Marine Air Ground Task Force (MAGTF) participating. This exercise generally includes infantry, tanks, artillery, and aircraft. It is designed to exercise everyone from the Colonel in command to the lowliest Private and across all the military occupational specialties (MOSs), from supply to medical, maintenance to paymasters, and of course the trigger pullers. The enemy is imaginary but there are targets everywhere in the nine hundred-square miles of range, from plastic, pop-up, man-sized targets to tank and aircraft hulks. There are several mock airfields and a couple of combat towns where live fire is allowed to practice clearing buildings and fighting in an urban environment. The main goal of the CAX is to have infantry, surface fires (artillery and mortars), and aviation fires (aircraft-delivered rockets, bombs, and guns), all maneuvering and firing at the same time as if it were a real conflict.

Our jobs at the 23rd Marines Headquarters Company were the same as always, but we were setting up, operating, and relocating our CPs in the steep desert terrain of the Twentynine Palms ranges. As a Corporal now, I was running the antenna farm, usually with two other Marines working for me. I loved it! I was out away from the "head shed" and in charge of my own little world. As long as I kept the radio nets running, no one messed with me. Our only interaction with anyone else was when I ordered supplies like chow, water, batteries, or fuel, and usually we could carry a week's worth of supplies. We always had one Marine standing by the hotline phone and monitoring the equipment and one Marine sleeping. The third guy was usually someone who was getting trained and would often just shadow me.

My best friend in the unit, Sgt Morgan, was the radio watch supervisor/chief at the CP, so I would chat with him on the hotline frequently. First Sgt Bricca would come out in a Humvee every few days to check on us. He also used this as an opportunity to rotate out some of the Marines working for me, to give guys a break or a chance to train on something else. Those were two more leadership techniques I learned from 1st Sgt Bricca: visit your Marines often and vary their training.

The local wildlife provided quite a bit of excitement during the CAX. On the first night in the field, I found three scorpions hidden in a stack of boxes of supplies. The second night a sidewinder slithered under our camo netting – only a few feet from where my Marines were sleeping. I woke the guys up and had them sit in the trailer while I chased it away with an extra antenna mast. Then, on the third night, while I was settling into my favorite sleeping spot on top of the Humvee, I felt the vehicle shake a little. The truck shook again and I heard a strange scratching sound from the front of the vehicle. When I sat up and leaned over to see what was going on, I came face to face with a coyote! Earlier that night we had put all our MRE trash in a bag, tied it off, and put it on the hood in an attempt to keep it away from the critters. Well, it wasn't enough to deter this guy! As soon as I yelled, the coyote jumped down, slid under the edge of the camo netting, and scampered off. We started keeping our trash in a hard-sided trunk after that.

After five or six days, it started getting a bit boring out there. One night, I took a backup PRC-104 (the HF AM radio) and set up a custom long wire antenna. I started flipping through the frequencies. I found BBC India broadcast! I don't know if it was timing or the ionosphere changing with the heat during the day, but we could only get reception at night. I hooked up an external speaker and we listened to the news and to the Top 40 countdown a few nights.

And so that's how we learned that Iraq had invaded Kuwait. At first it didn't even seem real – it was like a story that had somehow gotten lost in the airwaves. But as we listened closer, it sounded more real. And it sounded like the conflict had been going on for a while.

The next day we got a visit from 1st Sgt Bricca, who confirmed the story. He added some detail and told us that the US military was sending troops to Saudi Arabia. He said that they might even activate some Reserve Units, but he doubted that 23rd Marines would be activated.

We continued on with the CAX, but of course all the talk now was about Kuwait. Everyone had their own opinions about what the United States should do, whether the Marines should be involved or not, and whether our unit would be activated. To me it seemed to make sense that we should be on the list of units most likely to go – after all, we were in the desert, doing desert training. But I was just a young Corporal with very little knowledge of the Marine Corps and all the other factors at work. We knew very little about Iraq, Saddam Hussein, or his forces, but we did know they had just fought an eight-year war with Iran and that the US had backed Iraq during that conflict. We heard that Iraq had the fourth largest army in the world with close to one million battle-hardened troops. We also had heard that Iraq didn't hesitate to use chemical or biological weapons.

This was the beginning of a mental shift for all of us. Even though the Berlin Wall had fallen, we were still studying, training, and preparing to fight Soviet-trained forces in major land conflicts. The Iraqis had lots of Soviet equipment but their techniques, tactics, and procedures (TTPs) didn't follow Soviet doctrine. The Marine Corps has always devoted some time preparing for small wars and insurgencies, but this seemed to be the first time we had started to consider that our next fight might not be against the Soviet Doctrine. This mental shift took years. In fact, up to summer of 2001, the CAXs I participated in were still designed around a Soviet doctrine-based enemy.

Soon we returned to our lives and the "real world," and I resumed my preparations to transfer to Cal Poly and 3rd ANGLICO. There still wasn't a lot of talk of activating reserve units but I started following the news a little more closely. I did a little reading on the Iran-Iraq war and focused my study on Iraqi weapons and vehicles. I followed as the United States deployed more and more units to Saudi Arabia. But on a day-to-day basis, I still went about my life as college student in a pretty normal manner.

Christy left for USC about two weeks before I left for Cal Poly and I didn't talk to her for several days. She didn't call, and when I called her dorm room, she was never there. I'd heard from many people how relationships didn't survive going away to college and I felt I was losing Christy already.

I was still excited to start at Cal Poly. I planned to live in the dorms the first semester while I got acclimated to university life. I loaded up my little Ford Fiesta and headed down to Pomona. I was lucky to get another transfer student for a roommate. We were close in age and soon became friends.

Although I was a bit intimidated at first, I got into the school routine quite easily. Classes weren't much different than Foothill. Most of the twenty thousand students lived locally and commuted to school. There wasn't much school spirit and we didn't even have a football team, but that was okay with me. I made a few friends in the dorms but for the most part, they seemed young and immature.

I went to see Christy at USC a few times and even set up a romantic dinner in her dorm room while her roommate was out. But it wasn't the same. There was definitely a distance between us. We talked about it and Christy told me nothing was different, but I knew it was different. USC was only thirty miles away from Cal Poly, but with LA traffic it was always at least an hour drive. I made it over to see her every few weeks. She came to visit me once.

Meanwhile, I had started at 3rd ANGLICO. ANGLICO stands for Air Naval Gunfire Liaison Company. The unit's mission is to provide small teams of forward observers to friendly forces to enable them to use Marine and Navy supporting arms. A firepower control team (FCT) is six to eight Marines and has the ability to control Marine and Naval aircraft, Naval gunfire, artillery and mortars.

The unit was only forty-five miles away, but in afternoon LA traffic it took two hours to get there. When I first checked into the unit, they didn't have a full complement of field gear. I got issued a flack jacket, helmet, shelter half, rucksack, field belt and suspenders, a first aid kit, and one canteen – not much for going to the field. No sleeping mat and no sleeping bag. Supply promised me that I would get the rest of my gear soon.

I got the schedule for upcoming drills and a few publications on the missions and duties of ANGLICO. Normally they ran an Indoctrination

Platoon (Indoc Plt), but they didn't have enough new guys right then so I was assigned straight into 1st Platoon. I was relieved – I had heard some horror stories about the pain of Indoc Plt.

The guys in 1st Platoon seemed excited to hear I already had my military driver's license and knew my comm gear pretty well. I had expected to be treated as an outsider and a boot, but the fact that half of 1st Platoon hadn't been to jump school yet and that I was a Corporal with some experience improved my standing. They were more casual with rank than my last unit. There were plenty of guys going to school but there were also a lot of guys who were on police or sheriff's forces. A few were firefighters and others worked private security. In general, this group was more enthusiastic about going to the field than my previous unit and I was happy to join them.

We had formation and then started preparing for the weekend's activities. Marines who were jump qualified went off to prepare for a night jump. The rest of us loaded gear on five-ton trucks and rode down to Camp Pendleton.

We set up on the edge of the drop zone, and while we waited I got to know some of the other guys while we ate MREs. After the jumpers landed, we recovered all their gear and bedded down for the night.

I was surprised that no one set up any tents or shelter halves. I took off my boots and stuck my feet in my rucksack and wrapped my extra T-shirt around my head. I rolled up my flak jacket and tried to use it as a pillow. I got pretty cold that night when the damp cloud layer rolled in from the ocean, but I survived.

We got up at 0530 the next morning, packed our gear, shaved, and ate MREs. Then we broke into two groups to rotate through various field classes. We sat on the ground in a semicircle while members of the platoon taught hour-long classes on controlling aircraft, directing ordnance, calling artillery strikes, and using different radio equipment. I was glad to have gotten into the habit of always carrying a small notebook and a pen. I took notes furiously. Between classes we'd have a few minutes' break to go pee in the bushes, fill up a canteen, or have a smoke.

The typical ANGLICO team has a team leader, an officer who is a forward air controller (FAC), a team chief (senior sergeant or staff sergeant), two or three Marines who have been to artillery observers school, and then two or three Marines who have been to comm school.

With controlling supporting arms, it doesn't matter how good you are if you can't get the supporting agency on the radio – you have to be able to maintain good radio communications. That was something I could bring to the team.

We did a lot of cross-training. The comm guys would teach everyone about comm stuff, the artillery guys would teach about artillery, and the officers and some of the experienced sergeants and staff sergeants would teach aviation. I loved all of it.

On Saturday afternoon, we humped our gear several miles to Observation Post Alpha and set up bivouac there. OP A is a single conical-shaped hill with a flat top overlooking the ranges where aviation can shoot ordnance on Camp Pendleton. That's when I learned that we would have Cobras and Hueys coming in to shoot for us. We each wrote up a strike mission (called a nine-line) and had one of the officers review it. The nine-line format gave the pilots what they needed to know to strike the correct target and not endanger friendlies. Back before the days of GPS, this was a bit tricky. Usually the officer reviewing your nine-line would have you read it just like you were talking on the radio and they would pretend to be the aircraft. They'd make a few suggestions or corrections and then you'd do it again. When they were satisfied, you would get in line to wait for an aircraft.

When it was your turn, the officer running the range would hand you a radio handset and you would check in with the aircraft. The range officer had another radio and if you flubbed something, he would quickly correct it so the pilots got the correct info. The usual format was for the pilots to give you their callsign and type of aircraft, how much time they had, and what ordnance they had. You would then give them your nine-line in a slow, steady pace, taking pauses so they could write it down. Then you'd give them a time hack – basically starting a timer so you both knew exactly when the ordnance would impact.

When it was my turn I gave the aircraft the coordinates to a tank hulk out on the range and successfully got a good time hack. Moments later the pilots reported, "initial point inbound," meaning they had flown over the starting point I had given them and were now heading toward their firing point. The range officer interrupted with a quick "visual," telling the pilots he could see them, then slapped my shoulder and pointed to where the two helicopters were coming into view just past a hill behind us. Part of the art of controlling air is geometry and knowing where to look in the sky when you need to see your aircraft. The range officer held his handset away from his ear and said, "Tell them continue." I keyed my handset and said, "Continue."

The pilot came back with, "Viper 21 wings level," which meant they were ready to pull the trigger or "pickle" the bomb to hit the target. I could see the Cobras and they looked like they were pointed roughly at the target. Still, I was nervous about the next call and looked at the range officer. He said, "Hurry up! Clear 'em hot!" So then I got to utter my favorite phrase in the Marine Corps. I keyed my handset and shouted, "CLEARED HOT!"

I stood with my jaw open as the rockets came off the Cobra, leaving a smoke trail down the range. They impacted and threw a huge dust cloud into the air. The impacts were two to three kilometers away, so it took a few seconds for the sound concussion to hit us. They didn't hit the hulk I was aiming for, but they came pretty close!

The range officer was slapping my shoulder again. "Dash two! Dash two!" The second aircraft is usually thirty seconds in trail, calling "wings level" about twenty seconds after the lead's shot. The range officer was pointing so I could pick them out of the sky. Sure enough the radio squawked, "Dash two, wings level." My mind froze. I was supposed to give them a correction from the lead's impacts, but estimating distance and direction had me flummoxed, so I spit out, "Dash two, cleared hot, hit leads hits!"

Again smoke trails, impacts, and a big dust cloud. Then a few seconds later the roar of the rockets firing and the concussion of the impacts hit our ears. It was insanely loud. I was frozen in a state of awe when the range officer said, "Not bad. Next!" I got out of the way to let the next guy have a turn.

One of the other officers came to debrief me on my mission. I was shaking and excited but felt like I had messed up because I'd frozen on the radio. He talked over each phase of the evolution with me with very constructive criticism, from figuring out the right part of the sky to look for the aircraft, to giving the aircraft more description of the target after the nine-line – what he called "talking them on" – to estimating distance and direction for a correction to dash two. Calling "hit leads hits" is a last resort. If the lead aircraft already shot there, you can generally assume they destroyed their target and that you should shift the next impacts to something else. When I told him that it was my first time, he grinned and slapped my back. "Outstanding! Maybe you have a knack for this!" I still couldn't believe I was getting to control aircraft as a Corporal – and all this on my first trip to the field with 3rd ANGLICO.

We each wrote up another mission and then spent the rest of the afternoon watching other guys run them, quietly critiquing each mission amongst ourselves. It was an awesome spectacle – exactly why I had joined the Marine Corps.

When the last mission was complete, the range officer said something into the radio about checking panels and then hollered back, "Stand by for a panel check!" I didn't know what this meant but followed everyone else up to the front of the observation area. A bunch of guys were digging out disposable cameras. Just then, a Cobra and Huey came scorching up the hill from the range side, probably seventy-five feet off the ground. I could feel the individual whops of the rotor blades in my chest, and I swear I could see individual rivets and oil streaks on the bottom of the aircraft as they flew directly over us. Then they turned a hard ninety degrees and flew off over the hills, gaining altitude as they went. It was an impressive show to end an impressive day.

Chapter 7

Getting the Call

I headed home to my parents' house for Thanksgiving. After Thanksgiving Cal Poly would have "dead week" with no classes, followed by finals during the first week of December. I was looking forward to having a short break and then planned to hit the books fresh on Monday.

Things weren't going well with Christy. We didn't talk or see each other much, and when we did everything seemed a bit forced. She was always talking about her activities with her new friends at school, which made me jealous. I was really hurt when she told me she wasn't going home for Thanksgiving, but was instead going with some friends to Arizona. I had hoped that seeing her at home in our old surroundings would help us reconnect, but apparently that wasn't going to happen.

My parents welcomed me home late Wednesday night. My old room was cluttered with some of my mother's stuff, but she had cleared off my old bed and made it up with fresh sheets. There was a thick stack of mail waiting for me. I took off the rubber band and started to go through it, but it was late and I was tired, so I set it aside and went to bed.

The next morning on Thanksgiving day, I headed over to a friend's house for what had become an annual flag football game. It was good to see old friends and it was fun playing semi-competitive football. After the game, it was back to my parents' house for the big Thanksgiving meal.

There was quite a crew at my parents' already – my brother Hew and his wife Cathy, my sister Anne and her husband Al and their two-year-old daughter Emily, my other sister Sara, and a younger foster sister named Sarah. It was great to see them all and we had a grand time catching up and telling stories.

After we finished a traditional Thanksgiving feast, things slowed down a bit and I remembered my pile of mail. I went back to my old room and started thumbing through it. A lot of it was catalogs and ads, which went straight into the trash. When I started going through the business-size envelopes I was surprised to see a letter from 3rd ANGLICO. I'd only been with the unit three months. I realized that when I checked in, I had given them my parents' address since I didn't have mail set up at school yet. My parents' address is also part of my formal Marine Corps record as my official "home of record."

I opened the envelope. There were four pages stapled together. The first page was an official business form letter, the second page a set of orders, the third page a roster of everyone in 1st Platoon, and page four was a gear list. I started scanning the first page and my heart skipped a beat. This was notice of activation! I read it again more carefully. It said the members of 1st Platoon on the attached roster were being called to active duty in support of Operation Desert Shield. I reviewed the platoon roster and yes, there was my name. I looked through it all again. The orders said to report on 3 December 1990 to the Reserve Center in Long Beach. Usually orders will have a duration noted, either the number of days or an end date. But these simply said "in excess of 180 days." The cover letter said to expect deployment to "an overseas location."

I didn't know how to react. For a while I just sat on the edge of my old bed in the back bedroom. I was excited to be invited, to go on active duty and deploy, and finally put all my training to test. But I was nervous and a little scared, too. I was shaking as I read it over again, searching for answers to all the questions forming in my mind. The gear list contained items like "(3) M-16 magazines" and "M-17 field protective mask," which indicated I might be going to combat. The phrase "expect to deploy to an overseas location" didn't guarantee that I was going, but it was a strong indicator. I figured in the most extreme case I would go to Kuwait to fight the Iraqis for at least six months and probably longer, while in the least extreme case I would go sit on my butt in Camp Pendleton.

I wanted to go. I wanted to do what Marines have done since November 10, 1775. I wanted to be a part of going to fight and winning a battle. But then I started to think about the other aspects of my life. Did I just waste an entire quarter of school? What would I do with all my stuff in Pomona? December 3 was less than two weeks away. I thought through it all a bit more and then steeled myself to go tell my family.

Most of my family was sitting in the living room. I asked my mother to come in from the kitchen for a moment. When she walked in wiping her hands on her apron, I told them I was going to Desert Shield. Mom responded with her typical, "Oh, Andrew!" She had the same tone in her voice that she always had when I told her I had done something wrong. I know she didn't mean it that way, but that's how it sounded to me. There was a brief silence and then they all started peppering me with questions.

My family is not very knowledgeable about the military, so I answered their questions the best that I could – though most of my answers were along the lines of "it could mean…or it could be…" or "we might…or we might…"

But everyone was very helpful when it came to some of my more immediate issues, like finishing the quarter at school. Anne suggested that I talk to my professors and ask to take my finals early to still get credit for the quarter. Hew offered me a ride back down to Pomona so I could leave my car at my parents' house. All of this really helped me focus on the task at hand.

My announcement definitely put a damper on the jovial Thanksgiving mood. I didn't want to admit that I was excited to go, that I had been hoping for an opportunity like this since before I had joined the Marine Corps. In my mind I was going to go help fight tyranny and the bad guys of the world. Hopefully, I would prove myself a man. Thoughts of politics or oil did not cross my mind.

On Saturday I drove back to Cal Poly. The rest of that week was a blur of begging professors to give me an early final and visiting various university offices to get my student status held. Everyone I dealt with was very helpful. The admissions office put me on a hold status and refunded my deposit for the next quarter. The housing office arranged for me to check out of the dorms on Sunday, December 2. I managed to take three finals early and got an A and two Bs. I even managed to swing by the bike shop and let them know I was deploying but would love to work for them when I got back.

That next Sunday afternoon I packed everything in my car, got checked out of the dorms, and said goodbye to friends. Pat Tule, a friend from the unit, let me stay with him that night. Early the next morning, we headed to the unit to check in.

There were about forty-five guys in 1st Platoon, ranging from Major to several new PFCs. Overall the mood was fairly jovial, but there were some negative comments, too. The next few days were filled with paperwork, forms, medical exams, lots of shots (again), gear inspections, writing up new wills, creating powers of attorney for those that needed them, and classes on what to expect in the Middle East, including different aspects of Arabic language and customs. About half of us stayed at the transient billeting – which is like a cheap motel – and the other half went home each night.

After a week we boarded a plane for Camp Lejeune, North Carolina. This is where we would prepare to deploy to Saudi Arabia and participate in Operation Desert Shield. I was finally leaving the West Coast. Soon I would be in a foreign land for the first time in my life.

Part II

The Gulf War (1991)

Chapter 8

Camp Lejeune

Normally there are about 35,000 Marines stationed on the 246 square miles that make up Camp Lejeune. But in December 1990, more than half the Marines stationed there were deployed elsewhere, mostly to Saudi Arabia. And many of the families of the young deployed Marines had moved back home for support and assistance while their Marines were gone. So the base and neighboring town of Jacksonville North Carolina were practically empty.

Of approximately 23,000 Marine Reserves called to active duty at this point, six thousand or so of us were scheduled to deploy to the Combat Operations Area. Those of us in ANGLICO didn't really see ourselves as reservists, though. And reasonably so: ANGLICO units do more training, schools, deployments, and exercises than typical reserve units.

We stayed in four-man rooms in brick, two-story barracks. During the next six weeks we continued training on everything from calling in aircraft and mortars to combat first aid. We got issued a lot of gear, including desert camouflage utilities, which we called chocolate chips because of the small dark brown spots mixed into the normal tan camo patterns.

We were issued pyridostigmine bromide tablets that supposedly countered the effect of Soman gas, which we expected the Iraqis to use. We continued receiving shots, which included anthrax and botulism vaccines. Some people were a bit freaked out about all the shots, and we heard stories about Army guys refusing them. We also did plenty of nuclear, biological, chemical (NBC) training and practiced performing normal tasks in protective equipment such as charcoal impregnated suits, gas masks, and rubber boots and gloves. Donning all this gear wasn't too bad in the cool North Carolina winter, but we worried we would die of heat and dehydration wearing that stuff in the desert.

Although the news was full of stories about the political efforts to get Saddam to back down, none of us believed it was going to happen. We all fully expected that we were going to end up going to war to kick Saddam out of Kuwait. And so everyone was taking the training very seriously. We did a lot of conditioning humps and we made a few visits to the range and did a lot of aircraft controls. One day I even got to control a flight of A-6s under Capt Smith's watchful eye. The A-6 was an impressive old aircraft that could carry a TON of ordnance. We quizzed each other constantly on recognition and capabilities of US and Iraqi weapons, vehicles, and aircraft.

Military Operations in Urban Terrain (MOUT) was in its infancy at this point. We were fortunate to have a Los Angeles SWAT trainer in our midst. Chief Warrant Officer 4 (CWO-4) Sid Heal gave us a crash course on urban SWAT tactics and we spent three days at the small fake town on Camp Lejeune, training for MOUT. We learned simple things like never letting your weapon protrude from a window or around a corner, to more advanced things like "stacking" your team and making dynamic entry into an unknown building. Much of his training stuck with me twenty years later.

At any other time in history, a bunch of reservists rolling into Camp Lejeune for training would be largely ignored or even shunned. But with the town half deserted, the tattoo shops, pool halls, bars, and strip clubs welcomed us with open arms. So after working hard all day, we went out and partied hard every night.

Still, I wasn't really in a party mood. Every night for the first four or five days I had tried to call Christy from the cluster of payphones near the barracks. But each time I just ended up talking to her answering machine. I was pretty sure she was out meeting other guys and having more fun than she could ever have with me. One night while drinking, I spilled my guts to my buddy Glenn Walsh. Glenn was a lot more sure of himself than I was, and I trusted his opinions on things. Glenn listened to my story, then outlined my options. He told me that I should tell Christy that if we couldn't be exclusive we should break up. In my inebriated state, this sounded like a great idea. With a handful of quarters, I struck off in search of a payphone.

This time I actually managed to get through. I promptly issued my ultimatum. Of course it didn't go the way I had hoped. To be fair, she didn't say she wanted to break up, but she didn't agree to be exclusive, either. So we broke up, on the phone, three weeks before I left for Desert Storm.

I was devastated. I had been expecting this for months, but now it was real. I had just lost the most beautiful girl that ever paid attention to me. So after that I was ready to go do some drinking and partying. I already had the "I'm going off to war and might not come back" attitude, but now I really felt I had nothing to lose.

One evening out drinking, Mansfield and I met a couple of girls playing pool. The girls were attractive and must have been at least twenty-one. Things were going great and the girls asked us to come back to the house with them. We all piled into a big '80s-era Bronco and headed to one girl's house.

While everyone got settled in with a fresh beer, I looked around the living room. On the mantel I spotted a framed photo of a Marine in dress blues with a woman in a fancy dress. It looked like the typical Marine Corps Ball picture. I asked, "Who's this?" The girl whom I was unofficially paired off with walked over, turned the picture down, and said, "It's my husband, but don't worry. He's deployed."

I was shocked. I stammered something and then walked out the front door. A moment later Mansfield followed me outside, asking what was wrong.

"What's wrong?" I said. "These girls are married! Their husbands are already in Saudi Arabia and we are back here thinking we're going to get lucky! That's what's wrong!"

Mansfield hadn't seen the picture or heard the conversation. I didn't feel like I could even go back in the house – I just wanted to get the hell out of there. Mansfield went back in, called us a cab, and we vacated that position as fast as we could.

That situation was depressing and disgusted me. It definitely changed the way I acted around girls in the bars. I understood why everyone says don't date women from Jacksonville, North Carolina. They are either some Marine's daughter or married to one. Either way, you don't want to be messing with her. My attitude toward women was pretty negative at that point.

After a few weeks, one of the Motor Transport Companies put on a two-night NVG (night vision goggles) driving course. Obviously, you don't want to use headlights in tactical situations because it gives away your position. Without NVGs you have to drive really slowly, and often you need to have someone walk in front – what we call a ground guide. I'd done this plenty of times and it was no fun. So I was very keen to be certified to drive using NVGs. I also knew I probably wouldn't get to drive in Kuwait if I wasn't.

The NVGs we had back in the early '90s (AN/PVS-5s) are fairly primitive by today's standards, but they seemed pretty high-tech at the time. Basically, NVGs amplify the available energy in the near-infrared spectrum about 20,000 times. This was pretty useful in most conditions, but they were still very awkward to use. Imagine a swim mask painted all black except for two small toilet paper tubes sticking out the front. Inside each tube was what equated to a thirty-millimeter TV screen that only displayed in shades of green. Even with optimal conditions, the images displayed were very grainy. And while technically the NVGs had stereoscopic vision, there was basically no depth perception. Focusing NVGs was a challenge as well – you had to focus each tube individually, which wasn't something you could do quickly. As a result, we mostly just left them focused to infinity, which meant everything inside thirty feet was out of focus. Finally, if you looked at a light or heat source, it made a huge bright green spot that "bloomed" out the rest of the image. Eventually we learned to keep light sources out of our field of view.

After we'd learned the NVG basics, we started driving (slowly) on the gravel and sand roads out in the woods of Camp Lejeune. With NVGs, the best clarity is when there is some contrast. Driving in the woods was fairly easy since the dark pine forest contrasted dramatically with the light-colored gravel and sand roads. Still, if you had any speed, it was tricky to time your turns for the twists in the roads. By the end of the first night I was exhausted – I got cramps from tensing my legs and butt, which made it difficult to be smooth on the throttle and brake.

The second night, we headed out to the more open areas and then out to the beach. In the big open fields, we didn't have the contrast of the trees so it was more challenging. And on the beach, it was even worse. I learned to move my head around to build some lateral situational awareness to substitute for peripheral vision. It amazed me how far I wandered just trying to drive straight across an open field.

On the final day we had the driving test. The instructors laid out a five mile course through the forest and out to the dunes on the edge of the beach, placing chemlights at various points to help us keep on track. The course was timed and we had an instructor riding shotgun to grade us.

I carefully inspected the Humvee with my mini Maglite, then settled in the driver's seat, adjusted everything, and focused my NVGs. I was ready. My instructor warned me not to look over at him – he had a chemlight in his lap so he could take notes, and if I looked in his direction, the NVGs would bloom out.

We left in five-minute intervals so we wouldn't see each other on the course. I was nervous but excited when we finally rolled out. The first half of the course was pretty easy, and I was generally able to see the next chemlight marking each turn in plenty of time. I was getting fairly comfortable driving while looking through the tubes. I maintained a speed of about 25 or 30 mph and was doing fine on time.

When we got to the sand dunes, everything just blended together and I had to slow way down. It was tough to pick out the track. The instructor warned me that the left turn coming up was the hardest part of the course. He said, "Just trust me, and I'll tell you when to turn." Sure enough, the turn came up and I couldn't tell the dunes on the far side from the dunes on the close side. Just as I was able to discern a slight gap in the dunes, the instructor barked, "Now! Left turn!" I turned on his call. My timing wasn't perfect and the left wheels rode up the dune to our left and the Humvee tilted sharply right. But when I made a small correction, the Humvee slowly came back to level and I was able to see the rest of the track.

"Good, good," the instructor said. "Not perfect, but you didn't panic."

I didn't reply. I was concentrating on staying on the track and keeping my speed up a little. There were a few more twists and then the track straightened out and I could see two lines of Humvees that had finished. As we passed between the two chemlights marking the finish line, the instructor looked at his watch and said, "You pass!"

Wahoo! I passed! NVG qualified!

Then the instructor said, "Now just pull up behind the last Hummer on the right."

As I slowed down and pulled up to the last Humvee, the instructor hollered, "Stop! Stop! Stop!"

I started applying the brake but on his third "Stop!" there was a crunch and a shock through the vehicle. I'd hit the Humvee in front of me – not too hard, but enough to crack the one-piece hood and fenders.

I'd let my guard down and the lack of depth perception had gotten me. Later, I learned that this happens fairly often. Still, the instructor was pissed and I was embarrassed. Luckily, I still passed and got my NVG driving qualification. But in all the driving I've done with the Marines, this is still the worst damage I've caused that was directly my fault.

Christmas and New Year's were coming up and the usual "port and starboard" leave schedule was established, which meant that half of us got four days off for Christmas and the other half got four days off for New Year.

I've always been a bit of a romantic about Christmas, but with the breakup with Christy, I didn't really want to go home. And since practically everyone wanted the first leave period for Christmas, I volunteered for the New Year period.

With half of the crew gone by the evening of December 23, it was pretty quiet around the barracks. I went fishing by myself on Christmas Eve and then met up with a couple of guys to go to a movie that evening. But afterwards they went out to find an open bar, and I caught a cab back to the barracks by myself.

On Christmas morning I went to a service at the Protestant chapel on base, then spent the day halfheartedly fishing the banks of the river again. It was cold and drizzling and I didn't catch a damn thing. That night I drank beers with some of the guys in the TV lounge and watched a few movies. So that was my first experience of being "deployed" for Christmas.

As soon as I was cut loose on December 29, I changed out of my uniform, grabbed my bag, and met up with a couple of guys to cab share to the airport. Most of the other guys were from SoCal, so none of my buddies were on my flight. It was a redeye anyway, so I slept most of the way.

My sister picked me up and dropped me off at my parents'. I slept late the next day then called some of my old friends to see what was going on that night. I wanted to go out and party a bit but they just wanted to go see a movie.

It all felt surreal and like I wasn't really there. I hadn't hung out with these friends since I had moved to Pomona the previous August. It was good to see them but I wasn't terribly sad to go back to North Carolina a few days later.

Once everyone was back, it was all business. Our flight was scheduled for January 6. We must have written out fifty rosters of everyone and a hundred rosters of the limited gear we were taking.

On the morning of January 6, we stood in formation at 0400 with our rifles, a seabag, a rucksack, and a small carry-on bag. We loaded all our gear onto the big open-bed trucks and went over the roster again. Then everyone boarded the white school bus for the hour-long drive up to Marine Corps Air Station Cherry Point. When we arrived, we proceeded through the usual goatrope of unloading gear, checking the rosters, and checking the weapons' serial numbers. Then we proceeded to wait in an empty hangar for eight hours.

The initial excitement had worn off and the bright eyes were now droopy. Fatigued, most everyone was lying on the floor with their heads resting on their carry-on bag. Some were reading, some listening to Walkmans or playing on a Gameboy, but most were sleeping.

The contract airline plane showed up and we went through our roster and weapons serial numbers again. Then we loaded into the plane, which looked just like a civilian airliner complete with flight attendants.

The next thirty-six hours was a blur of sleeping, watching movies, and eating airline food. I'd like to say I had some profound thoughts about what was ahead of me, but mostly it was just painful to sit that long and kind of weird to be on the plane with our M-16s. We stopped three times to switch crews, refuel, and resupply the galley, but we never left the plane. We saw some stuff from the air but could never really see anything when we were on the ground. Just airfields. And it always seemed to be night when we were on the ground.

During the night of January 9, 1991, we landed somewhere in Saudi Arabia. No one really knew exactly where we were. Again, we waited. Then, after what seemed like hours, they finally opened the aircraft doors and a set of portable stairs were pushed up to the door. As we deplaned, a Staff Sergeant stood by the door, checking names off a roster and verifying the weapon serial numbers.

Even though it was dark, it was probably ninety degrees out. I couldn't see anything except some lights in the distance. But for the first time in my life, I was on foreign soil. The adventure was about to begin.

Chapter 9

Arrival in Saudi

After unloading our gear from the plane, we each got issued sixty rounds of ammunition – fifty rounds of standard and ten rounds of tracer. Most of us loaded five rounds of tracer and then twenty-five rounds of standard in each magazine. The idea was that if we got in a firefight, when we started to shoot tracer rounds we'd know we were about to empty the magazine. This was before we learned that putting thirty rounds in a thirty-round magazine made by the lowest bidder was a bad idea – it tended to fatigue the spring and cause jams. Later we all loaded magazines to twenty-eight rounds. In any case, getting ammo was a sure sign that we were getting close to a fight.

Two odd-looking compact buses pulled up. Finally, something that didn't look like the stuff we had back home! The buses were very boxy and low to the ground and sounded like they were powered by diesel engines. A stack of mattresses was tied on the top of each.

We stuffed as many seabags and packs as we could underneath, then boarded the buses and shoved the rest of our gear down the aisles and under the seats. The buses had reclining seats covered in real cloth with a subdued checkered pattern. Fancy curtains with fringed edging were tied back with a twisted cord. While this seemed to be rather luxurious, they were designed for people smaller than us – when the guy in front of me reclined his seat, the headrest went straight into my chest!

After another thirty minutes of waiting around, we finally pulled away from the airport. We were all glued to the windows as we started down the Saudi version of an interstate. The road was a four-lane divided highway with a large median. Powerful streetlights along the highway illuminated the flat sand for twenty or thirty meters on either side. The highway was empty and there wasn't much of anything resembling terrain. I could detect a slight rolling from the headlights ahead of us, but the elevation gains and losses were in the tens of feet at most.

The street signs were in Arabic and English, but the English really didn't help because there were too many consonants. Most of the numbers were in two different styles. There were the standard numbers and then the Arabic numbers. I remember my high school math teacher telling me that our numbers were actually Arabic numbers. So what were these numbers?

At one point we saw a camel headed down the middle of the three lanes going the other direction. That drew a chuckle from most everyone. A minute later we saw a tan Land Cruiser with blue flashing lights headed after the camel. Must have been the camel police.

After about an hour we pulled through the gates of Camp 5, our home for the next few weeks. It was a cinderblock walled compound, about a city block square with guard towers draped in camo netting on each corner. Trailers with skirting were arranged in groups of four, creating a perfect grid.

The driver stopped the bus and we were instructed to unload all the gear onto the sidewalk. Afterwards, we formed into a platoon formation of three ranks to wait. Somebody asked about making head call – it had been two or three hours since we'd had the opportunity. Gunnery Sergeant Megas told us to make a "tactical leak" in the hedge behind us. Since I was in the back row, I just turned around and started peeing. Relief! But while I was pissing, I felt my right calf and foot getting warmer. I looked over my shoulder to see Cpl Monarrez talking to the guy on his right and pissing down my leg!

"What the hell, Monarrez? You're pissing in my boot!"

"Oh, heh heh. Sorry, man."

"Watch what the hell you are doing, man! That's uncool!"

"I said I was sorry. What the hell you want me to do now?"

I was ticked off but there really wasn't much I could do about it. I took off my boot, dumped it out, wrung out my sock, then put them back on. Then I washed my hands with a little water from my canteen. First chance I'd get, I planned to take my boots in the shower and do some laundry.

We were roomed by rank instead of teams, so I was in a room with three other Corporals. I considered all of them to be my friends so it was fine. I dug out my hygiene kit and towel and headed for the showers.

After so much time in the same clothes it was great to finally get clean! Afterwards, I went to the other end of the head and noticed that half of the stalls didn't have a toilet. Instead, there was hole in the floor with foot-shaped tread on either side. There was a hose on the wall with a valve to wash off your left hand when you were done. I'd heard about this kind of head and how toilet paper was foreign to this culture. I planned to just wait for one of the two US-style toilets when it came time.

The bunks were functional but small. The mattresses were just two-inch foam with fabric stretched over it. We dragged out our blankets and hit the rack. After about twenty minutes the barracks were silent save for snoring.

The next few days were filled with briefings, classes, and lots of physical training. We also had at least one Scud alert each day, sometimes two or three. When the alert sounded, we all grabbed our gas masks, flak jackets, helmets, and ammo and ran to observation positions on the perimeter wall.

Those first few Scud alerts were scary as hell. For the first time in my life, I was in harm's way and it felt very real – much different than training. My heart felt like it was bouncing off the inside of my flak jacket and my panting would fog up my gas mask. I'd strain to hear over the loud thumping of my pulse, my panting, and the rushing in my ears. Then slowly I would relax. Everything would normalize and I would get so sleepy I could hardly keep my eyes open.

After the first few alerts where nothing happened, we stopped rushing to man the walls. The Marines from another unit that had guard duty on the wall had just laughed at us anyway. Word came down that when a Scud alert was called, we were simply to put on our gas mask, flak jacket, and helmet and go to our rooms. Soon Scud alerts started to seem more like drills. We'd wait in our rooms until the all-clear, get accountability for everyone, and then get back to business. I got pretty good at sleeping in my gas mask and helmet.

Among the Corporals in my room, we had many conversations about where we were going, when the war would really start, how long President Bush would give Saddam, etc. Truth was, we didn't really know anything.

There were a couple of guys who just wanted to go and fight. While guys like that are generally good to have on your side, that was not my feeling, and I didn't really like that attitude. Others voiced the opinion that the conflict was just about oil. While I felt there was some truth to this argument, I also felt that the atrocities by Hussein and his crew needed to be stopped. So even if the main goal was oil, it seemed to me that the war was worth it for humanitarian reasons.

Five or six platoons of ANGLICO had been in Saudi since late August. Most of the 2nd ANGLICO teams were working with US Army units to help them utilize Navy aircraft and USMC artillery. But ANGLICO was spread thin and the Army was screaming for more of us – they wanted an ANGLICO team with each battalion.

The 1st ANGLICO teams were working with units that comprised the Joint Forces Command East (JFCE). These units were from Saudi Arabia, Kuwait, Qatar, Oman, United Arab Emirates, Bahrain, Syria, Morocco, Spain, and the French Foreign Legion. Typical of ANGLICO units, they were doing more than providing liaison to supporting arms – they were also training the newly formed volunteer Kuwaiti units and providing communication to the US heavy Coalition headquarters. By most accounts, the ANGLICO units were instrumental in bringing these Coalition partners into the fold. Still, the 1st Marine Division was very nervous about having the Coalition units cover their eastern flank and wanted more density of ANGLICO teams in the JFCE.

We learned that we would be split up and that three of our teams would fall under 2nd ANGLICO and move to the "elbow" with the Army units there. (The "elbow," was the area on the southern border of Kuwait about fifty miles from the Persian Gulf, where the border turns west after a thirty-five mile north/south stretch.) The other four teams would fall under 1st ANGLICO and support the JFCE units. These units were responsible for the area from the Persian Gulf to approximately thirty-five miles west along the southern Kuwaiti border. When the ground war commenced, they would cover the right or eastern flank of the 1st Marine Division north to Kuwait City.

We were all a bit nervous about working with Arab forces. It was hard to know what to expect in terms of their training, discipline, or motivation. And to make things more confusing, JFCE units had equipment and vehicles from just about every major exporter of arms. We had been studying all the Soviet vehicles and weapons as threats, but now we were trying to get our heads around the fact that friendly forces would have the same equipment. We knew that this would make for some dangerous and confusing situations once the shooting started.

Meanwhile, we had been trying out the little bit of Arabic we had learned on garbagemen, truck drivers, and laundry attendants. But we soon learned they weren't even Arabs! Turns out most of the manual labor in Saudi Arabia was done by what we referred to as Third Country Nationals or TCNs from India, Sri Lanka, Bangladesh, Thailand, Myanmar, etc.

After a few days at Camp 5, about fifteen of us got sent down to the port in Jubail to help unload gear from the ships. We stayed in one of the enormous warehouses that was wall-to-wall cots. There must have been five hundred guys in each warehouse. I've never had so much trouble finding my own rack.

Huge pallets of cases of water bottles were everywhere. That was important because it was HOT! Most days it was over 110 degrees – an oven-baking dry heat that sapped us of our energy and appetite. Most of the time I felt half asleep – I didn't want to move, didn't want to do anything. White salt stains showed up on our clothing – the sweat evaporated so fast I never noticed being damp. And in the middle of the night, the warm breeze blowing across the desert was like a giant hair dryer. The bottled water was hot, too, but having a dehydration headache in those conditions was brutal, so we all forced ourselves to drink.

The days were long and tiring, and for the most part we were moving vehicles and shipping containers so another crew could hook them up to a crane and hoist them out. Typical to Marine Corps life, you go to school to learn a job, but then spend most of your time doing other jobs and just learn as you go. We joked that we should all get the longshoreman rating after that week.

By the time we returned to Camp 5 a few days later, we had started receiving some unit gear, including vehicles. Each team got one Humvee except the Brigade Air Teams, who got two. Keep in mind that each team had at least six guys. Humvees look big but they don't have much interior room, and only have four seats. Factor in individual gear plus team gear like radios, ammo, NBC suits, fuel and water cans, and boxes of MREs, and things get cramped pretty quick.

We immediately started working on ways to strap gear to the outside of the Humvees. We scored sheets of plywood and lashed them to the roll bars under the canvas tops so we could load gear on the roof. Concertina wire and cammie netting got lashed to the hood. We cut little slits in the canvas sides and tied loops of wire or paracord through them so we could hang our packs down the sides. After several days all the vehicles looked like something out of *The Grapes of Wrath*.

By now it was mid-January and we were all aware of President Bush's January 17 deadline. We were ready to move out and join the other ANGLICO teams up on the border. One by one, the teams were getting their assignments and moving out. We were assured that our gear would be fine at Camp 5, so we each only took a pack with us. That meant a hygiene kit, three or four pairs of skivvies and socks, a couple pieces of snivel gear, and maybe a little bit extra chow. It had started to cool off and were all wishing we had brought some warmer gear. When it's one hundred degrees in the daytime, seventy-five degrees at night feels downright cold.

About half the teams had rolled out by January 16. The rest of us sat around that evening, trying to find some news on the radio. We wondered if the deadline would be moved again as it had been postponed from January 15 to 17 already. At around 0200. the next morning, we were awakened by the sounds of aircraft flying north over our heads. Cheers went up all across the camp. I could even hear cheers from the other nearby camps.

Within the hour, we could hear the concussions of the bombing taking place fifty miles north of us. This became the norm for the next few nights. We heard aircraft flying overhead and the distant thumps of their payloads hitting their targets.

To me the start of the air war was a relief. No more waiting or wondering – it was really happening. It also signaled to Hussein and the rest of the world that when pushed, the United States would not back down. And it meant that when we finally did move into Kuwait, there would be much less enemy to contend with. I was confident that US military airpower would put a significant dent in the forces facing us to the north. Little did I know how significant that dent would be.

Even after six months of buildup, we still didn't have good maps. The most commonly available map was a JOG-AIR map, with 1:250,000 scale. That was great for pilots, but not so great for those of us on the ground. For targeting, we preferred and usually worked with 1:50,000 scale maps, where one inch on the map represents 0.8 miles on the ground – which is much better for when you need to find roads or buildings.

Also, most of the maps were based on data from the 1940s. In fifty years many of the dunes and sabkhas (marshy area) and wadis (sand wash or old riverbeds) had changed significantly. And of course the man-made features had changed dramatically.

Finally, there was the classic military supply situation. The S-2 Intel department was responsible for dispensing maps, but they were classic rice bowlers and never wanted to give anything away. Imagine going to 7-Eleven to get a Slushy but the clerk won't sell it to you because then he wouldn't have one to sell to someone else. So basically I had to cajole a bit and do a few favors to get our team some outdated maps meant for the Air Force.

A few days later, it was my team's turn to head out. We had eight on our team and two Humvees so we were more comfortable than teams that had to cram six into one Humvee. Pat Tule and I were the drivers. We went over our vehicles and lists a hundred times. And Maj Sheffield must have gone over our list an additional hundred times.

"Did you check the fuel cans? Are they all full?"

"Yes, Sir."

"How about the water cans?"

"Yes, Sir."

"Got every battery you could lay your hands on?"

"Yes, Sir."

"Do we have ammo already loaded?"

"Yes, Sir."

"Is it where we can get to it easily?"

"Yes, Sir, it is strapped in the middle right behind the radios."

"Do you have your frequency lists?"

"Yes, Sir. Right here, custom laminated with the plastic I brought."

"Maps?"

"Just this crappy one I talked the intel guys out of."

"Yeah, that's the best one we have so far."

Finally, we rolled out the gate and headed north in our mini convoy of two Humvees, looking to join up with the Kuwaiti "Al Fatah Brigade."

Game on.

Chapter 10

Moving North

The Kuwaiti-Saudi border was defined by a tall sand berm. It was about ten feet high and wide enough to drive a vehicle on top. The berm wasn't continuous – there were gaps, and in some places there were two berms. It also wasn't the legally defined border, but with the lack of reference in the flat landscape, it was considered the border. An Iraqi obstacle belt of oil-filled trenches, land mines, concertina wire, pits with spikes, and other nasty stuff was reported to be just north of the berm. So when someone said they were going "up to the berm," it meant they were getting closer to the action.

An assortment of small buildings stood at odd intervals along the berm. These "police stations" varied in size, but generally were four- or six-room, flat-roofed, cinder block buildings. Sometimes they were two stories, and sometimes they consisted of a collection of three or four buildings. We'd heard that the berms and police stations had been built by the Saudis in the early '80s to combat the drug flow from Kuwait into Saudi Arabia. Several coalition teams had set up in police stations on the berm to observe the Iraqis to the north, and rumor had it that a few of them had actually called air strikes and artillery missions on enemy vehicles.

We learned that our team was going to reinforce a 1st ANGLICO team that had been operating five miles south of the berm for the past six months. It was disappointing to learn that we would be playing a supporting role. But we were still working off the original intel on the size and experience of the Iraqi army, so we figured that when the war started there would still be plenty of action to go around.

We headed out with sketchy directions and a new Magellan GPS device velcroed to the dash – basically just a green box with a location readout. You could plug in coordinates and it would give you a heading. Or you could just set it to display your current location. But there were no maps, overhead views, or turn-by-turn directions like we have today.

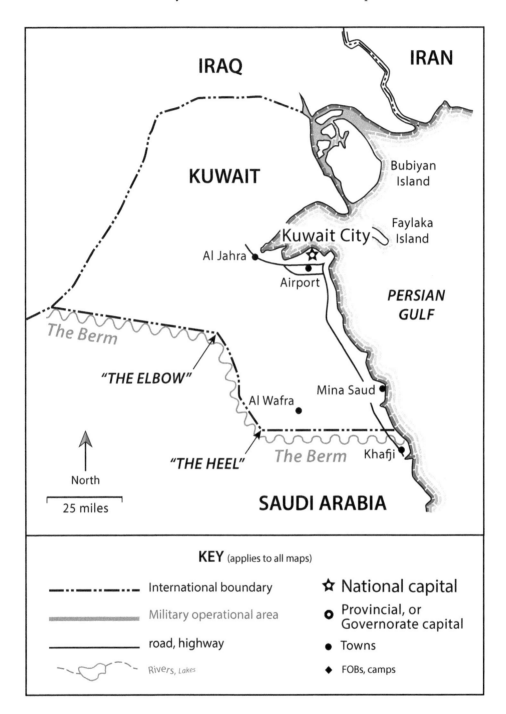

I was driving with Navy Lt Commander (LCDR) Moore in the right seat. He had the directions and was messing with the GPS. Sgt Miller and PFC Fillerton were in the back seats. Tuler was driving with Maj Sheffield behind us with Gunny Falkner and PFC Chu in the back.

The first ten miles or so were on Highway 1 along the coast, which was slightly elevated and one lane each way. Every mile or so there was a mangled wreck of a car on the shoulder. The wrecks were hardly recognizable as vehicles.

The directions told us to take a dirt road off the highway where a tailpipe was sticking up out of the ground. It sounded sketchy, but sure enough, a little ways down the road, we spotted a tailpipe sticking up out of the ground, muffler and all. Just past the tailpipe we saw where other vehicles had driven down the embankment and out onto the sand. We followed the tracks.

As I headed out into the sand, LCDR Moore yelled, "No No No! Not through the sabkha!" We had all been briefed about the sabkhas but I'd never seen one so I didn't know what I was looking for. A sabkha is like an almost dried-up lakebed. The surface sand is dry, but underneath the sand is wet and very soft. If the surface was thick enough, it formed a hard crust you could drive across – sometimes. But often the crust wasn't thick enough and a vehicle would sink to its axles. If the crust was thick enough to drive one vehicle across, it would not support a second vehicle, so you did not want to follow in previous tracks (in most terrain you'd follow tracks because of the landmine threat). I guessed that the sabkha was the slightly different colored sand and drove around it and picked up the track on the other side. Tuler followed me in the second Humvee but offset a couple of wheel widths just in case. We both successfully circumnavigated our first sabkha.

Then we were just driving across open desert, guided by our compass heading and occasionally seeing other vehicle tracks. The terrain was gentle rolling mounds – not quite hills but just big enough that you couldn't always see past them. LCDR Moore was working the GPS and giving me directions. It seemed like the GPS wasn't getting good signal from the satellites – it kept swinging the heading back and forth. We drove for several hours, zigzagging across the desert.

After a while someone called a tally on a large berm with a tan vehicle parked on top. LCDR had a quick conversation with Maj Sheffield on the radio then told me to head for that berm. It was great to finally have a reference point to drive toward!

As we got closer we could see that the berm was a large ring around a slight hill with V-150s (Fahd armored personnel carriers) of the Saudi National Guard positioned in the revetments inside the ring. As we got closer we could see the bulldozer marks left from pushing up the berm and making the revetments. There were several more tents and a few other vehicles.

We drove around the ring shape of the berm to the right and found the entrance. It had concertina wire across the front and was guarded by a Jeep with a machine gun mount. A hard-looking, dark-skinned soldier in strange desert cammies stood next to the Jeep. Sgt Miller said, "Those are the Moroccans!"

We had heard about the Moroccans and their simple but bold tactics. According to rumor, when the Moroccans attacked, they put their machine gun jeeps in a column and drove toward the enemy as fast as they could, with only the first few jeeps firing. If one of the front jeeps was hit or became disabled, the next jeep simply drove around it. Once through the enemy's defenses, the column would split, making ninety-degree turns left or right. Once the entire column was through the turn, they would turn back toward the enemy and attack back through the enemy. Generally the enemy would still be oriented in the original direction so the Moroccans would be attacking them from their rear. Gutsy moves.

The Moroccans also carried HK MP5s, a weapon we all lusted after. While it is a high-quality weapon, it really wasn't an ideal weapon for us. They are chambered in 9mm, which is useless for any distance, but it is a great weapon in an urban environment where most shots are twenty meters or less and there is less worry about the round penetrating a wall and hitting something you didn't intend to hit.

In any case, these Moroccans looked stoic and fearless and we were impressed.

Maj Sheffield walked up and did some "pointy talkie" with the gate guard, who pulled back the concertina wire and waved us through. We drove around a few small berms and pulled up at a large green canvas tent positioned about eight feet deep in a revetment with a berm around three sides. This was their command post.

The officers went inside and after a few minutes, came back out and directed us to another revetment, which had room for several vehicles next to a 16 x 32 tent with a wood floor. There was plenty of room for the eight of us and there were already twelve cots set up. This would be our home for the next few weeks. We pulled our gear out of the trucks and started to set up our housing area.

After we had gotten somewhat situated, Maj Sheffield had us gather by the front door. Five of our most junior guys would augment the other team's radio watches eight hours at a time. The other four not on radio watch would set up a couple of radios to communicate with our other teams, work on building a bunker, and maintain the vehicles. Maj Sheffield was planning on making some trips to check on the other teams and would need one of us to drive him. Between radio watch, one guy on the road with Maj Sheffield and the things we needed to set up, we would be staying fairly busy.

The next few days were spent getting snapped in with the 1st ANGLICO team and the ways of duty and life around the camp. The 1st ANGLICO guys were all active duty and they regarded us with a bit of disdain. Several of them referred to us as "tourists," which I found amusing. It was fairly accurate, though – we all had cameras tucked into our battle gear and often stopped to take pictures of stuff that was pretty mundane to them.

The 1st ANGLICO guys had been working hard since August but they were bored. There wasn't much of anything to do for entertainment, though I felt they lacked creativity. When I asked one of the guys which dunes were best for sledding, his eyes lit up and he said, "That's a great idea!" I couldn't believe they hadn't tried it already. With the revetments dug ten feet deep and the resulting sand pile stacked up fifteen feet or so, we had a good twenty-five-foot drop behind our tent that would be perfect for sledding.

Between duty and improving our defenses, Tule and I spent several hours one day amusing ourselves by sliding down the hill on various sleds we'd made out of MRE boxes. We even tried making some rudimentary skis. It was good for some laughs and we had a pretty good time just screwing around.

But most of the time we sat around listening to the radios, waiting for one of the teams on the berm to call in. There were hourly reports, four-hour reports, twelve-hour reports, etc., but since no one was really moving yet, they were pretty dull. Every now and then we had to go change batteries or do a little preventative maintenance on a piece of gear.

There were several new pieces of radio gear I hadn't seen or used and I was intrigued learning those. I particularly liked the tactical fax, which was pretty advanced for that time. It was basically a fax machine hooked up to the radio. It reduced errors because the message sender could write everything out in the message and fax it in, eliminating transmission, translation, and recording errors.

Every now and then there was a bit of excitement in the COC when one of the teams spotted something to shoot. They would talk straight to the firing agency, either aircraft or artillery, but we monitored and double-checked all their geometry, positioning, and targeting. Silence was consent, so we only spoke up if something didn't look right, and that was very rare. Occasionally, they would have trouble talking to another agency and we would relay information back and forth. Every time there was a "cleared hot" (aircraft) or "fire for effect" (artillery) we fist-pumped or high-fived. This wasn't often but when it did happen we were amped up for hours afterwards. We could always hear when artillery shot and sometimes we could even hear the aircraft ordnance impacts. Sometimes after dark, you could see light flashes on the horizon looking north. It reminded us that this was real and that there was a war on.

We didn't interact with the Kuwaitis and Saudis very much, but occasionally I would have some reason to go ask them for fuel or something and they would always want to sit down and have tea first. I enjoyed that. They had tents very similar to ours but usually just had a few carpets on the ground inside. They'd invite you in to sit while someone went and got a tray of tea. We'd talk about families, show each other pictures, talk about jobs, schools, movies, music – all kinds of stuff.

A few times we were invited for dinner. Everyone would sit on the edges of the carpet and they would place a large silver tray in the center, piled high with rice and bits of meat and vegetables. I watched them eat first to figure out what I was supposed to do. You made a scoop shape with your right hand (never the left; that's the "dirty" hand!) and scooped a handful out of the pile. Then you just just sat back and ate out of your hand. It was a very communal meal experience. The meat was pretty tender but didn't taste quite like any other meat I'd had – turns out it was goat meat. The rumors I'd heard about the eyes being a delicacy offered to the guests was true – and they weren't too bad once you got past the fear of putting eyeballs in your mouth.

I got to be friends with a Kuwaiti Corpsman who had gone to medical school in Chicago. He spoke English better than me. He had a striking resemblance to Magic Johnson. He was a lot smaller, slighter of build, but his facial structure and coloring looked a lot like Magic. On a few occasions we sat on the pile of sand behind the tents sipping tea or Kool-Aid. One night I asked him about the rumor we had heard that Muslims just wanted to die for Allah. He said that was bullshit! He didn't want to die at all. If he did die, he wanted it to be in service of Allah but that didn't mean he wanted to die. I could connect with that. That wasn't so strange.

Another night I asked, "Hey, do you know who Magic Johnson is?"

"Sure, LA Lakers!"

"Anyone ever tell you you look a bit like him?"

"Yes, I've been told that frequently. That's why I wear this…" He rolled down the brim of his worn purple beanie, and there was an LA Lakers patch!

While we were back at Camp 5, I had written several letters to family, to friends, and even to the dorm at Cal Poly. My mother had passed out my address to the entire church, a female friend had given it to the members of her sorority, and the RA in the dorms had posted my address on the bulletin board. Of course, my close friends were sending me stuff, too. Soon I started getting all kinds of mail. The way military mail works, it piles up somewhere in the system until it reaches some critical mass, then gets sent out. So you only got mail two or three times a week, but when you do, you get several days' worth. If you were disciplined, you opened a couple items and then spaced the rest out for a few days.

I got some pretty cool stuff in the mail. Lots of people had asked what we wanted or needed and it was the usual list: drink mix (to keep the high intake of water from being so boring), AA batteries (for flashlights, field razors, and of course Gameboys and Walkmans), beef jerky or other non-melting snacks, pantyhose and small balloons (to protect equipment from the sand), magazines, and of course baby wipes. Since we were taking field showers (pouring a water can over your head) baby wipes were critical.

A few things I added were cotton swabs and one-inch paintbrushes for cleaning weapons and radios. The sorority from SDSU sent me a box of five hundred Q-tips with little messages and hearts written on each one! Then there were the boxes and boxes of candy, snacks, and drink mix. I had more AA batteries than I could use in a lifetime – but that worked out well because we had started using batteries as currency.

Soon Maj S wanted to start making trips to visit our other teams. I'd check in with the teams on the radio the night before to ask what they needed. Then I'd prepare a care package out of the pile of supplies.

Our first visit was to Wild Eagle Two Eight out in the elbow. They were supporting Task Force Troy. Named for the city that received the Trojan Horse, Task Force Troy was made up of members of Marines, British Army, and the 4th Psychological Operations Group (Airborne). They only had five tanks and a few wheeled vehicles, but with inflatables, fake tanks, and arty pieces spaced all around, they appeared to be a 460-man unit. To top it off, psyops would drive around with loudspeakers playing the sounds of vehicles driving and helos landing and taking off.

Wild Eagle Two Eight was very thankful for the goodies. One Sgt there gave me a badly needed haircut. He had a hair clipper that ran on AAs – his price for a haircut was one AA battery.

On some of these visits to other teams, we would stay overnight. When that happened, I did all I could to help out. Sometimes I would pull a radio watch or sometimes just clean and repair radio gear. Soon it seemed that I was away more than I was back with my team.

Chapter 11

Up to the Berm

Wild Eagle Two Five was just a few miles south of the berm, and they seemed to get into more action than anyone else. They had been doing patrols up to the berm at night and spotting for targets. They had even called artillery on some enemy vehicles. Maj S took both Chu and me there one time and left me with them for a few days.

So it was with Eagle Two Five that I finally got to go out to one of the police stations on the berm. I was excited, nervous, and a little scared. I was more nervous that I wouldn't do the right thing or be in the right place or screw something up than I was scared about meeting the enemy. It's always a strange feeling when part of you is hoping to get into a fight and part of you is scared to get into a fight.

We went through our gear, did our PCIs (pre-combat inspections) and PCCs (pre-combat checks) on everything, but focused on the radios, weapons, vehicles and the MULE (modular universal laser equipment) used to help direct laser-guided munitions from aircraft into their target.

About an hour after sunset we loaded into the vehicles and headed north. They had a Humvee and a M113 armored personnel carrier. Peterson and the captain were up front in the Hummvee and I was in back. Everyone else was riding in the M113.

We followed the 113, driving slowly. The driver of the 113 had the team's only pair of NVGs so Peterson was just following the little Cateye light on the back of the 113. I covered the left side of the vehicle but all I could see was black.

When we got close to the berm we stopped and called the Special Forces guys, who had recently occupied the place, so we wouldn't surprise them. Made sense to me! A few minutes later, the Captain jumped back in the truck and we took the lead up to the berm.

The police station was a flat-roofed cinderblock building with another small building to the west. Most of it was one story, but about a third of it had a second story, making it look like a small castle. There were two

Humvees parked at the bottom of the berm right next to a ramp that went up to the police station. Peterson backed into the berm next to the other two Humvees while the 113 drove up the ramp and pulled up on the north side of the building. We grabbed our gear and walked up the ramp.

As we got to the top, I got my first glimpse into Kuwait. It was pretty dark and there weren't any features to see, but it looked just like everything else I had seen in Saudi Arabia. I couldn't see any obstacles or ditches.

Thompson and Howsen started setting up the MULE on the roof of the 113. Sgt Shue came out and directed me to set up the HF radio with a longwire antenna to talk back to Brigade.

I ran a longwire antenna from the top of the ladderwell down to the ground between the Humvees, then ran a coax cable from the top back down to the 113. I hooked into the HF radio and got a quick radio check back with Brigade, then updated our position with them. Soon everyone had their tasks completed and we were all set up.

Two of the Special Forces guys came down and introduced themselves as Bob and Tom. That was new to me. I'd always been introduced to other military guys by rank and last name or maybe even an MOS or job title thrown in. But these guys were Bob and Tom. Typical of Special Forces, they were wearing tri-color cammies but had on personal boots and ball caps. One guy had a shemagh (Arabic scarf) wrapped around his neck. They both had weapons that weren't issued to any standard forces. Basically it was like they were straight out of the movies and they seemed to play it up a bit. I didn't really have any problem with it – in fact, I was a bit jealous. They asked about our missions, experience, and jobs but never offered any info back and didn't really answer any of the questions we asked them. I asked them how many were on their team there tonight and Bob replied, "We've got a few operators here."

Sgt Shue had a watch schedule worked out. Two would be on watch, one on the radio and one spotting through the MULE thermal sights. We would rotate every two hours. Peterson and Foust had first watch, Thompson and I would have second. I was starting to come down off the adrenaline I had built up on the drive and felt like I could sleep. I lay down with my sleeping bag draped over me, my flak jacket on the ground under my hip and my pack as a pillow.

I swear I had just fallen asleep when there was a loud "WHOMP!"

I threw off my sleeping bag, pulled on my vest and helmet, and grabbed my rifle. Sgt Shue was already up and on top of the vehicle talking with Foust. Everyone else was gearing up.

Shue told us that artillery was impacting about 800 meters to our north. I got on the radio to Brigade to see if friendly arty was shooting near us. Brigade said no friendlies were shooting, but they were starting to hear some radio chatter. I told them the impacts were just north of us and that we'd update them when we had more info.

"WHOMP, WHOMP, WHOMP!" Several more rounds impacted to our north. This time I saw the flashes from the impacts.

Shue started working up an arty mission to counterfire but he didn't have a good enough location yet. Peterson and Foust were scanning with thermals and binos to see if they could see anything. I got on the radio back to the DASC (Direct Air Support Center) to see if they had any aircraft that could come help us out.

"WHOMP WHOMP WHOMP WHOMP!" Four more impacts, still to our north but closer than the last. It was loud and felt like someone was punching me in the chest. Shue was getting a little worked up. Based on the two sets of impacts and the flash on the horizon when they fired, he could now estimate their position.

There was another series of impacts, this time behind us. That was worrisome because it meant the Iraqis had us bracketed. All they had to do was drop half the elevation they had added and they would be dropping steel rain right on us! Shue called in an immediate arty mission based on his estimated plot of the enemy position.

Meanwhile, I could hear some activity on the roof. Then all of the sudden the Special Forces guys came running down the ladderwell and dashed straight to their Humvees hollering, "You better get the hell out of here!" They fired up their vehicles, switched on their headlights, and went blazing south across the desert. We all started laughing. Watching their headlights bounce across the desert and out of view, they seemed just like the Keystone Cops.

Sgt Shue gave the "fire when ready" command into the VHF radio on top of the 113. This let the arty guys know that we needed these rounds going downrange as soon as possible.

We were on pins and needles for a couple minutes. Shue relayed some of the info he was getting on the radio. "TOF 15" meant that the time of flight for the arty rounds was fifteen seconds. "Shot" meant they were firing. And then there was a faint "thump thump thu-thump thu-thump" to our southwest. Shue said, "Rounds complete," which meant they had fired all the rounds he had asked for. Sure enough, about fifteen seconds later, we could see and hear the impacts a few miles to our north. Peterson asked Shue how many rounds they'd fired. Shue replied "Battery one," meaning six guns of the battery, each firing one round for a total of six rounds. Peterson insisted he saw more than six explosions on the thermals.

"We must have hit something because I saw at least ten explosions," he said. "Some of them must have been secondaries."

The captain was confident we wouldn't hear any more from the Iraqi arty. We all took off our helmets, scratched our heads, and breathed a big sigh of relief. This was my first close contact. On one hand it seemed pretty impersonal, just lobbing arty rounds at each other like that. But I had been picturing the spotter, the loaders, and the gunners of the Iraqi arty and it didn't feel impersonal at all to me.

We sent out several reports to various agencies to summarize the action. I got the target grid from Shue and gave the SPOTREP back to Brigade, then talked to the DASC to see if they could have someone fly over the target grid and see what was there. All of our reports ended with an unsatisfying, "Current Enemy Disposition: unknown."

The captain had gone back up to the roof of the building and hollered back down to us that the Special Forces guys had left all their gear! We had another good laugh at their expense. They had really bugged out. We were astounded that they had left radios with cryptological gear. Marines get threatened with jail time for stuff like that! We packed their kit up and put it in the back of the Humvee, chuckling the whole time. Shue told me that after we cleaned their gear tomorrow, he was going to put a ribbon on it and take it back to them. I looked at their radios as we were loading them into the vehicles and it was not the same stuff we had. I would have liked to have kept it and played with it a bit. It was some high-speed stuff.

We set back with me and Thompson on watch while everyone else bedded down for a bit. I was glad to be on watch because I was too amped up to sleep. But after thirty minutes, that wore off.

Thompson and I debated the security of staying put. We both agreed that it was not a good thing that the enemy seemed to know we were there. We couldn't fathom how the spotters had seen us but figured maybe the intel was wrong and they did have night vision devices. Or maybe they had plotted the police station the previous day and just fired on the building, figuring someone would likely occupy it at night.

After about forty-five minutes, we traded places – I got on the thermal sights and Thompson took over the radio. I sat on my helmet and peered through the sights, scanning back and forth out to the north. I could see some thermal variations that looked like small scrub brush. Then after a couple minutes I saw some bright white spots! That was definitely heat. Then one of them moved! My adrenaline started flowing again.

"Thompson, come here, look at this! There is someone moving around out there!"

"Really?"

"Yeah, four or five of them. Wait, no – six out there."

"Okay, let me see."

I scooted back so he could get behind the MULE.

"Oh shit, man, that's mice!"

"Mice?" I said.

"Yeah, the magnification is throwing you off. I saw that the first night and thought the same thing."

He went back to the radio and I sat back down behind the MULE. As I watched the movements of the white spots I began to see that he was right. I could tell from the way they moved that they were small rodents scampering from bush to bush.

The rest of our watch was quiet and for the last thirty minutes it was really hard to keep my eyes open. I was glad to see my watch turn 0400, which meant it was time to switch.

We woke everyone else up. Shue and the captain decided it was time to head back. We packed everything up, made sure we didn't leave anything behind, then retraced our tracks to the camp.

The next morning we turned to cleaning weapons, radios, and the rest of the gear. After I had cleaned the Special Forces radios, I handed them over to Sgt Shue, who promptly disappeared with them. When he got back, I was cleaning the antennas. He came and sat down next to me.

"Hesterman, I was wrong about you."

"Whadda ya mean, Sergeant?"

"Well, back in Lejeune, I thought you were a worthless piece of shit."

I was so surprised I didn't know what to say.

"You did great last night. I just wanted you to know I noticed and I'll trust you from now on. Some of the other guys were about to flip out last night and you were on task and getting stuff done without me telling you to."

It was great that he seemed to think highly of me now, but I hadn't been aware that he thought I was such a turd before. It did, however, explain some of the "one-sided" conversations we'd had in Lejeune. I also wasn't aware of anyone who was about to freak out the night before. I wondered who he was referring to.

After we finished cleaning the gear, we took a small lunch break to eat an MRE. Then we started prepping for that night's mission. Someone cranked up the newly released AC/DC album *Thunderstruck* on a cassette player and we started getting amped up. Six guys in a sand ditch, weapons and equipment spread out on ponchos, unloading and reloading magazines, checking batteries, loading frequencies and crypto fills into radios, repacking rucksacks – even someone sharpening a big knife. All the while, AC/DC was blaring through cheap speakers across the desert.

We never did hear if we had hit anything with that artillery mission.

Chapter 12

Lost in the Desert

The next few days and nights blurred together. Each night we patrolled up to one of the police stations on the berm. We'd park the vehicles seven hundred meters or so to the south of the police station and proceed on foot. We'd stack on the southern window or door, then bust through and clear the building from top to bottom. Someone would bring the vehicles up and we'd spend the night making radio checks and staring into the darkness to the north.

We never saw anything but desert rats scuttling from bush to bush. And we never found anything more than piles of trash and debris in the police stations. I was always surprised at the sheer quantity of garbage – an old boot, stinky articles of clothing, broken desks and chairs, small chunks of concrete, a couple of ripped mattresses, plastic bags, etc. Sometimes the trash would be knee deep.

It was cold now and I was already wearing everything I had. I kept my flak jacket on for the warmth even though it made my back ache. I started doing my watches wearing my sleeping bag. I'd cinch the hood tight around my face with the top two snaps done, then skip a snap so my forearms stuck out holding my weapon, then more snaps done up to my knees. The foot of the sleeping bag dragged behind me like some fat, shapeless tail. I'm sure I looked like something from Alice in Wonderland – a giant demented green worm with an M-16. It kept me warm, though, and if needed, I could simply push my arms out to my sides, pop all the snaps, and shrug my shoulders to be free and ready to fight.

One night we decided to mix it up a little to avoid being predictable. We planned to patrol to a spot on the berm about midway between two police stations and set up an OP on the berm for about six hours.

Foust, Thompson, and I rode in the back of the M113. We had the top hatch open so we could stick our heads out (and avoid some of the exhaust). When standing on the floor, the roof was about neck high.

This was fine when traveling on smooth surfaces, but while going cross country through the desert it took both hands on the edge of the hatch to keep from slamming my throat against it.

I was monitoring the Tactical Air Request Net and updating the DASC with our positions as we moved. I was doing my best to hear other teams and aircraft talking about other missions, and tried to keep our SA (situational awareness) fairly high – not always easy while riding in the back of a 26,000-pound, diesel-powered, tracked, armored personnel carrier.

I could still look over my rifle sights comfortably, although I really couldn't see much out across the desert. It was pretty dark and we were driving slowly on blackout lights. Every now and then we would cross vehicle tracks but that really didn't tell us anything. We drove along with the Humvee out front for an hour or so. I didn't mind driving slow because it kept down the dust and the cold wind. I was still freezing.

After a while we stopped and Sgt Shue jumped out of the gunner's turret and ran up to the Humvee to converse with the Captain. Then he jumped back in and we continued. I kept glancing forward expecting to see the berm emerge from the darkness but it never did.

At the next stop, Sgt Shue hollered back to us to set out 360 security. Without a word, Howsen climbed from the driver's seat to the gunner's turret and swung the 50-cal out to the right. I jumped out and went about ten meters straight back from the vehicle and laid down, watching our "six." Foust went ten meters out to the left and Thompson went up to split the front with Peterson, who was driving the Humvee. Shue and the Captain sat in the Humvee talking, looking at the map and the Magellan.

Time seemed to creep by. I couldn't see anything while lying down so I got up to one knee with my left elbow on my left knee propping up my rifle. It seemed that I could see another ten meters or so. I could just make out the horizon because the sky was a bit lighter than the ground but there was absolutely no detail to pick out. I hadn't heard anything on the radio in a while so I got a quick whispered radio check with the DASC. We had just driven up in two loud diesel vehicles so I didn't really need to whisper, but it seemed like the right thing to do tactically. The DASC heard me loud and clear so I had that covered. I just continued to visually scan the blackness out in front of me.

After an indeterminable period of time, Shue came trotting back to the 113 and gave the mount up call in a hushed voice. We all returned to our original positions in the 113. That's when Shue confirmed what we were starting to suspect.

"Listen up. Something isn't right. We are going to head due south from here for a few minutes until we hit Runner Road (an east-west vehicle track that parallels the berm a few miles to the south), recage, and then head up to the berm from there." His confident tone kept us from feeling like we were really lost, just "momentarily disoriented."

We cranked up the vehicles and headed south. Our previous tracks faded off to the left and we were in the void of the empty desert again, with no reference points. But at least now we were headed back to a friendly area instead of toward Saddam's juggernaut.

My fear of being lost out in the desert was that if we did get into a firefight, we couldn't direct any supporting arms (aircraft or artillery). You can't tell someone where to shoot if you don't even know where you are.

The terrain was exactly the same as it had been all night – flat, windswept sand with a dotting of small scrub brush. Suddenly a large shape loomed ahead of us. At first glance it seemed to be a shape directly in front of us, but soon it was recognizable as a large berm perpendicular to our path. My first thought was we had stumbled on another combat outpost and I was concerned that Saudis or Kuwaitis on the other side of this berm would shoot the living crap out of the unknown vehicles coming out of the darkness from the north.

As we crept closer I could see that this was not like the little scraped-up berms around the combat outposts. This was bigger and more solid. It was not just a pile of sand. This was THE berm! We were on the north side of THE berm! We had been driving around in Kuwait this whole time! If we weren't on our highest level of alert before, we were now!

We pulled up to the base of the berm. The Captain scrambled up and laid down, peering over the the top. After a few seconds, he stood up and scanned the horizon. Then he hopped back down and jumped back in the Humvee.

The Humvee turned left and paralleled the berm. We followed. I scanned to the left of the vehicle, toward the north, but I kept glancing forward and behind me up at the top of the berm. That was bad discipline because my job was observing the left side. But I was convinced that either we were going to drive into mines or someone was going to light us up from on top of the berm.

We continued on for a tense mile or so and then the berm just suddenly faded away. It was as if a giant housekeeper with an enormous broom had flicked the pile of sand back out into the desert. There was only a small hump now – resembling a small sand dune. We banged a hard right over the hump and resumed our southward drive.

A strange feeling washed over me. I kept saying to myself, "Can you believe that shit?" It was a huge relief but there remained a feeling of dread for what might have happened. It seems that on our initial turn north, we were off in our azimuth a few degrees to the west and by stupid chance stumbled through a break in the berm. In the dark, no one recognized the hump as remnants of the berm. Based on travel time, the Captain recognized something wasn't right and brought us back due south, which is where we bumped into the north side of the berm.

We continued south to Runner Road and then straight back to our outpost. We set back into our revetment, cleaned and stowed the gear, and hit the rack. I was finally snuggled up in my sleeping bag, warm for the first time since the previous day. No one had spoken of our little adventure. The Captain headed off to debrief the trip and Shue left us alone after telling us to get the gear taken care of and to hit the rack.

I lay there in my sleeping bag with the hood cinched around my face so that only my nose stuck out, with my rifle poking my ribs inside the bag with me. My flak jacket was draped over me and I was still wearing the same clothes I'd been wearing for three days straight. My closed eyes burned from how tired I was, but my mind was racing. I thought I'd never get to sleep. I kept thinking of what might have happened. I was amazed that we hadn't seen any mines or oil-filled trenches or any of the nasty obstacles that Intel had told us about. It was the first evidence I'd had that maybe the intel we had wasn't so accurate. All these thoughts whirled through my mind, entwining and raising more questions, and I just wanted to sleep.

Chapter 13

Point Man

I always took crap for wearing a KA-BAR knife inverted on the left front strap of my battle harness. I think most guys gave me shit because they were jealous they hadn't done it first. I used several wraps of green riggers tape around the scabbard and always made sure the pommel strap was fastened so it didn't fall out. Wearing a KA-BAR on your battle harness has its roots in the serious fights of history when getting into a knife fight in combat was a real possibility. But with the weapons systems and sensors of the 1990s, getting into a knife fight was highly unlikely. It was kind of showy to wear my knife there and I would admit that the most use my knife would ever get was opening an MRE bag. But a good knife is a valuable tool, and I wouldn't dream of going to the field without it.

The next trip up to the berm started like all the others. *Thunderstruck* blared from the tiny little speakers on the boom box while we unloaded, cleaned, and reloaded magazines, weapons, radios, NVGs, etc. Then we gathered around the captain on the ramp of the 113 just before sunset to get the final brief. We were headed to one of the police stations we'd been to previously. No one had been there in a couple days. We were going to clear it as usual except this time, I was going to get to lead the stack. I was amped.

The point man is usually the one who triggers the booby trap or the ambush, but it's a Marine bravado thing to be the first one and I'd been looking forward to getting my chance. It meant I got to wear one of the two pairs of NVGs for the night. It also meant I didn't have to hump a radio – the problem with being good with radios is that you always have to carry one.

The drive up went much the same and we parked the vehicles just inside a click south of the police station. It was a little lighter that night – maybe because the overcast was thinner – and we could see the moon and some stars. We dismounted the vehicles and I double-checked my NVG adjustments. I could see the outline of the mini castle of the police station on the horizon. I stayed on one knee in front of the Humvee for a few minutes watching the police station for movement. Thompson was next to me, my battle buddy for this go-round. Howsen and Peterson were staying with the vehicles and the rest were fanned out to our sides. In a hushed tone, the Captain said, "Whenever you are ready, Hesty."

I stood up and started my patrol walk toward the station. I watched the building outline carefully as I approached, then scanned down at the blurry ground in front of me. I walked in a slow, deliberate pace, placing my feet by starting with the outside of my heel, then rolling down the outside of my boot and then across the balls of my feet. I scanned the building, looked where my next footstep would land, then made a quick glance left and right back to the next Marine. The entire time, I had the rifle pointed at the building. Ten meters to my left, Thompson was doing the same thing. His distance was perfect because that was right where things came into focus with my NVGs. When I scanned over his way, I could see his facial expressions.

It was slow going but everything was nice and quiet and after a few minutes we stacked up at the bottom of the berm. I looked left and right to make sure everyone was in position, then gave Thompson the exaggerated double nod. He followed me up the berm as soon as I started moving. The berm was only six or eight feet high and the slope was fairly gentle. As soon as we cleared the edge, we covered the five meters to the south wall of the building, scanning the large window, then the roofline, the edges of the building, then back to the window.

The window was a black hole against the light-colored cinder blocks. It was about six feet wide and the bottom would be even with my gut if I were to stand straight up. There wasn't anything in the window. I crouched on the ground two feet from the wall, at the right edge of the window with my rifle pointed up. Thompson was in the same crouch under the left edge of the window, facing the left corner of the building. As Foust came up to the building, Thompson rotated to cover the window and Foust put his back to Thompson's, facing the corner. Simultaneously, the captain and Shue were doing the same thing behind me.

A double pat on my shoulder told me Captain and Shue were ready behind me. Thompson gave me a blurry left-handed thumbs-up. I did a quick leg extension to peek through the window and then dropped back to my crouch. I paused just a second to let what I saw sink in. The doorway was opposite the window and was open and clear. There was the usual debris on the floor but it was out of focus. That's about all I'd been able to take in.

I gave Thompson the double nod. He was on his left knee with his right foot on the ground giving me a step with his right knee. In one motion I stood up, put my left foot on Thompson's knee and left hand on his helmet, sprung up, and swung my right leg up and into the window. I half-rolled my back and butt across the sill and swung my legs down beneath me as I dropped down to a crouch inside.

I had intended to bounce off the inside wall and immediately run to the left corner. But I miscalculated the distance to the wall, so when I leaned back to push off it, I rocked back on my heels and lost my center of gravity. I was struggling to regain my balance when someone grabbed me from my right. A blurry hand was on my rifle and another hand gripped my right bicep. As I attempted to turn and face my threat, I slid down the wall and rolled onto my back. My attacker rolled on top of me and we wrestled with my rifle.

I couldn't see anything but flashes of green and dark green through my NVGs. I considered attempting a head butt but couldn't because of the way I was pinned on the floor. I wanted to punch him but I didn't want to let go of my weapon – a cardinal sin in the Marine Corps. It seemed that we wrestled for an eternity, pushing and thrusting back and forth with my rifle. Then I realized my KABAR was just inches from my right hand.

I released my grip on my rifle and in one motion, pulled down on my knife and thrust immediately back up and out. I thrust where I imagined the bottom of the attacker's ribcage would be. The resistance to my thrust gave way so quickly that at first thought I had missed. But the guttural moan that I both felt and heard, and the warmth running down my hand and arm, told me otherwise.

I was really pissed. Pissed and confused. I was supposed to be in the corner ready to fire on anyone coming through the door. Instead I was lying on my back, knees drawn up, with someone on top of me and I didn't even have proper control of my rifle.

I was on my second or third shove and twist – not really drawing the knife out, just pushing in harder – when my attacker was lifted off of me and disappeared like a rag doll through the window.

I scrambled to my feet and ran to the corner of the room. I sheathed the knife and got my right hand back on the pistol grip with my finger along the trigger well. A Marine dropped through the window and went to the right corner and then another came to my corner. I crossed to the next corner and then slid along the wall to the door. I was at the edge of the door frame, just off the wall. I choked up on my rifle like a batter going to bunt to keep it pointed through the doorway but not protrude through the doorway.

The rushing in my ears started to fade and I could begin to hear again. I heard a "Go!" from behind me. I crossed through the door headed for the right-hand corner this time, clearing in front of me and to the left.

We cleared the rest of the building without incident. No one else was there. We consolidated on the roof as usual and the captain told me to keep watch from the roof while everyone else brought the vehicles up and got set up.

As I stood there peering into the green darkness, everything started to sink in. I felt like I was covered in blood and really wanted to turn on my flashlight to see. But tactically that was a really bad idea so I just stood there staring out into the darkness, trying to shrink back from my clothing so the wetness wouldn't touch me.

After they got all set up, the Captain came back up to the roof and we sat down and talked for a bit. We didn't really talk about what had just happened, but I thought he was trying to determine if I knew how badly I had screwed up. I didn't apologize exactly, but I tried to let him know that I would be where I was supposed to be at all times. He told me I had nothing to worry about, that everything was fine and I should go back down and get in the watch rotation. As I walked down the ladderwell, the adrenaline wore off and I got a bad case of the quakey knees. I had to use the handrail and take one step at a time.

The other guys asked me how I was. It was kind of surreal – I don't remember what I said but I'm pretty sure we were having two completely different conversations. I finally got a chance to use my flashlight to check out how bloody I was. I was surprised and relieved to find that there wasn't much blood, mostly on my right sleeve and a bit on the front of my flak jacket. Thompson got a water can out and helped me wash it out. Then I cleaned my knife really well.

The rest of the night was fairly normal except I was in a bit of a fog. Nothing else happened, and around 0300 we packed up and returned to the outpost.

I never talked about what happened with those guys again. It wasn't until later that I began to ask myself the hard questions. I considered all kinds of scenarios. The most likely was that my attacker had been an Iraqi deserter who had camped out in the police station, waiting for the right time to walk south. Because I was wearing NVGs, I never really saw him, and in some ways that was a relief. When the stories about the conscripts and threatened families came out, I felt even worse about it.

I also thought about how it is every young Marine's wet dream to clear a building in enemy territory and kill with your bare hands. But the reality of it is something very different – something that no one would ever wish for.

I don't like this story. Through all the years, I never told my family about it. I probably told only three or four friends about it, only after three or four beers too many.

Chapter 14

Khafji

Next I was assigned to assist Wild Eagle 22. Their compound was located about twenty miles south of the border and about fifteen miles west of the coast. They were technically SALT Bravo (Supporting Arms Liaison Team "b"), but several of the guys on the team were overweight by USMC standards, so we affectionately referred to them as SALT Belly.

I didn't mention the knife incident to anyone. I tried to not think about it. Staying busy helped and I managed to occupy myself working on the radios and Humvees. There was always something to fix or improve. Still, from time to time I did think about the guy I had stabbed. I kept going through different scenarios, thinking about who the guy was and what he was doing there. I kept thinking that if somehow the situation had been different, he would have surrendered and lived. It's hard to explain, but somehow I felt more apologetic to his family than to him. I didn't know if he had a family but I imagined that there was someone. There always is.

After a few days, reports started coming in from teams along the border that were having contact with the enemy. These reports started from the "elbow" but slowly worked their way east along the berm. Some teams simply heard mechanized forces to the north, while others could actually see them. And several teams were taking and returning fire.

It was confusing and hard to put all the pieces together as the reporting trickled in. At first, it sounded like a large Iraqi mechanized force was driving along the border west to east and randomly engaging the teams in the police stations. But soon it became apparent that there were multiple enemy forces pushing across several places on the border.

Given our distance from the berm, we weren't in any immediate danger. But we did have a few buddies up there and recognized some of the voices on the radios.

The main enemy push was to the east near the coast. A few teams engaged in direct firefights but found themselves sorely outgunned against tanks and armored personnel carriers (APCs). Through the night I heard two Marine Cobras working for an ANGLICO team and several Air Force A-10s working for both the LAVs and the ANGLICO teams. It sounded like the aircraft had plenty to shoot at and killed several enemy vehicles.

But many of the teams started falling back – they just weren't equipped to fight mechanized forces. Even the LAVs lost a couple of vehicles and fell back. The LAVs had TOW missiles and 25mm Bushmaster chain guns, but their aluminum armor wasn't much against the Iraqi tanks and anti-armor missiles. The big bushmaster chain guns still couldn't penetrate the heavy rolled steel armor of the tanks.

To the west, US aircraft engaged the Iraqi tanks and armored vehicles and repulsed two large columns attacking south. The battle lines seemed a little simpler there – a forward observer could simply confirm that the aircraft saw the berm and clear them hot on anything to the north.

It was more confusing to the east, where two SANG (Saudi Arabian National Guard) APC battalions between the border and the small town of Khafji were heavily engaged. They lost a few vehicles and withdrew. From the initial reports, it sounded like they had been shot up pretty badly.

Soon the Iraqis had pushed all the way into Khafji, the small Saudi town five miles south of the border. We had debated whether the Iraqis would ever try to invade Saudi Arabia. Intel and higher headquarters had said it was highly unlikely, but here it was, happening.

With the SANG battalions gone, all that was left in Khafji were two six-man Marine Corps teams surrounded by hundreds of Iraqi tanks and APCs. One was a 1st ANGLICO team and one was a 3rd Recon Battalion team. Through the night, more aircraft trickled in, along with Marine artillery. Most of the calls for fire were coming from the teams pinned down in Khafji. It seemed like every mission they called was "Danger Close," meaning they were inside the casualty range of the weapons being fired.

It was a confusing and difficult situation for the observers and the aircrews alike. The Marines on the ground weren't sure where all the friendlies were, and the two teams weren't able to talk to each other. The aircrews were having trouble picking out friendly and enemy, given how entwined everything had become. No one had decent maps of Khafji, and the observers were low on radio batteries.

By this time an AC-130 gunship had rolled into the fight and was orbiting the town, eliminating targets called by the observers on the ground. The AC-130 is an impressive weapons system with a 105mm howitzer, 40mm BOFORs autocannon, and two 20mm Vulcan machine guns. They can stay "on station" for hours at a time. Usually AC-130s supported Special Operations Forces and it was rare for Marines to get them in support.

While the AC-130 is an effective aircraft/weapon system, it has no self-defense capabilities. It is relatively slow and a big target, so generally they only fly under the cover of darkness in order to protect themselves from anti-aircraft fire and surface-to-air missiles (SAMs). So we were surprised that they continued to operate over Khafji as the sky started to lighten. At 6:35 the AC-130 was hit by a SAM and crashed into the gulf. That was hard to listen to – we could hear the change in tone of all the aircrews on the radio. We later learned that all fourteen crew members of Spirit 03 were killed.

By the time it got light, the Iraqis occupied Khafji with hundreds of tanks and APCs. The two six-man teams were still trapped in the city, hiding on rooftops. Miraculously, through all the firefights, the only US casualties on the ground were the two LAV crews. We had heard that one of the LAVs had been shot by a USAF A-10 and that was another tough blow. Later we heard that the second destroyed LAV had been shot by another LAV in their own company. This wasn't hard to believe, given how confusing the situation had been.

There were two important reasons to retake Khafji. The first was to rescue the two teams that had been stranded there. The second was to stop the Iraqi advance. This was the first Iraqi offensive and it was important to mount a robust reply.

Throughout the day, our officers were gone in planning meetings with the units we were supporting. Looking back at it now, it amazes me just how little I knew about what was happening. I worked hard to keep up and follow what was going on in the bigger picture, but in reality I had no idea what was going on most of the time.

My team made sure everything was ready to roll at a moment's notice. That afternoon, one of the SANG battalions rolled out with a few companies of Qatari tanks in support. There were two or three 1st ANGLICO teams with them. We sat on the edges of our seats and listened to the radios.

The SANG battalion rolled up to the town gates and immediately came under heavy fire. They fired back from the APCs 90mm main guns and the Qatari tanks but got pushed back. They drove at the southern edge of the city again and again met heavy fire. This seesaw back and forth continued for a few hours while the observers called artillery and airstrikes on the outskirts. Since they still didn't have the exact location of the stranded teams, they couldn't call much within the city limits.

We were told to stand by to move to Khafji, and later that evening, we got the plan. Early the next morning, one SANG battalion supported by some Qatari tanks would circle west of Khafji and cut off the enemy from the north so they couldn't get reinforcements from Iraq. We would join another SANG battalion and a Qatari tank company going straight up Highway One from the south into Khafji.

It was important that Coalition forces retake their town for political and tactical reasons. We would support them however we could with aircraft and arty. Our officers were also coaching the SANG staff to ensure sound tactics in the attack. They were in planning conferences all day, which continued into the evening.

We made sure all our gear and vehicles were ready, studied our maps, and confirmed we had all the right frequencies, crypto info, etc. We checked the flight schedules for what aircraft would be airborne in the vicinity at what times. I wrote down their callsigns, types, and times on the back side of my map.

I updated my map from the big master map in the Command Center. The town was about six miles long north to south and a mile or so east to west. In the middle it narrowed to less than half a mile wide, dividing the town into northern and southern portions. It was a pretty straightforward grid pattern and the city was well defined. The roads on the edges of the city simply had buildings on one side and open desert on the other.

The teams that were hiding in the the town were in the southern portion, and the intel was based on their reporting. The positions of the US teams were marked on the map with big blue circles. We didn't know which buildings they were in, not even the exact blocks – just the general vicinity. One of the blue circles had a red box in it with a flag. This meant that there was an enemy headquarters very close to our guys, possibly even in the next building.

Finally it was time for our team to move out. We pulled out to the "driveway" and watched as eight or so Qatari AMX-30 tanks rolled by, followed by a long column of the big Saudi V-150 APCs. These were followed by a couple of tan Land Cruisers (presumably Saudi staff officers). We pulled into the column behind them. Another long column of V-150s followed us. We drove the dirt track across the desert for some time before finally reaching the asphalt highway.

I had always envisioned going into an attack with a little more tactical dispersion, but we drove straight up the highway in a two-by-two column. When we got within about a mile and could see the gates to the town, several of the last APCs and the land cruisers pulled off to the side of the road. We swung over and parked near them. The tanks and the first few APCs continued straight up to the gates to the town, driving two abreast on each side of the divided highway.

By the time the second set of tanks passed under the arches, the firing started. The tanks fired their main gun and coaxial machine gun. The V-150s fired their turret machine guns, and some of the troops fired out the little gunport/windows on the sides of the APCs.

I grabbed the big binos, climbed up on the hood, and propped my elbows on the roof, watching. It always cracks me up in the movies how people will stand there with high-power binos watching something. I don't care how steady you are, if you are looking through 10x or bigger, you have to have them propped on something to see a clear picture.

The town skyline was pretty level. Most the buildings were three stories high. Even from my position, I could make out damage to the buildings and see holes and black marks from the previous action.

I could see three or four burned-out vehicles off the side of the road in front of the arches. One was recognizable as a tank and the other two hulks were APCs.

Tanks and APCs continued to file through the arches, with some moving off on side roads. It wasn't a constant stream of fire from either side, but it was often enough that it was definitely a battle.

Propped up on the roof of my vehicle, looking through the binos, the whole thing seemed unreal. We were less than a mile from the action, just watching and waiting.

After a while Capt Johnson came jogging over to us. He told Sgt Meek to work up some arty calls for fire for a few intersections and buildings. Then he told me to work up a Naval gunfire call for fire for a building he suspected was the Iraqi headquarters.

Two 16-inch (Iowa class) battleships had been brought out of retirement to support Desert Shield/Desert Storm and we were supported by the USS *Wisconsin*. Back then, it was considered the "holy grail" for a forward observer to direct fire from a battleship with 16-inch guns, which fired a 2,800-pound explosive shell at 1,700 miles per hour. I was excited, but not without reservations. The casualty radius of a high-explosive shell that size is really big. In the open, it would be around 1,500 meters. There was no way I could ensure there were no friendlies in an area that large in Khafji.

I pulled out a black marker and started filling in the blanks on my laminated cheat sheet. When it came to position, I went back and forth between the map and what was out in front of me several times, confirming the correct grid by figuring it a couple of different ways. Soon I had my call for fire all ready.

The APCs that had been behind us started to come past us and head into the city. A few more Land Cruisers and Humvees pulled up and parked with us, and officers from those vehicles piled out and joined the group of officers already there. It was a classic scene comparing the two cultures. The Americans looked like a bunch of rednecks leaning on thier pickup truck, talking about who was going to go hunt where. The Saudis were doing their classic squat with their butts on their heels and their elbows tucked in between their knees, smoking and talking.

Soon a section of Cobras checked in and one of the teams started working the southern portion of the town. We watched and listened as the Marine on the ground talked them onto targets. They fired rockets and guns two or three times during the hour or so they were on station.

As the afternoon turned into evening, many vehicles had come and gone, and both Saudi and Marine officers had joined and left the huddle nearby. After a while it became clear that I wouldn't get to call the 16-inch guns mission. As much as I wanted to rain destruction down on the enemy, I was a bit relieved, too.

We finally mounted up and prepared to drive into the city. We had two APCs in the lead, followed by the Land Cruisers, a US Humvee, and then us. Since we were tail end charlie, Sanchez and I rolled up the back of the soft top and laid on top of the gear facing backwards with our rifles out the back, like tail gunners. We were weapons free, meaning we could engage anything not positively identified as friendly. Capt Johnson had warned us about not confusing Saudis for Iraqis. We were pretty confident we could tell the difference between the Saudi desert camo and the Iraqi olive drab uniforms. As soon as we drove under the arches over the divided highway, we went into hyper-vigilant mode.

As we entered the city, one of the APCs fired their machine gun into the top story of a four-story building. We craned our necks to see what they were shooting at but couldn't see anything. But all the vehicles continued forward, so we did, too.

Just as we passed the building, Sanchez hollered "FIRING" and capped off three or four rounds into the same spot. As soon as he did, he hollered "ALL GOOD!"

I was shocked. My ears were ringing and I was frantically searching through my sights to try to see what he had shot. Capt Johnson yelled something back at us, but I couldn't hear what he said.

I hollered at Sanchez, "What do you see? Where's the target?"

"Oh nothing, it's all good."

"What! What are you shooting at?"

"Nothing, man, just the building the SANG were shooting at."

"What the hell? Why did you do that?"

"Just wanted to make sure I fired my weapon in combat!"

I looked back over my shoulder to see what Capt Johnson was doing but he was looking straight ahead with a radio handset pressed to his ear. The two inch strip of his neck between his helmet and flak jacket was bright red. His head was shaking but I couldn't tell if he was laughing or pissed.

We started to wind our way through the town. Almost immediately I became disoriented. We passed SANG vehicles and SANG soldiers on foot. We saw several smoking vehicles. Buildings everywhere had sustained damage and there was rubble in the streets. We continued to hear small arms fire and larger weapons. It was hard to tell over the noise of the vehicles, but most of it sounded several blocks away.

At one intersection, SANG soldiers had rounded up several prisoners wearing the olive drab trousers of the Iraqi uniform and white T-shirts. It was a bit cold to be wearing just T-shirts, so I assumed they were getting searched.

We pulled into a large parking lot surrounded by three buildings making a "U." Everyone pulled into the parking spaces correctly, which seemed kind of funny. Suarez killed the engine and Capt Johnson turned in his seat to brief us.

"The Saudis are going to clear the center building and the one to the right. They will be setting up their command post in the center building. We are going to clear the building to the left and set up an OP on the roof and our CP on the top floor. I want it slow and methodical. Two by two. Full communication. Clear the bottom floor and work up room by room, floor by floor. You all know your challenge and reply?"

In unison: "Yes, Sir!"

We piled out and went to work. It was a large building. At first I had thought it was a hospital, but as we started going through it, it became clear it was a school. Each floor had a main hallway going down the middle with classrooms coming off both sides. Most of the classrooms had a bunch of one-piece desks/chairs piled up in the corner. There was clutter and debris everywhere – books and binders, an occasional foam mattress, various clothing, an odd piece of plywood, and tons of loose papers. We worked in pairs, checking each classroom, each closet, and the occasional office. It probably took us an hour to cover the entire building but we did so without incident.

After we had cleared the building, we started schlepping our gear to set up the OP on the roof. We set up antennas and ran wires and cables down to the vehicle parked against the building. Sgt Meek and Lopez cleared out the classroom closest to the large stairwell facing the parking lot and set up a small CP.

The roof was flat with a three-foot wall around the edges. There were A/C units and a few vents scattered here and there. Soon Sanchez and I got radio checks on our new setup and started looking around the town from the roof.

Now that I had a clear view, I could see that we were in the southeastern section of the town. From time to time we would hear some firing in the distance but it was very sporadic. It started to drizzle so we grabbed a couple of ponchos and strung them up with some stacked-up desks, a piece of plywood, and a pole we had scavenged to make a lean-to.

Capt Johnson came up and we all gathered in the new CP area. He related the good news that the two teams had been recovered and were all okay. He also briefed us that most of the town had been cleared, but still wasn't secure. Most of the Iraqis were surrendering but there still hostilities going on, so we should stay alert. We would be spending at least the next day or two there, maybe a little longer.

Sgt Meek divided out the tasks and we turned to getting them done. The adrenaline of the day was wearing off and I really wanted to go to sleep. Luckily it wasn't long before we had everything set up. I didn't have watch for the next six hours so I took off my boots and vest and curled up in the CP with my rifle in my sleeping bag. It was warm and dark and I was exhausted so I soon slipped into the black of deep sleep.

Chapter 15

Little Red Corvette

The next day consisted primarily of radio watch and observing from the roof. For the most part Khafji was considered retaken, but the SANG and Qataris were still searching and clearing. Most of the Iraqis were surrendering and we only heard a few incidents of small arms fire. We had been advised to avoid being involved in the taking of any prisoners – we didn't have manpower or facilities to deal with any EPWs and I think there was also the fear that if Saudi, Kuwaiti, Qatari, or other forces mistreated the prisoners we turned over to them, we would be complicit in the violations. So we stayed on the roof, monitoring radios and observing what we could see.

We also spent much of the day working to improve our setup and rummaging through the rubble in the building to see what we could use. We found a few pieces of plywood, which was always in short supply. Tables, map boards, shelves, boxes to hold gear, roofing for the Humvees so we could stow gear – it all needed plywood.

That evening we got an update brief from Capt Towne. The area was cleared. It was considered safe but we were instructed to be "heads on a swivel" when moving about the town. Several more battalions would be moving up to Khafji in the next few days, which meant that at least one more of our teams would be joining us at the same spot.

We all knew it from the frequent sound of jets flying overhead, but Capt Towne told us the air war was continuing and going very well. We still didn't have a timetable for crossing the berm but we had to stay ready.

Capt Johnson asked us to work on fortifications the following day. He wanted sandbags or something more significant for protection on the roof. He also wanted us to secure the other entrances to the building and to do something about all the windows. "Cover them up with some plywood or something!" There was a collective groan.

That night on radio watch, I sat on the roof under a full moon. I was smoking a cheap cigar someone had sent me from home and was really enjoying it. I hadn't had a chance to relax in several days. I wondered if people back home had heard about Khafji. Did my family hear about it? Did Christy hear about it? I also wondered what the rest of the US forces had been dealing with in the meantime. We hadn't heard or talked about anything besides Khafji for several days now. Had there been attacks on other parts of the border? And what did the other US guys think of our battle? Were they going to scoff and tell us that it "wasn't really a battle"? I hadn't played much of a role in the Battle of Khafji, but I felt some ownership and was proud of it.

What did Khafji indicate about the Iraqi forces? It had been a bold move that caught us unprepared, but once we got focused, we pushed them back fairly easily. I didn't know the numbers but I had heard we lost twenty-five American personnel and the Saudi/Qatari forces had lost about twenty. We had lost two LAVs, two Qatari tanks, and about ten Saudi APCs. How many vehicles had the Iraqis lost? It had to be sixty or seventy at least. I had only seen the southern portion of the town and there were burnt-out vehicles everywhere. I had seen what looked like hundreds of Iraqi prisoners. While tragic, two vehicles and eleven Americans were lost due to our own mistakes – friendly fire. The remaining fourteen were all due to one lucky SAM shot on the AC-130. In addition, the Saudis had done much better than most people expected. It hadn't been an easy battle by any means, but overall the Coalition did pretty well.

So did this all mean that the Iraqi forces weren't as imposing as Intel had been telling us? Or were the Iraqi forces we had encountered just flunkies, the speed bumps the Iraqi Army had sent to soften up the Coalition before they rolled into the attack?

The next morning Suarez and I set out to find materials to help improve our position. Plywood was priority number one. Sandbags, or something similar, were on the list, too, and any salvageable lumber would be useful as well. I drove the Humvee in an expanding box search pattern centered on our combat outpost while Sanchez spotted. We stopped frequently and tried to keep heads up at all times while we scanned rubble piles and trash for anything useful.

We found a couple of large signs and threw them in the back of the Humvee. We drove past several burnt-out vehicles and stopped at the first few to see if there was anything useful. Walking up to the back hatch and looking in was kind of like watching a scary scene in a horror movie through your fingers – you want to see it to know what happened, but at the same time you are afraid to see it. We half expected to see charred skeletons but never did. I don't know if it was because no one had been in the vehicles or if the fire had burned hot enough to burn bone. But they were all so badly burned, there weren't even seat frames left.

So after a while we didn't stop at any more vehicle hulks. There were a few civilian vehicles around but most of them were damaged and I was surprised at how many were missing wheels. It reminded me of the stolen car you would see dumped in some of the rougher areas of Los Angeles.

We drove through one area that looked like a shopping district and scored several more plywood signs. There were more signs hanging up on the front of the buildings, but we decided against pulling those down. We also found a pile of empty gallon jugs and debated picking those up to fill with sand, but decided it would be too labor intensive for the small volume.

The next street was houses – mostly flat-roofed, two-story buildings. Some of the houses had carports on the ground floor, with the second story extending over the carport. Many of the walls had sections knocked down, leaving piles of brick and concrete in the street and the courtyards. A few had collapsed exterior walls so you could see right into the home. From what we could see, they looked pretty normal inside.

There was plenty of rubble and trash around but nothing looked salvageable or useful. I was beginning to think we would be better off in the more commercial zone. I was just about to tell Suarez that we should skip this area entirely when he hollered, "STOP!"

"What?" I said. "What do you see?" I pulled up my rifle and was trying to point it out the window.

"Look at that! HOO LEEE SHIT!"

"What? What?" I was looking in the direction he was looking but didn't see anything.

Suarez was transfixed. "I don't believe it!"

We were idling in front of a typical house, which appeared to be fairly intact. Then I saw it. Parked in the carport, and covered in so much dust that you almost couldn't see the color, was a red Corvette. It was a newer fourth-generation Corvette, just like the one owned by my high school buddy's mom – probably an '84 or '85.

"Come on," Suarez said. "We gotta go check it out."

"Uh, okay," I said.

I backed the Humvee into the driveway, right up behind the Vette. We hopped out and did a quick check around but didn't see anyone or anything.

Suarez said, "Think we could get it hotwired?"

The thought excited me but I didn't really know how to hotwire a car. Then again, I'd changed a few ignitions, so maybe I could figure it out.

I tried the driver's door and was surprised to find that it was open. This was insane.

"Suarez, you go keep lookout while I try to get the ignition wires out."

"Okay, but if you need my help let me know."

"You just keep us covered."

Suarez went back to the corner of the carport so he could see both ways down the street. I got out my pocket multi-tool and started working off the steering column and surrounding covers. I hadn't worked on a car this new before and the fasteners and clips were different from what I was used to. When I finally got the wires exposed there were more than I expected and I couldn't get enough slack in them to really get them out. I didn't want to start cutting any of them until I was sure which ones to use. I was looking for the classic fat yellow, red, and black wires.

Suarez appeared back by the side of the car. "Come on, man! If you haven't got it yet, let me have a turn. I can get it."

"Okay," I said reluctantly.

I had wanted to hotwire it, but mostly for bragging rights. Suarez was right – I'd been playing with it for probably ten or fifteen minutes and didn't know what I was doing. I wriggled my way out from under the dash and went back to the corner of the carport to cover us. Suarez popped the back hatch and rummaged around in the trunk.

I looked up and down the street but still didn't see anyone. I was starting to have second thoughts. Were we just stealing? We had heard from both the Saudi and the Kuwaiti governments that we could use whatever we needed and to not worry about collateral damage. Our team did need another vehicle. And Sgt Shue had commandeered an old Chevy pickup. But a Corvette wasn't exactly practical. Then again, those wide tires would probably be good on the sand...

Suarez started banging something inside the car. A moment later he called out asking for a screwdriver. I tossed him the flat-blade screwdriver from my little tool kit. He ducked back in the car and started banging again. A second later the engine turned over. Suarez laughed. "Oh yeah!"

He cranked it again, but it was just turning over – not catching. I started to wonder about things like power to the fuel pump and how that connected to the ignition when the V8 fired up. The deep, throaty growl of a Vette is impressive even if you aren't a Chevy fan.

"It's even full of fuel!"

"Awesome!"

I walked over to see what Suarez had done to get it going. He had hammered most of the ignition cover off, then jammed the screwdriver down the key slot. You simply turn the screwdriver like turning a key to start it. Genius.

We started arguing over who got to drive. But Suarez had gotten it started, so I quickly acquiesced. I fired up the Humvee and pulled out into the street. Suarez backed out the Vette and pulled up behind me. Of course he chirped the tires as he did this – which wasn't hard with the sand on the asphalt. As we wound our way back to the school, I could see him kick out the rear at every turn.

We pulled into the CP parking lot as casually as we could and then trotted upstairs to get some help unloading the plywood. Sgt Meek and Cpl Lopez came down to help.

They both went nuts when they saw the Vette. We immediately popped the hood and started checking it out like we were at a Saturday night cruise. They were very impressed.

We started talking about how to make it more combat capable. I had an image in my mind of me driving it with the top removed and Suarez standing on the passenger seat, firing an M-60 from the hip as we rode into battle. We knew we were going to have to do something about the bright red color. And somehow we were going to have to convince the officers that a Corvette was a useful addition.

We hauled all the wood and signs back up to the third floor and completed our tasks as quickly as we could – covering windows and filling sandbags for a small bunker on the roof. And the whole time we just wanted to get it done so we could go mess with the Vette.

After some discussion we elected Sgt Meek to tell the officers about the Vette since he was the most senior. I was nervous that Capt Towne was going to go ballistic.

We had gotten about half the windows covered with the plywood and aluminum when Capt Johnson and Capt Towne came up. Without hesitating, Sgt Meek told them we had acquired another vehicle.

"Great! What'd you get?"

"Sir, just look out the window. It's parked next to the Humvee."

Capt Johnson and Capt Towne walked over to the window and looked down at the parking lot. There was a brief, stunned pause. Then came the flood of questions, with Capt Towne and Capt Johnson talking in unison. I could tell by the look on Capt Johnson's face that he was excited about it, but the tone in Capt Towne's voice said, "No way, you little criminals." I had hoped to gloss over the part about hotwiring it, but Suarez was straight up about it and simply said he'd cracked the ignition and jimmied it.

Capt Towne and Capt Johnson paused for a moment, then agreed that they'd discuss it further in private. Capt Johnson said, "But we have to do something about the red. There is no way can we drive it around red."

We all shouted in unison: "We are going to paint it!"

The next morning the officers left without telling us yay or nay on the Vette. We decided we'd better fix it up to help them decide we should keep it. Sgt Meek headed off to meet his supply contact while we removed the back hatch and sunroof. We stripped everything out of the trunk and test-fit several fuel and water cans, which worked quite well.

A short while later Sgt Meek came limping across the parking lot with a five-gallon bucket. He had scored us some paint! Only problem was, it was white. Maybe that was a little bit better than red, but not much? We joked about making it striped like a big candy cane. It was also interior house paint. We talked about trying to add shoe dye or something to tint it. Then I remembered making redneck non-skid.

I said, "Hey, all we need to do is coat it in paint and then throw sand all over it while the paint is still wet!"

"Yeah, that will make it sand-colored!"

"Sounds like a plan!"

We didn't have brushes or rollers or paint cans, so we simply dipped cut-off water bottles in the five-gallon bucket, dribbled paint onto the car, and then spread it around with pieces of cardboard. It quickly became obvious that it would take a lot more sand than we had imagined, so we had to take a break from painting to gather more dry sand. But soon we got a pretty good system going: Sgt Meek poured paint, I spread it, and Suarez threw on the sand while Cpl Lopez fed Suarez's dry sand supply.

The interior paint was very thick and made a good base to hold the sand. And fortunately, there weren't too many tricky sections. The windshield frame was already black. The most challenging sections were the front bumper and the B-pillar that formed the arch over the headrests.

After a while the car was covered in sand. We stood back and admired our handiwork. I wasn't sure how it would hold up when dry but we got it pretty well covered – there wasn't any red showing and not much white. It definitely wasn't pretty. In fact it looked kind of sad. But still, the idea of a tactical assault Vette was pretty awesome and we were excited.

We never did hear an official yes or no from the officers so we drove the Corvette around for the next few days on our scouting trips. No one ever yelled at us but we got some really strange looks from the Saudis.

I got several chances behind the wheel. I loved the way the seats cradled your body, the snappy gearbox, and the low seating position. The real joy came from punching the throttle and feeling the power throw you back in the seat. Sadly, I never found a long enough straightaway to really open it up, so I probably never got it above sixty, and even then only for a couple of seconds. But it was a kick to drive into the empty sand lots and do a bunch of donuts. I bet we took half the tread off the tires.

My theory about the wide tires on the sand was proven correct when we took the Vette and the old Chevy pickup to get fuel for our generators. The Vette did just fine in the soft and rutted sand lot of the Saudi fuel dump, but the old pickup bogged down twice and had to be rescued by the Vette!

A few days later, another team showed up with Maj S and Chu. I headed back to the Brigade Air Team with them and never saw the Vette again. Next time I talked with SALT Belly, they told me that they had left the Corvette in Khafji. Probably for the best – it surely would have raised a few eyebrows if we'd shown up on CNN driving an "acquired" sand-covered Vette into Kuwait City.

Chapter 16

Crossing the Berm

After Khafji I went back to the Brigade Air Team. I was just getting back into the swing of things when we got briefed on the start of the ground war. The air war had been going on for over a month now. The plan was to cross the berm to liberate Kuwait on February 24 – just three days away.

Intel indicated that several of the Iraqi brigades just north of us were attrited to the point of being combat ineffective. But I wasn't so sure. While I was impressed with the amount of sorties and ordnance that the air war, TLAMs (cruise missiles), and naval gunfire had dumped on the enemy, I also knew that throughout history, it was always surprising how many troops survived bombardment. The Iraqis had had months to prepare bunkers, fighting positions, and protection. I was also concerned by the lack of updates on the obstacle belts (minefield, trenches, etc). With all the aircraft flying over them, I thought we'd have better reports on all the obstacles.

We were also still concerned about chemical weapons and other weapons of mass destruction. It was thought that Saddam would probably use them as a last defense, so we were told to expect it when we crossed the border – especially if we got tied up in an obstacle belt. We were to enter Kuwait wearing our NBC suits with our masks, overboots, and gloves immediately accessible – known as MOPP (Mission Oriented Protective Posture) level 2. Fortunately, the weather was still quite cool, so it wouldn't be too awful, but the thick, charcoal-lined suits were bulky and kind of a pain.

I had expected the attack to take place in the wee hours of the morning, but it was planned for 0800. The night before, we packed up everything and slept on the ground next to our vehicles. It was hard to sleep, thinking about what tomorrow might hold. Tule and I whispered long into the night. The thing we kept coming back to was how nice it would be to have a couple of beers, or some Jack on ice.

We got up at zero dark thirty and ate a cold MRE. We did our PCC and PCIs, checking and rechecking batteries, ammo, frequencies, etc. The plan was simply to drive our vehicles in the middle of the combined SANG and Kuwaiti column we were supporting and wait for something to happen. I don't know if the simplicity of the attack was Saudi driven or if it was simply our response to the Saudi tactics.

The sky was getting pink and starting to lighten when we rolled our vehicles into position in the column of SANG V-150s. Tule was driving Humvee No. 1 with Maj S, Sgt Miller, Gunny Falkner, and LCpl Gonzales. I was driving Humvee No. 2 with LCDR Moore in shotgun and LCpl Chu and PFC Fillerton in the back. We had broken open the big foil bales of our MOPP suits and had put them on. It cracked me up that we had all this nice desert camo but then covered everything with woodland green cammie MOPP suits.

We sat in line, locked and loaded, with our engines idling for what seemed like hours. Everyone was amped up – nervous, excited, and scared all at the same time. All the information we had received was so contradictory we really didn't know what to expect – we might roll across the berm and hit a mine or be vaporized instantly by some weapon system. Or maybe we would just be out for a nice morning drive. The uncertainty of battle is one of the worst things. Once you get started, you focus on correct actions and training, which keeps you occupied and generally prevents you from thinking about bad things. But waiting beforehand – with your brain cycling through all worst-case scenarios – is torture.

Finally, the five lead vehicles started pulling away. Tule followed at about a fifteen-meter interval and I followed ten meters behind him. Fifteen or twenty meters behind me were the first of ten or more V-150s, followed by several Kuwaiti BMPs. It was still weird seeing the BMPs. They were a Soviet APC that we had studied as a threat for years. Here they were the good guys (although we had been briefed that the Iraqis had BMPs, too). The potential for confusion once the shooting started was one of the things that had kept Tule and me from getting much sleep the night before.

Mixed in the column were several tan CJ-7 jeeps, a couple of fuel tankers, and the tan Land Cruisers that carried the Saudi and Kuwaiti officers. Every single one of the V-150s had a flag on it. Most of them had Kuwaiti flags, though there were a few Saudi flags, too. Tule and I had put flags on the antennas on our Humvees. I had an 8 x 10 American flag on top of the right antenna and I had traded a Zippo lighter with one of the Kuwaitis for a large Kuwaiti flag, which I mounted right below it. I was impressed with the sight of all these military vehicles rumbling across the desert, flags flying. But I was also a little jealous of the APC's armor – our fabric-topped Humvees felt kind of vulnerable.

We drove for a while doing about 30 KPH across the desert until we arrived at the berm, at which point the column turned left and drove parallel to the berm. Soon we pulled up behind another group of Coalition vehicles waiting behind the berm. After a few minutes, another column of vehicles pulled up behind us and it wasn't long before there were vehicles as far as I could see to the east and the west.

It was almost 0700; we weren't crossing the LOD (Line of Departure) until 0800. Even though we were mounted or motorized, we still called it "stepping." I suppose that is adopted from the old infantry "stepping off from the LOD" at the prescribed time. Waiting there for an hour with all the vehicles bunched up seemed like a bad idea to me, but no one seemed concerned about our vulnerability. Maybe recon aircraft had confirmed there wasn't any Iraqi artillery in range of our position.

I looked east up the line of vehicles and watched as a D-7 bulldozer moved back and forth, digging a cut in the berm. It was almost time to roll. By 0745 the notch in the berm was big enough to drive through, so we mounted up, got one more radio check with everyone, and then followed the rest of the column through the berm and into Kuwait.

Although I had "accidentally" crossed the border on that dark night with Wild Eagle Two Three, the rest of this team had not been into Kuwait yet, so it was a big deal to be finally driving onto Kuwaiti soil. As expected, Kuwait was the same flat open desert spotted with small scrub brush. With so many big vehicles in front of us, there was a pretty well-defined vehicle track to follow. Every now and then, I could see where a vehicle had branched off from the main track, which didn't seem very smart. We had seen a few mines just a few meters off the track – the winds had blown the sand away, exposing the pie plate-sized disks. But that was it in terms of hazards. We never did see any oil-filled trenches, concertina wire, or holes filled with punji stakes.

We drove in the spaced-out column, moving quite a bit slower than before for about an hour. When we came to the top of a small rise, the column halted. Behind us, I could see our track back to the berm, which was now barely discernible in the distance. To the west, I could see the columns of black smoke coming from the oil fires in the Al Wafra oil fields. To the east, I thought I could see the coast, but I couldn't tell for sure if it was actually water or just the horizon melting away.

While we idled there, I debated whether or not I should stay in the vehicle and monitor the radios or if I should get out and help form a security perimeter. Everyone else was staying in their vehicles except for a small conference of officers just ahead of us.

And that's when I noticed a strange smell. It wasn't the familiar diesel exhaust or the now familiar smell of burning oil fields. It stung my nose a little bit. Gas! Sure enough, the alerts were being shouted up and down the line and I could see the officers putting on their masks. I relayed the alert, yelling, "GAS GAS GAS!" as I pulled out my mask, put it on, and cleared it. I checked Chu, Fillerton, and Gonzales and they all had their masks on. Good. I grabbed the radio handset and was about to report a suspected NBC attack. I pulled out my notebook with the format for an NBC attack and was checking the GPS for our current position when someone else started the report. I listened in to double-check the position. Sure enough, they reported a position within a mile of ours.

After about twenty minutes of listening to non-conclusive radio traffic, Maj S came walking back to our Humvee with his mask off.

"Nothing to be alarmed about. Go ahead and stow your masks."

Muffled through my mask I said, "Sir, are you sure? How do we know?"

"Hesty, just have everyone put their masks away and get ready to step off again."

"Uh, okay, Sir."

I wasn't convinced. This contradicted the procedure we'd learned in a myriad of NBC classes. I hated wearing that damn mask but I was confident in the protection it offered. But everyone one else was removing their masks so I removed mine – though I made sure to get it all set up to put back on quickly if needed. LCDR Moore came trotting back to the vehicle, and shortly after that the entire column began to move again.

As we crept along across the desert, we discussed what the smell might have been and tried to convince ourselves that we hadn't been exposed.

"Out here in the open, with the breeze blowing, you'd have to have a ton of gas to make a lethal dose."

"Yeah, and I didn't hear any booms, so how was Saddam delivering it?"

"If that was some kind of booby trap, there is no way it had enough gas in it."

I found myself checking the chemical detection tape around each wrist to see if it had turned color. It never did.

We never heard anything else about the smell and I still don't know what it was. When we got back to the States, our Corpsman wrote a specific entry in our medical books that detailed our exposures while we were there. He gave us each a hard copy and told us to safeguard it in case it was removed from our medical records. Outstanding Corpsman – thinking ahead!

We were now back on lower ground and had lost the ability to see very far. We came across an abandoned Iraqi fighting position that had two tanks and two APCs partially dug in. The column stopped and we jumped out to have a look. I reminded the other guys to watch out for booby traps. The Saudis just watched us as we went about our business.

There was an amazing amount of crap strewn about near the vehicles. There were olive drab uniform items, civilian clothes, empty wooden boxes, empty fuel cans, and even a doll still in a cellophane wrapper.

We proceeded slowly and covered each other as we swept each vehicle and searched inside. The vehicles weren't burned out, just abandoned, with the same random assortment of stuff strewn about inside. The two things we didn't find were fuel or ammo. We checked the last vehicle, then reported back to Maj S what we saw. He told us good job and to mount back up.

The column moved out. We continued the slow crawl through the open desert until we joined a divided blacktop highway and our speed increased a bit. Pretty soon we saw road signs – once again we were on the highway that paralleled the coast. We passed a destroyed tank hulk and a little later we saw an APC that was still smoking. The column stretched as far as I could see in front and behind us as we continued along the coast.

Chapter 17

The Tank

The column paused again on the coast highway and Maj S gave us the signal to rally between our vehicles. He told us we were about to head into Mina Su'ud, a small industrial coastal town. We didn't expect many civilians – the town had been occupied by an Iraqi armor unit for several months. We were to prepare for a fight.

Helmet straps were buttoned, flak jackets were fastened, and weapons were locked and loaded. I checked my notes as we waited in the vehicles. I couldn't see any aircraft that would be airborne in our area. Then again, the flight schedule was confusing to read. I doubted that any artillery was set up to range Mina Su'ud and I didn't know how to find out if the *Missouri* or the *Wisconsin* were on station or would be ready to fire. I'd need to set up the HF radio to talk to them but it was in the other vehicle. I felt frustrated that I wasn't ready to bring in any supporting arms if we found targets. Still, it was the officers' job to control air and naval gunfire. So contrary to my usual attitude, I decided to simply be ready on my rifle and stand by on the radio if one of the officers told me to do something. But I knew how to control air; I had done it and I wanted to contribute to winning the coming fight.

We started moving again. Soon we passed a road that could almost be described as an exit. I watched in the rearview mirror as part of the column branched off behind us and took that road to the east. A mile or two later, the lead of the column turned off in front of us. We made the turn as well and headed down the two-lane road to the east. There were a few buildings fairly close to the road on the left and a few more buildings much further from the road to our right. That must be Mina Su'ud.

The column slowed as we approached a large three-story building and I heard small arms fire. Suddenly the vehicles in front of us stopped and I saw muzzle flashes in the windows from the building one hundred meters to our left. They were shooting at us!

I slapped the Humvee into park, pointed my rifle out the window, and yelled "FIRING" as I let two rounds fly into the window of the building where I had seen the last muzzle flash. That didn't work out so well. The hot brass bounced off the windshield and into my collar. Ouch, that stung! I slumped down and writhed around in the Humvee, trying to swat the brass out of the right side of my neck and shake it out all at the same time.

The Saudis opened up on the building with their mounted machine guns. Everyone from my vehicle had bailed out and was vying for a spot behind the Humvee to return fire. Except Fillerton. Fillerton was on the hood, sitting crosslegged and wrapping his rifle sling around his left bicep to make a tight shooting position.

"Fillerton!" I yelled. "What the hell are you doing?!"

"Making a tight sling!"

"Get the hell off the truck!"

"But I was just getting a good shooting position!"

"Get behind the truck!"

"Yes, Corporal." He slid off the hood and took a position behind the Humvee.

Good shooting positions had been ingrained in us since boot camp, but unfortunately our training had focused on range shooting, not combat shooting. The tight sling and cross-legged position was a good shooting position but not a smart move in this situation. Besides the fact that he was exposed, he was blocking the rest of us from being able to shoot over the hood.

The firing from the building seemed to have stopped and slowly our firing died down. It appeared that the Iraqis hadn't hit anything. A few moments later, white pieces of cloth showed up in a few of the windows. One looked like it was tied to the barrel of a rifle; others were waved by hand.

There was a lot of shouting in Arabic as several Saudis advanced toward the building on foot. We stayed hunkered down behind the Humvee as a second squad of Saudis headed into the building and joined the first group clearing the building.

A few minutes later the Saudis came out of the building with about ten Iraqis with their hands on their heads. A V-150 came up from behind us and drove over to meet them. Meanwhile, Sgt Miller hollered back to us from the first Humvee to mount up. We climbed back in and followed the other vehicles in front as they began to pull away. My neck was still throbbing from where the brass had burned me. My blood was really pumping and my legs were a bit shaky.

We continued up the road. The buildings were increasing in density to our left and there were crossroads now making city blocks. Some of the buildings looked like houses but many of them looked more commercial. There was still open desert to our right for a few hundred meters until the buildings we could see in the distance. We stayed focused on the buildings to our left.

The column stopped again. LCDR Moore got out and walked up to meet Maj S. Together, they walked along the right side of the idling vehicles. We got out and stood on the right side of the Humvee watching the buildings to the left. There were so many windows and rooftops to watch. We could see the Saudi gunners on top of their vehicles scanning the buildings, too, so we focused on the buildings closest to us.

After a few minutes, the officers came back and we all gathered behind the front Humvee. The plan was to sweep through the town on foot to the canal that was a few blocks to our north. We were not going to clear the buildings, just sweep up the streets. Gunny Falkner, Sgt Miller, and Chu were going to take the next street up. I was going to take Fillerton and Gonzales up the street directly in front of us. Tule was going to stay with the radios in the vehicles, and the officers were going to stay with the SANG staff two vehicles up. Red smoke or a red star cluster meant you needed help, and yellow meant rally back at the vehicles as fast as you could. And we had to be careful with our fire because SANG was sweeping a block to our left and our other guys would be a block to our right. That meant we had to confirm targets shooting east or west before returning fire. Maj S estimated that it was less than a mile to the canal so we should be able to sweep and then return to the vehicle in the next hour. If we ran into any serious resistance, we would disengage and withdraw back to the column to regroup.

Fillerton, Gonzales, and I trotted up to the next road and started up the street. We leapfrogged along, covering the open spaces quickly and lingering near cover while we visually swept the buildings ahead for movement or any signs of enemy. Some of the buildings had overhangs with nice big pillars that provided a good spot to assess the surroundings while being at least partially protected.

As we followed the street around a bend, a large open area appeared to the north. I figured that must be the canal. As we got closer, it started to look like a traffic circle with a raised hump in the middle. That's when I first heard a diesel engine idling. But I couldn't tell where it was coming from because of the way the sound reverberated off the buildings.

Gonzales waved at me and pointed toward the circle. I looked toward where he was pointing but didn't see anything noteworthy. He waved me over so I trotted across to where he was kneeling. That's when I saw it – a T-62 tank sitting in the middle of the traffic circle! It was pointed to our left, toward the west.

This was a strange situation. Every Iraqi vehicle we had seen so far had been burned out or abandoned. None of them had fuel or ammo on board. But this one was idling. Obviously it was in operating condition.

I was torn. I wanted to complete our mission, but taking three guys against a tank wasn't very smart. Then again, I'd rather approach a tank on foot than in an APC. On foot you could move laterally much faster than in a vehicle. And you'd probably stand a better chance of surviving the tank firing out in the open than in an APC.

Gonzales and I trotted back across the street to talk with Fillerton. Maybe it was the adrenalin or maybe it was a sense of strength from not having had any serious challenges yet, but we decided we should go clear it. The top hatch was closed so it could only fire the main gun or the coaxial machine guns in the direction of the turret. If the tank started to move or swing the turret, we would evade laterally and then hustle back into the buildings and head south to rally with the column. If someone popped out of the hatch, we would simply light him up before he could bring the hatch machine gun into action. I had been in a T-55 before and the manual turret was really slow. I imagined the T-62 to be the same.

We continued leapfrogging along the right side of the street until we got to the last building and had the tank directly in view. There was a row of jersey barriers between the last building and the traffic circle. We snuck along the side of the building, then crawled up behind the barriers.

I whispered instructions one more time to the others. "If it starts to move or traverse, evade back in between the buildings. Get out of his line of sight. If we get separated, first rally point is the intersection where the road bends; backup rally point is the vehicle column. If you are evading, get a building between you and the tank and head south. Make sure you don't wander into the other team's sectors! And if the hatch opens before I get to the tank, SHOOT HIM!"

I leaned my back against the barrier and steeled myself. I couldn't believe we were doing this. I was going to walk up to the tank. I knew I had to do it because I couldn't make one of the other guys do it. I don't know why, but something told me it was all going to be okay.

I nodded at Fillerton and Gonzales, who then poked their weapons over the top of the wall and found good shooting positions. I swung around the end of the wall and started toward the tank.

I did my best "combat glide," walking a slow, deliberate pace with my rifle tucked tight into my chest and trained on the top hatch of the tank. My steps were smooth and slow to keep my rifle from bouncing as I crossed the road and into the center of the circle. I continued to aim steadily at the top hatch. My heart was in my throat and I could hear the banging of its beat over the tank engine.

Nothing moved on the tank. It dawned on me that I didn't know what I was going to do when I got there. What if I couldn't open the hatch? Why hadn't I thought of this before?

I was still approaching slowly, trying to decide if I should back away or continue, when the top hatch swung up with a clang. A bearded face appeared and everything went into slow motion. This man seemed to be rising out of the hatch as if on an elevator. His cold-weather hat and beard were as clear as day, but the other details were a blur. As his elbows cleared the edge of the hatch, I saw he had something in his hands.

Why was it taking me so long to pull the trigger? It seemed like I had started to pull it minutes ago! Several shots rang out simultaneously and a pink mist erupted from the back of the man's head. He jerked back against the vertical hatch and then slid back into the tank.

I don't know how long I stood there looking through my rifle sights at the empty hatch. It seemed like five minutes yet it seemed like half a second. Nothing else moved. Awareness of my surroundings slowly broadened back out to normal.

I continued my approach. I moved to the back of the tank and covered the hatches while Gonzales and Fillerton took turns moving up to the tank. And then we were all on top of the still-idling tank, peering over our rifles and down into the hatch.

The Iraqi had a fatal bullet wound to the face. He was slumped back, half on the floor and half on the standing platform for the hatch. A dark pool of blood bloomed behind his head like a gruesome halo, reaching the edge of the platform and then running onto the floor.

You can't really search a tank from outside, but none of us wanted to go inside. We did our best to see everything we could. There was no evidence of anyone else in the tank. I wanted to turn the engine off, but the driver's hatch was closed in front of the turret and I wasn't about to crawl around inside.

Then the bravado kicked in.

"See that? What a shot! I got him straight between the running lights!"

"No way man, that was my shot!"

"What are you smoking? I hit him!"

The truth is that I probably didn't hit him. Shooting in the offhand position, pumped on adrenaline, I probably shot high. I wasn't even sure if I fired once or twice. If the three of us were in a bar tomorrow, though, we would probably argue about who hit him.

The whole thing was kind of odd. For several weeks now Psychological Operations (PYSOPS) had been air-dropping different kinds of pamphlets, including ones on how to surrender. We had even seen some of them in the trash piles.

"What the hell was he thinking just jumping up like that?"

"Everyone knows how to surrender."

"He wasn't trying to surrender."

"What the hell was he going to do then? Look, the hatch gun only has a belt of like three rounds."

"There is no way he could have got that on us fast enough."

"Why didn't he just drive away?"

"I dunno. It doesn't make any sense."

"Looks like he was holding his helmet."

"Yeah, that's what I thought I saw when he jumped up but I wasn't sure."

"Just doesn't make any sense."

"Yeah, jus' don' make no sense." Chuckles all around

Standing there on the tank, I cold see the canal five meters to our north on the other side of a small dirt berm. To the east I could sort of make out where the next street met the canal street. Due to the barriers and a slight bend in the canal and the road, I wasn't sure if the other guys would be able to see the tank when they hit the canal. And when I looked to the west it suddenly dawned on me that standing on top of a running Iraqi tank with armed SANG and Kuwait forces to our west was not a good idea.

"C'mon guys, time to get back."

Gonzales said, "Hold up a minute." He laid down on the top of the turret and reached down into the tank.

"What are you doing"?

He held up a 9mm pistol. "Everyone needs to go home with one of these!"

"Oh, cool!"

"Okay, let's get outta here!"

I was a little jealous that I hadn't noticed the pistol and grabbed it for myself.

Chapter 18

The Water Tower

We returned to the vehicle column and went looking for Maj S to report the tank. I found him standing beside one of the Land Cruisers talking with a couple of the Saudi officers. I figured he was going to be pissed so I abbreviated the story a little bit. I told him we had seen a tank with an Iraqi in the hatch so we shot him. Then when nothing else happened we approached and searched the tank. The important thing was to let the Saudis know there was a still-idling tank sitting up on the canal road, but we didn't think there was anyone else in it. Maj S didn't seem too upset about us approaching the tank and paraphrased it to the translator, who relayed it to the other officers.

I accompanied Maj S and LCDR Moore back to our vehicle. We mounted up and headed further east along that same road. I was following Chu again. After a while they pulled through an open chain-link gate and into a walled compound that was just off the road. An eight-foot cinder block wall surrounded a small building and two water towers. The total enclosed area was almost a city block and there was a lot of open space. The water towers were cylinder-shaped with four legs and were each about forty feet high.

We parked the Humvees by the ladder leg of one of the towers and started setting up the mobile command post on Maj S's direction. This simply consisted of a folding desk by the Humvee and the large map board hanging on the side of the Humvee. We covered the desk and map board by stringing a poncho from the roof of the Humvee to the water tower. I also hung a few antennas off the ladder about halfway up the water tower to get a little more height and better range.

Maj S briefed us that the ground war was going much better than anticipated and that we would be spending the night here. Maj S wanted the map board updated with all the teams' current positions.

I sat down at the desk with the radios remoted from the vehicles and got radio checks and position reports on all the nets and frequencies we were supposed to be monitoring. Sgt Miller updated the positions on the board.

There were two teams I couldn't reach – these were teams that had started out much further west of us in the elbow. I told Maj S I could reach them if I hung a longwire HF antenna off the top of the water tower. He waved me off. He had a conversation with higher headquarters and got their positions. He gave me the coordinates and told me not to worry about the longer-range antennas.

I sat down to the first radio watch while the other guys set up the rest of camp for the night. I hadn't eaten since breakfast so I broke out an MRE and ate it while I listened to the chatter on the radios.

I found my mind wandering back to the Iraqi in the tank. One of the slang terms used frequently in ANGLICO was "alone and unafraid." I wondered what the hell that Iraqi thought he was doing facing such a large force. The Kuwaiti doctor had dispelled the myth that these guys just wanted to go see Allah, so I didn't think it was that. The best explanation I could come up with was that he had been told he'd be shot if he left his post. He must have been more afraid of the Iraqi commanders than the Coalition bearing down on him.

Later we would hear about some of the threats made to Iraqi soldiers' families. When I heard those horrific stories, I figured the guy in the tank had probably been told his family would be tortured and killed if he didn't die attacking the Coalition. It was the only thing that made sense.

After a while I just tried to put the guy in the tank out of my mind. I found that the only way I could keep some of these events from churning in my mind was to think of them as stories I had been told. It wasn't all that difficult because of the strange feeling of detachment I'd had during the little action we had seen. It was almost like I hadn't even been there. The more I thought of them as stories, the less real they seemed and the more foggy the events became in my mind.

We had been monitoring the radios most of the day but we were starting to hear more chatter now. Maybe it was because we had our antennas better elevated. Gunny Falkner started his little stove and a pot of coffee. I was looking forward to getting a cup.

There was nothing directly affecting us on the radios, but I started to follow a series of reports about Iraqi gunboats along the coast. I plotted the last known location and was surprised to see they were pretty close to us. We were on a fairly significant point and only two or three blocks from the coastline. No one had any updated info on the boats and everyone was asking where they were. There weren't any US aircraft in the area to go check, but someone was trying to get some Kuwaiti Gazelles to go take a look (a Gazelle is a small two-seater helicopter that has rockets and forward-firing machine guns).

I asked Sgt Miller to come over and briefed him on what I was hearing. Then I told him my plan. I was pretty sure I'd be able to see the boats from on top of the water tower. So if he could stay on the radios, I would climb up the tower, take an azimuth from our position to the gunboats, and then holler the info back down to him. The DASC could probably get us in touch with the Gazelles and we could run them on the gunboats between me spotting and relaying the info to Sgt Miller on the radio.

Sgt Miller hadn't really been involved in any action yet and I could tell he was excited. I grabbed the big spotters binos, my compass, and my rifle and started up the water tower. It was a long way up and was a bit unnerving crawling off the top of ladder and onto the flat, featureless circle that was the top of the water tower.

From the top of the tower I could easily see the coastline, the point, and much of the coastline on the north side of the point. And then, almost like it was for my benefit, three boats appeared and started rounding the point. I don't know if I would call them gunboats – they looked like open pangas with an outboard on them. I was looking at them through the binos when Sgt Miller shouted up to me.

"You see 'em?"

I had to hang my head off the tower to really hear him and for him to hear me.

"Yup!" I shouted. "Looks like three of them. Can't tell how many troops are in each one, though. Hang on a minute – let me shoot an azmuith."

I swung back around and shot an azmuith with my lensatic compass. This would allow me to estimate the distance from our location and then approximate a grid for targeting the boats. But I was having trouble getting a reading. The compass was acting kind of crazy and the needle wouldn't settle down. I pushed my rifle a little ways away from me so the metal wouldn't affect the compass. That's when it hit me – I was laying on a steel water tower! How would I ever know if the azmuith was

My squad doing some MILES training in the field at Camp Pendleton. Marines love to pose with their weapons! July 1989.

Wild Eagle Two Five, just south of the Kuwaiti border. This team probably saw more action than all the other teams put together. January 1991.

Row of Kuwaiti and SANG Fahd APCs and Jeeps on the coastal highway, getting ready to drive into Kuwait. February 1991.

My boys of Salt Bravo, affectionately known as SALT Belly. Kuwait, February 1991.

Posing with my AK-47 in front of the captured ZPU-4, wearing my newly traded keffiyeh (or shemagh). Kuwait International Airport. February 1991.

Mounted patrol in an AMTRAC. Me manning the M-240.

With my father at my commissioning. Quantico, Virginia. March 1994.

Posing with the cool paint job T-34C at flight school. I love helos, but that plane was a blast to fly. Whiting Field, Florida. 1995.

Huey pilots of HMLA-269 at CAX-10 1998. L to R, front row, CUT (wanna be Huey guy), Catfish (OIC), Cooter, KW. Back row, Hesty (me), Mange, Flounder, Bull, Mute.

Coming in to land at my favorite LZ in 29 Palms. Hueys were they only ones that could fit so it was "our" LZ. Had to watch your blade tips on the two peaks of rocks on either side of the LZ.

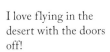

I love flying in the desert with the doors off!

Posing with Donna in front of my Huey. She painted the nose art. The nose panel is now hanging in my shop. Kosovo, February 2000.

Dawg and me getting ready to go fly in Kosovo. This is before he beat me up for coloring his sneakers pink. March 2000.

Can't ask for a better "office" view! Flying a SAR Huey in Guantanamo Bay, Cuba. GTMO terrain is strikingly similar to SoCal.

L to R, S-4 (Brent), S-6 (BK) and me. 3/5ths of the bitter majors club, just outside Hit, Iraq. October 2004.

Enemy weapons recovered from a captured Mosque.

Fallujah mosque before and after precision bombing the minaret. Note the limited damage to adjacent building. November 2004.

Met up with former students in Afghanistan. L to R: me, Jon, Jake, Rob. I had the honor and pleasure of promoting these three to Staff Sergeant then commissioning them as 2nd Lts at Auburn. While in AFG, I had the privilege of promoting two of them again to 1st Lt. War Eagle! Camp Leatherneck, AFG. December 2009.

Homecoming hugs after 14 months in Afghanistan. My last deployment. April 2010.

Rob and Andy in 2021.

accurate? I felt like a total dumbass. Still, I really didn't have any other options.

That's when I heard a booming voice from below: "HESTY! GET DOWN!"

I hung my head back over the side of the tower. Maj S was staring up at me, and even from this height I could tell he was angry.

I started to try to explain: "Yeah, but Sir, I can see the boats! I can spot them for a mission!"

"NO YEAHBUTS – GET DOWN NOW! GET OFF THAT WATER TOWER!"

"Yes, Sir!"

I slung my rifle, took one last look at the boats, and inched my way back onto the ladder. I was kind of pissed. Here was a target that we could hit. Several stations on the radio had been asking for someone with "eyes on" and I had eyes on! Maj S was just being too cautious.

As I backed down the ladder, I looked around a little bit more. On the climb up, I had been focused on climbing up the ladder and making it to the top of the water tower. But now, looking down made the feeling of being up so high a bit unnerving. As I looked over my shoulder, I could see across the town and into the desert. I could even see across the open desert into the southern portion of the town where most of the Kuwaiti and Saudi forces were located. There were even some plumes of smoke from burning vehicles. I realized how exposed I was and what a great target I would make for the enemy.

Maj S read me the riot act when I got to the ground. Toward the end of his tirade, he softened a little and admitted that I was just trying to do the right thing and that it could be a good opportunity.

"It's just too much risk," he said. "The town hasn't been cleared yet and it would be too easy for a sniper to pick you off. We wouldn't have any idea where the shot even came from behind this wall. If you need to go back up the ladder to work on these antennas, check with me before you go up."

As soon as he walked away, I looked at the map board and estimated a position from what I had seen on top of the water tower. I reported to the DASC the estimated position of the gunboats and time and that we no longer had visual. Of course they came back with a bunch of questions I couldn't answer, but I did my best.

About thirty minutes later, we heard helicopters and some shooting off to our southeast. It could have been one of the other teams working a target in southern Mina Su'ud, but I was pretty sure it was the gunboats and felt somewhat vindicated for my efforts.

I did a watch cycle on the radio, then a watch at the chain-link gate, then a watch standing on a small electrical box peering over the wall at the opposite corner of the compound.

Later I relieved Gonzales at the corner, standing on the electrical box. Gonzales was worried about having the 9mm from the tank. I told him to not worry about it, that a couple guys on the other teams had them as well. Capt Jones was even walking around with an AK-47.

"I dunno, man, I just don't wanna get strung up for it. It's not worth it. They told us no war trophies."

"Yeah, but this isn't really a war trophy. And anyway, you couldn't just leave it there." I didn't mention that we'd left a machine gun with rounds in it. I should have at least taken the ammo out of it.

"Here," he said. "Why don't you take it? Besides, you made the walk, so you should have it." (He was referring to me walking up to the tank with no cover.)

"Well, okay, but if I carry it around and take it back to Saudi I'm not going to give it back to you then."

"Yeah, I know, that's fair."

"All right," I said. "Thanks." I took the 9mm and tucked it into my flak jacket.

It was about 0200 before I got a turn to sleep. Tule had set up a cot and told me to use it as he took over watch from me. I dragged it under the tailgate of the Humvee to provide a little bit of overhead cover and fell asleep in an instant.

I woke up later to whispering and gear getting packed up and tried to sit up on the cot. Bang! Oh yeah, the tailgate. Oye, that hurt, right on my forehead.

We got everyone up, packed up all our gear, and drove out of the compound to link up with the Saudi column. It was about 0530 and still dark.

Chapter 19

Attacking North

It was just starting to get light when we rolled out and took our place in the column. The sky was overcast and the sun barely penetrated the thick haze, giving everything an orange glow. Every now and then it would drizzle for a bit. The drizzle was oily from all the soot in the air.

The column left Mina Su'ud behind and turned north along the highway heading toward Kuwait City. We were driving at a slow, steady pace, about 40 KPH. From time to time a military vehicle would come past us in the fast lane at a high rate of speed. Usually it was a Jeep or Land Cruiser. We drove under a typical road sign bridge that had the Arabic names on top and English translations beneath them. I tried to snap a photo of the sign for Kuwait City with a disposable camera through a windshield – no surprise that didn't come out.

We passed burned-out Iraqi tanks and APCs every now and then, and if the column was stopped, we'd jump out and ratfuck the abandoned vehicles. I found a dark blue beret like the one Saddam wore. I was disappointed it didn't have the Iraqi Army pin on it but it was in good shape, so I stuffed it in my cargo pocket as a souvenir. Later I found a tanker helmet – an old Soviet-style one that looked just like the ones the Russians always wore in the movies. I kept that as well.

The radios had been fairly quiet all day with just a few updates on positions as we moved north. Two of our other teams were somewhere in the column behind us. There had been a few minor incidents with shots fired at the Coalition, but as soon as anyone returned fire the white flags came out and the Iraqis surrendered.

We were still heading north up the coast highway when once again the convoy slowed to a stop. There were about fifteen vehicles in our section of the convoy now. Maj S told us that he and Gunny Falkner were going to meet with the Kuwaiti and Saudi staff. We should just stay with the vehicle and monitor the radios.

Watching in the rearview mirror, I noticed a white Land Cruiser coming up the column behind us. Every couple of vehicles, it would stop and a few people would jump out and approach the vehicles. Oh great, it looked like the press. We'd had so many briefs and classes on what we could and couldn't say to the press that I really didn't want to deal with them. I was almost scared of them – scared I would say something I shouldn't.

I put in a big fresh dip and turned to clean the contacts on the radios. This just entails unplugging a cord and using a pencil eraser on the contacts to remove any corrosion. The little brass contacts seemed to corrode incredibly fast. I usually cleaned all the contacts at least once or twice per day. Each of the connectors had an o-ring seal. When you plugged it back in, it would twist back on much easier if you wetted the o-ring. Any Marine that has messed with radios does this out of habit – you lick your finger, then run it along the o-ring inside the connector. Push and twist and the connector slides right on.

I was just getting a handset back on one of the radios when I heard Wild Eagle Two One calling Blacklist (the callsign for the DASC). They were pretty faint. I hadn't seen those guys in quite a while. I didn't recognize the voice on the radio but I was pretty good friends with most of the guys on that team.

The voice called Blacklist again.

"Blacklist Blacklist, this is Wild Eagle Two One, over."

No reply.

"Blacklist Blacklist, this is Wild Eagle Two One, over."

No reply.

After three or four more attempts, it was obvious Blacklist wasn't hearing them.

I keyed the handset, "Blacklist, this is Wild Eagle Two, over."

"Wild Eagle Two, Blacklist, go."

"Blacklist, Wild Eagle Two One is trying to establish comm with your station, over."

"Break break, Wild Eagle Two One, this is Blacklist."

"Blacklist, Wild Eagle Two One, we have enemy mortars firing on our position. Request any available air, over."

No reply.

It was now clear to me that Blacklist couldn't hear Two One, but Two One could hear Blacklist. I rolled the other radio to our inter-team frequency and called Wild Eagle Two One. The same voice answered me on the other radio and I could now recognize it was Cpl Jensen. I could hear in his voice that things were pretty tense on his end. I explained what I knew and offered to act as a radio relay for them since I could talk to Blacklist and he couldn't. Jensen told me do it.

Jensen fed me the information on one radio and I relayed it to Blacklist on the other radio. Then Jensen would tell me on the inter-team radio that I had relayed it correctly and that he had heard Blacklist's reply. I wrote the grid for their position on the corner of a page in my notebook. I ripped it off and handed it to Gonzales, who was now in the front passenger seat with the map. I told Gonzales to plot their position and then gave him the grid for the enemy mortars.

Blacklist had a section of A-6 Intruders that were vectoring toward Wild Eagle Two One, but it was going to be ten minutes before they were in radio range. I copied down their callsigns, weapons load, and frequency for contact. It took me a minute to decrypt all the numbers using our manual decryption sheet. Our radios were not encrypted so we had been encrypting numbers manually. It was a pain in the ass.

I hollered at Gonzales to get the PRC-113 out of the back and get it set up. Aircraft worked on UHF frequencies and the radios we had in this Humvee were VHF. If we wanted to talk with the aircraft or follow what they were doing, we had to get the 113 out. Gonzales handed me the map and jumped out of the vehicle.

I had the map laid out over the steering wheel, my notebook in my lap and a radio handset in each hand. Jensen was passing me some more information to relay to Blacklist to build the pilot's situation awareness as they made their way to the target area. It was mostly information about friendlies, type, and number of vehicles, how they were marked, how they were positioned, etc. He passed a little bit about what they could see of the enemy position. There were two or three mortar pits that were dropping mortar rounds very close to their position.

I knew I was letting the anxiety in Jensen's voice get me worked up, too. I needed to be calm and methodical. I was feeling a little frazzled trying to keep track of everything and was struggling to find my zen state of mind. My best state for these kind of situations is when I almost have the feeling of being very tired – very calm and detached.

Gonzales had just hopped back in the passenger's seat with the 113 when a face and a camera appeared in my zipped-down window. The voice was high-pitched and penetrating. And the face seemed to pay no attention to my attempts to wave it away. It took me a minute to realize I couldn't understand what the guy was saying because he was speaking French. But then he switched to heavily accented English: "What iz ze situation?"

"Get outta here!" I yelled. "I'm working!"

"But what ez going on? What can you tell me about ze hostilities?"

I was tempted to give him a smartass comment about getting hostile on him. I needed to pass some more information to Blacklist but I didn't want to talk on the radio if this guy or his cameraman could hear me. The cameraman kept pushing this large lens through the window, and I kept pushing it out with my left hand. I didn't want them filming the map with our marked positions and then put it on the nightly news. I continued yelling at them to get lost and gave the camera a firm stiff-arm out of the window.

In my increasing anxiety and yelling, I had swallowed some of my dip and now had a lump in my throat. Usually I'm a pretty controlled dipper. I rarely spit and almost never have a problem. I have run full physical fitness tests with a pinch stowed between by lip and gum. Now I was frazzled, pissed, feeling sick, really worried about my buddies and giving away classified information. I spat the remainder of my dip out the window just as the camera came back. It was completely unintentional, but I nailed the lens square in the middle. Both the Frenchmen took a step back.

"You have to get out of here! I will use force if I have to! Go find the adjutant or something!"

They both stormed off. My blood pressure immediately lowered. I was almost back to my cool meditative operating state when there was a large explosion a few hundred meters off to the east. It was close enough that we could feel the concussion and it made my ears ring a bit. Gonzales yelled at me to get off the road. He was right – sitting up here on the raised road bed, right next to all the Saudi APCs, made us a great target. The Humvee was still idling so I slapped it into gear and drove down the left side of the embankment. We were now down between the two raised road beds of the northbound and southbound sides of the highway. I asked Jensen how they were doing as I buckled my helmet back on. Wild Eagle was still taking mortar rounds but they hadn't actually been hit or had any casualties. I told him that we were taking arty rounds now but I was still here to help however I could.

Gonzales had the 113 out and ready. I was starting to consider stealing the A-6s to come find whoever was shooting at us. We had only had one round impact, though, and it wasn't anywhere near us. And we were in a pretty good spot now – they'd have to land a round within twenty-five meters of us to have any effect because of the highway berms on either side.

I was copying down a nine-line (the format for giving an aircraft attack directions) from Jensen when Gunny Falkner came jogging up and started talking to Gonzales. He didn't seem too concerned.

"Gunny, Two One is taking some mortar rounds and Blacklist is sending them a section of A-6s. Should I redirect them or ask Blacklist for more air?"

"No, make sure Two One gets the air."

"Should I see if we have any US arty that can range us?"

"No, don't worry about it. The Saudis are working their own arty on it."

"Do we need to move? Shouldn't we move a klick or so?"

"Nope, stay put and follow along with Two One. We're good. Make sure they get what they need."

As always, Gunny was a calming influence. It almost seemed lackadaisical how calm he always was. I don't think I ever saw him pissed off, either.

Back on the radio with Jensen, they were still okay but hadn't talked to the aircraft yet. Gonzales had been monitoring the 113 and hadn't heard anything.

I told Jensen that I was going to try the aircraft, but as soon as he thought he could talk to them he should break in and I'd shut up. I didn't want to confuse the aircrew or get in the way of Jensen trying to run a nine-line.

Gonzales handed me a third handset, the one to the 113.

"Jackal 61, this is Wild Eagle Two."

"Jackal 61." Aircrew used different techniques on the radio.

"61, I've got a nine-line for you from Wild Eagle Two One. I've got your load out from Blacklist – confirm flight of two?"

"Affirm."

"What's your ETA and time on station?"

"ETA five mikes. We've got one plus 45." This meant he'd be in the target area in five minutes and had an hour and 45 minutes before he'd have to go get fuel from a tanker.

"Roger 61, advise when you are ready to copy nine-line."

"Ready to copy."

I hollered at Gonzales to tell Jensen that Jackal 61 would be overhead in five minutes on the other radio while I started to read the attack information to Jackal on the 113. I had to pause in my radio transmission because there was another explosion off to our right. It sounded about the same distance as the last one. But I was in my groove and didn't let it bother me.

About the time I got to the remarks section of the nine-line, I heard Wild Eagle Two One come up faintly on the 113. It wasn't Jensen and I didn't recognize the voice. Jackal responded to him, so at the next pause in transmissions, I transmitted "Wild Eagle Two out" letting them know I was done talking and they could now get down to business.

I listened to the conversations and followed their attacks. I couldn't always hear Two One but it didn't matter. I copied down anything important I heard from Jackal 61. They could see the mortar positions and made two runs dropping bombs on them. The BDA (Bomb Damage Assessment) was three mortar tubes destroyed, eight enemy KIA, the rest surrendering. Jackal 61 made a couple of passes looking around the area and couldn't see anything else. Wild Eagle Two One must have then released them because all I heard was, "Thanks for the work, Wild Eagle, go get 'em, switching." Switching meant that the aircraft were switching frequencies to talk to someone else.

Jensen came back up on the inter-team radio. "Echo Four Hotel, you still there?"

Jensen was using a little cheater technique to speak directly to me. Echo Four meant E-4 or Corporal, and Hotel is my last initial. In effect he was saying Cpl H. It is a major no-no to use names on the radio.

"Yeah, brother, I'm here. You guys all good?"

"No casualties, no damage. All good. Thanks for your help." His voice sounded normal now.

"You bet, here for you. Want me to pass BDA to Blacklist for you?"

"Affirm."

The last part of a mission was passing the results up the chain of command, in this case to Blacklist. The aircraft would pass the BDA up, too, and at some point they would get compared and it all got tallied.

Gonzales was sitting on the edge of his seat peering over the radios at me. I hadn't even looked over at him in a few minutes. I'd been writing, reading, and looking at the map. Gunny Falkner was standing outside his window, smoking a cigarette and sipping coffee from his canteen cup. He leaned into the window.

"Nice job, Hesty. Want some coffee? Get your cup."

I climbed out of the vehicle and stood up. It felt good to stretch my legs. I hadn't realized how tense I had been holding them. I got my cup and joined Gunny and Gonzales on the other side of the vehicle. Gunny poured some of his coffee from his cup into mine and then gave me a cigarette. I didn't really smoke much but occasionally I did. Right then it felt really good to drag on a smoke and sip some good coffee. We didn't really say anything – just kind of nodded at each other.

After a few minutes, I remembered the artillery we'd been having. Gonzales and Gunny told me that the Saudi artillery had shot at them and the Iraqis took off. Gunny then mentioned the French reporters were from French CNN. I don't know if he meant the actual CNN or just a French version of it. I was a little worried about spitting dip on the camera. I didn't want my family to see that on the news but more importantly, it wasn't how we were supposed to handle the press. It honestly was an accident, but who would believe that?

We dug "ranger graves," which is a small depression just big enough to sleep in and keep your body below the level of the ground. Fortunately the damp sand was easy to dig but firm enough it didn't cave in on you. I stretched my poncho out over my ranger grave and staked it down so my head would be the only thing that would get wet if it rained. It had been drizzling on and off all day.

I was shaving in the mirror of the Humvee when Maj S walked over and told us to come with him. Gunny Falkner was going to stay and watch the radios. Maj S took us over between two Land Cruisers that had a tarp stretched over them. The Saudi officers were sitting in a circle, having dinner. They had a large carpet spread out under the tarp and there was a big silver tray piled with rice and pieces of meat. They waved at us to come sit down and eat with them.

We sat down with them and reached into the pile of rice and meat. The hot chow was really good. We hadn't had anything but MREs for a few days now. The Saudis were all smiling at us, some chattering in Arabic. Every now and then someone would say something in English about how the Iraqis were no match, Allah's will, and a few other comments about how well things were going. I smiled, ate, ate some more, smiled, and said, "Yes," "Shukran" (thank you), and very little else. I was relaxing and had to fight to keep my eyelids open.

When we got back to the Humvee, Maj S said we could ditch our NBC suits. I had taken off my boots for a couple hours the previous night, but other than that, we had all been wearing the same stuff since the morning we crossed the berm. It felt good to shed the oversized suits. Underneath, our tan-colored cammies were black from the charcoal on the inside of the suits.

After I cleaned my weapon, checked the vehicle, and cleaned the radios, I stood there in the dark next to the Humvee, boots and socks off, smoking another cigarette and feeling almost human again.

Chapter 20

Kuwait City

The column started moving again. It went much as the previous day: drive for forty minutes, then sit on the side of the road for fifteen, drive forty, sit for fifteen. And whenever there was an overpass close to our stop, we drove up on top to get a full view.

The landscape was changing. There were buildings now and they were getting more frequent. Sometimes there were even civilians standing in front of the buildings waving. The women were in the traditional garb – long black robes with scarves over their heads. Most of them didn't have their faces covered, but a few did. And there were always kids with them, usually wearing sweatpants and some type of soccer T-shirt.

At the next stop several cars drove by with pictures of a guy in a traditional Arabic scarf and flags plastered all over the outside of the vehicle. There were people hanging out of the windows and sunroofs waving and shouting. I figured this must be the welcome wagon.

At one point, we could see the coastline and the beach. Even from the distance, it was quite obvious that there were fortifications, obstacles, and weapons on the beach to defend against an amphibious landing. I later learned that the Navy had run a big deception operation. Amphibious Battle Group (three to five Navy ships with a battalion reinforced of Marines on board) had sailed up and down in the gulf and even did some practice landings on the Saudi coastline. The objective was to convince the Iraqis that the attack would come from the sea. That way, when the real attack came from the south, we would be attacking the Iraqis' flank instead of dead into their defenses. From the evidence on the beach, it seemed to have worked.

At the next stop, we pulled up on an overpass and were rapidly surrounded by civilians. "WELCOME! WELCOME! THANK YOU!"

I was a bit unnerved. I didn't suspect that any of them were Iraqi spies, but all the yelling and the women yelling "LA LA LA LA LA" really fast and high-pitched was nerve-wracking.

Even though I was totally on guard, one young man walked straight up to me with no hesitation. His hand was outstretched and he was repeating, "Thank you, thank you, thank you. Welcome, welcome."

I shook his outstretched hand and said, "You're welcome." I wasn't sure if that was the correct response.

Then, in a thick Arabic accent but with excellent diction he asked me a couple questions.

"Where are you from?"

"Um." I wasn't sure if I should tell him and I didn't know how much he knew of American geography. So I said, "California," thinking that was pretty nondescript.

"Ah! San Diego! Lots of Marines in San Diego. Beautiful there."

"Yeah, yes it is." What would it hurt if he thought I was from Camp Pendleton? Lots of Marines here were from Pendleton. It was all over the news.

"So tell me..uh… Why do you have the Kuwaiti flag upside down?" He was gesturing at my Humvee with the big Kuwaiti flag on the left antenna.

Holy crap! This whole time! I looked around at all the Kuwaiti flags everywhere around me and sure enough, I had mine upside down. Their flag was horizontally symmetrical with a black triangle on the left and a horizontal white stripe in the middle, but one edge had a red stripe and the other a green stripe. For some reason when I put it on, I just figured the red went on top. I could see now I was mistaken and felt like the ugly American.

"Oh, I'm so sorry! It was an accident. I'm so sorry, I didn't realize."

I wanted to fix it immediately, I was so embarrassed. I walked over to the back of the Humvee and he followed me, jabbering away. I bent the spring-loaded antenna over so I could slide the flag off and flip it. He was trying to help me and was talking about how beautiful Kuwait was, and did I like it? Had I been to see the beaches yet? I didn't know what to say. I didn't want to explain that this wasn't exactly a vacation trip for me. We got the flag flipped to the correct orientation and then luckily it was time to roll. He was still talking as we drove away, saying, "Thank you" and "Welcome." The crowd parted for us as we started to drive down the overpass to rejoin the column.

As we drove on, the crowds got thicker alongside the road and the cars whizzing past us became a regular thing. All of the cars had flags and pictures pasted on them, with people hanging out the windows shouting and waving. I didn't know who was depicted in the picture on most of the cars, but I figured it was probably the Emir of Kuwait. And everywhere the people were waving and shouting, "Welcome" and "Thank you." I even heard a few yell, "Oorge Boosh!"

At the next stop, we pulled up on an overpass that was labeled "10." The crowd collapsed around us as soon as we stopped moving. It was much the same as the previous stop but with even more people. Another young man started a similar conversation with me with the "Welcome to Kuwait. Thank you!" and "Have you seen our beautiful beaches?"

I realized that I had come to another country and still didn't have any foreign money. My father used to give me his pocket change when he came home from overseas business trips and it was always my favorite gift. I asked the young man talking at me to exchange some money. I pulled out my wallet and dug out a few dollar bills. He thought it was a great idea and exchanged some Kuwaiti bills with me. Then he asked me to sign one. I pulled out the Sharpie from my vest and signed my name on one of the bills. He was excited. He snatched one of the Kuwaiti bills out of my hand along with my Sharpie and started writing on it. He smiled when he gave it back to me. He had written, "We in Kuwait thank everybody in USA and Mr. Bush." I thought that was pretty cool. That bill is still in my treasure box.

Another Humvee came idling up through the crowd and pulled up next to us. It was Wild Eagle Two Three – the guys I had patrolled up to the border with a few weeks prior! They had the back canvas off their Humvee and it was in pickup form, with bench seats down the sides of the bed. Sgt Shue, Thompson, Foust, and Howsen were all crammed in the back with a big pile of gear.

We immediately exchanged the usual manly greetings, back slaps, and what's ups. It was a classic military bro's picture – with them sitting up in the bed and on the tailgate – so I snapped several pictures with my disposable camera. But it was tough to frame the shot with the crowd pressing in. One lady with a baby in her arms was trying to hug Peterson. I told Peterson to give her a hug and asked her if he could hold the baby. He gave me a look like, "What the hell?"

"It'll be great!" I said. "The classic liberators being welcomed by the indigenous peoples!"

He agreed and the lady excitedly pushed the baby into his arms. Then she pulled her toddler over and pointee-talkied Peterson to hold the toddler as well. Thompson slid down off the tailgate and took the baby and Peterson picked up the toddler. The toddler was waving a flag with pictures of Kuwaiti royalty on it. The lady draped a satin Kuwaiti flag over the toddler in Peterson's arms. I snapped a few more pictures and could hear several other cameras clicking too. I really wished I had brought a better camera. It was a great pic, though. You could see the flat desert in the background, a Kuwait City roadsign, the crowd all around and the guys all geared up in their desert cammies and weapons, with Peterson holding this cute Kuwaiti baby.

I didn't realize it at the time but there must have been a professional photographer in the crowd. *Soldier of Fortune* magazine printed that exact picture in the June 1991 issue. Yeah, I composed that shot. Among other pictures in that issue is one of Robert K Brown, the editor, sitting on a D-9 bulldozer. I could have sworn I'd seen him when we drove through the cut in the berm.

Soon it was time to move out again so we loaded back up and joined the column.

It was even slower going on the highway now. We were just crawling. Crowds lined the sides of the road and the decorated cars zoomed up and down the highway. The column of military vehicles stretched back as far as I could see. The crowds were shouting and the women were trilling. Some were even throwing or offering candies, cigarettes, and other goodies. Groups of small children would jog along beside us for a little while.

I was still on edge and starting to worry that there was still Iraqi resistance in the heart of Kuwait City and that all the civilians out celebrating might be in danger.

We went under an overpass labeled "8." We were definitely getting closer to the center of Kuwait City. Pretty soon we couldn't see open desert beyond the buildings anymore.

Then as we were crawling along, with thick crowds on either side of the highway and civilian vehicles mixed into the convoy, we heard gunfire. It wasn't just one or two shots – it was full automatic from lots of weapons! I just about sucked the seat cushion up my butt. I started trying to get my weapon up and pointed out the window with my left hand while driving with my right.

Maj S shouted, "IT'S OKAY, IT'S OKAY. Relax! Relax!"

"What the fuck, Sir? What's going on?"

"It's the Kuwaitis and the Saudis – they are celebrating. They do that sometimes. They fire into the air when they celebrate".

"WHAT? Don't they know that those rounds gotta come down?"

"Just relax – these guys are gonna do their thing. We'll be okay. We can't stop them now anyway."

Looking ahead and in the rearview, I could see that the soldiers in and on the vehicles in front and behind us were firing their AKs into the air and waving and shouting to the crowd. This was extremely unnerving. It was a lot of gunfire. I was really hoping we wouldn't get into a real firefight now because these guys were going to be out of ammo. I also imagined a family standing outside their house a mile or two away suddenly being struck down by bullets falling from the sky. We all made sure our helmets were securely fastened.

It was a real party now, with guys firing into the air, women shrieking "Lalalalalalala," people throwing cigarettes and candy to us. The only thing missing was some beer!

We continued on at our snail's pace. We weren't stopping anymore but our rate of forward movement was a walking speed.

After a few more overpasses the highway turned into more of an expressway and we started to see commercial buildings and businesses. We even caught a glimpse of the American Embassy across an open field. I wouldn't have known it was the Embassy compound except that the US flag was flying and Maj S pointed it out. The interchanges were now giant traffic circles instead of off-ramps with overpasses. And the traffic circles were almost the size of a city block – one even had a mosque in the center. All of them were crowded with people and decorated cars.

At the third or fourth giant traffic circle, we went three-quarters of the way around it instead of just halfway around it. We were now headed west. Five or six vehicles behind us, the rest of the column went one-quarter of the way around and headed east. I wasn't sure what was going on, but when I glanced over at Maj S, he just gave me the hand wave gesture to stay straight ahead and follow the rest of the column.

We were definitely in Kuwait City proper now. There were skyscrapers and space needle-looking buildings sprinkled in between the more traditional Arabic-style buildings. It felt like we were in a downtown parade. We took another left and it seemed like we were headed south again, but I wasn't really sure. The buildings turned more industrial and there were fewer crowds. Five or six blocks later the crowds were gone and we were in a shipping district or something. It was kind of a relief. All the crowds had been friendly and positive but it was a bit overwhelming and difficult to scan out to the surroundings.

After a few more blocks we turned through an open gate in a high chain-link fence into an area that looked like the edge of an airport. We had heard a little chatter on the radio about some fighting going on at the Kuwait City airport but I didn't know where that was (or where we were for that matter). I went back into high alert mode as we drove across what looked like taxiways. Behind us and off to the right were some large buildings that could be terminals. We were zigzagging a little, making our way to the left toward what looked like small warehouses and trailers. I noticed that the Saudis who had been riding on top of the vehicles in front of us had slid back down into their vehicles.

Maj S finally spoke up. "Okay, this area has not been completely cleared. There is still some fighting going on somewhere out here. There are friendlies on the western and northern sides of the airport. I think we are going to clear the buildings on the south end of the airport."

Wow, maybe we could have talked about this a little earlier? It would have been nice to know. I guess it really wouldn't have mattered. I don't know when Maj S found out about it but I assumed it had been at our last stop, over an hour ago.

We drove in a diagonal toward the low metal buildings to the south. I was mentally reviewing how unprepared I was. I didn't have any idea about what aircraft were flying and I was pretty sure there wasn't any artillery set up that could support us if we needed it. As I was thinking about it, I wasn't sure if the daily codes and passwords had changed. I hated the feeling of being unprepared. I didn't even know where the closest friendlies were. There was no way I'd be able to call any supporting arms if we needed any.

Maj S leaned over and rolled a new frequency into one of the radios and made a couple of calls. I didn't recognize the callsign of the other station but the conversation was basically just notification that we were approaching the southern buildings.

As we neared the buildings, the column slowed down and started to fan out a little bit. We were now in five or six short columns, driving parallel to each other. Maj S told me to just follow the APC in front of me. I thought I heard some gunfire and was just about to say something when I saw the unmistakable flashes of weapons being fired from the metal warehouse in front of us. The vehicle machine guns responded with authority.

In an elevated voice, Maj S said, "Hold on, hold on. We're Okay."

The firing trickled off quickly and the white flags appeared. Moments later three Iraqis came out of a small trailer just to the right of the warehouse. They had their hands up and were holding white T-shirts in their hands. The Saudis started dismounting rapidly and sweeping up the numerous Iraqis who continued to come out of the warehouse and the trailer.

Chu pulled up next to us on the right. Maj S told us to stay put and jumped out of the Humvee. He waved LCDR Moore to follow him and headed over to the circle of tan Landcruisers.

We sat in the vehicle and watched the Saudis round up the prisoners, search them, and put them in a circle surrounded by soldiers. The Iraqi prisoners were pretty beat looking. Many of them didn't have shoes or jackets. It was drizzling lightly again and still pretty cool out. They all hung their heads and walked a shuffle of shame as the Saudis moved them around. A few of the APCs and jeeps took off to circle around the back of the building.

Maj S came walking back toward us in his long-legged lope. He waved at us all to dismount. We gathered around in a semicircle to listen to his brief.

"The Saudis are going to continue sweeping these buildings. We are going to wait here with their command element and a couple of their squads holding the prisoners. Gunny, I want you with me over by the command element. Sgt Miller, Hesty, take the rest of the guys over and help the Saudis handle the EPWs. We are just going to help guard them so don't get involved if there is any mishandling. DON'T put yourselves in jeopardy and DON'T let your guard down."

"Yes Sir," in unison.

"Back the Humvees up to the building there. I think they are going to use this one as a temporary holding facility."

"Yes Sir," in unison again.

Gunny walked off with the Major. We jumped back in the Humvees and drove around the growing circle of EPWs. We then backed up to the building across from the big double doors. The Saudis were starting to push the EPWs into the building in a single file line. We fanned out in a line behind the line of Saudi soldiers who were on either side of the EPWs. It was obviously a reinforcing move. We were in alert posture, meaning we all had the stock of our rifles in our shoulder but the barrel was pointed down at the ground. You could sort of hook your left elbow on your ammo pouch or belt to help you hold your rifle so it wasn't too tiring a position. If you did need to fire, all you had to do was raise your left arm and put your finger on the trigger.

As the last of the EPWs filed into the building, we followed with the last of the Saudis. The building was empty inside – just a big metal warehouse with a row of small rooms down one wall. The offices around the perimeter were dark but the main area was well lit by the large circular lights hanging from the ceiling.

The Saudis had constructed what I would call a corral in the center. It was mostly barriers that looked like long sawhorses, but mixed in were a few tables and shelving units. They had obviously used whatever they could find. It wasn't so much for security as it was to let the Iraqis know where they should stay.

There must have been twenty-five or thirty EPWs in the corral now. Most of them were standing there or sort of milling about, but a few of them were sitting down on the concrete floor. The Saudi soldiers had made a circle around the corral with a meter or two between them. We spread out and stood in the bigger gaps between the Saudis. The Saudis all nodded and smiled at us as we stepped into the circle. I had a momentary fright that they might start shooting into the EPW circle but nothing liked that happened.

We had learned the mnemonic five Ss of handling EPWs: Search, Segregate, Silence, Speed, and Safeguard. The Saudis had searched them already. We didn't have facilities to segregate them just yet. They were all staying silent for the most part. Speed meant getting EPWs to the rear area. We couldn't do that just yet. Safeguard meant protect them from any harm. We were doing that the best we could. They were inside out of the rain and there didn't seem to be any immediate threat of combat. We didn't have any extra food or clothing to give them. It was pretty rudimentary but we were covering the basics the best we could for the moment.

A few more Saudis came in with about ten more EPWs. They had them in a single-file line and brought them up to the edge of the corral. After a bit of Arabic conversation and a few commands shouted, the circle opened up to include the new group. The squad that had just brought them in headed back out the door. Two of the Saudi soldiers stepped up to the front of the line and started searching the new EPWs, then gestured them inside the corral.

A few of the EPWs were whispering to each other but in general they were silent. So I was quite surprised when one of them walked up to the barrier directly in front of me. He looked me in the eye briefly, then looked down at my feet and said, "When will I be deported to the US?" He spoke English well, although he did have a thick Arabic accent.

"What do you mean?" I said.

"I was a medical student at the University of Pennsylvania. I came home to visit my family and I was forced into the Army. I just want to go back to my home at University."

I stammered a bit. "Uh, well, this is going to take some time to sort out. I'm not sure how all this will be handled. It's going to be a while before anyone goes anywhere."

"Okay, thank you."

I was still reeling from this short conversation when another Iraqi stepped up next to the first and said, "Who did you kill?"

Oh crap, what have I started? And he couldn't actually know about any of the incidents I had been involved in, could he? What was he talking about?

"Whadda you mean who did I kill?"

"Who did you kill to become a US Marine? We know that you have to kill someone in your family to be accepted. And that the Gunnys? The Gunnys have to kill their parents?"

Now I understood. I had heard that Psychological Operations had dropped leaflets that described some fearsome (but untrue) things about the Marines to intimidate the Iraqis into surrendering. This story must have come from those leaflets.

I was interested in talking with some of these guys but they were EPWs. We didn't have them secured yet and moments ago they had been shooting at us. A few more had started to gather around the first two talkers. I had to get this fixed – this was not how handling EPWs was supposed to go. If they believed some of the stuff from PsyOps then maybe I should just use it.

"You don't need to know," I said. "Don't you worry about it. Just stay in the circle and keep quiet. If all goes well, you might get something to eat tonight."

I didn't want to come off as completely heartless. I also didn't want to promise anything, positive or negative, that I couldn't make sure happened. I was pretty sure we were gonna find some way to feed these guys, so it wasn't an empty promise.

One of the Iraqis muttered, "So sorry," and then they turned around and shuffled toward the center of the circle.

A few more squads came in at irregular intervals, bringing more EPWs. The same process repeated itself with a single-file line, search, then into the corral. Then the squads would head back out. The group of EPWs must have grown to seventy-five or so. It was getting so they were pretty dense in the corral. If we got many more, they weren't going to fit.

Several of the officers came in and headed over to the offices. As they walked past, Maj S shot me an "Everything okay?" glance. I gave him a thumbs-up and a nod. They walked over and set up in one of the offices that still had glass in the window. The lights in the office even worked.

The next few squads that came in only had two or three EPWs. After those EPWs got searched and shuffled into the corral, the Saudi soldiers joined into the security circle. There was plenty of security now.

Maj S stepped out of the office and waved me over. I trotted over.

"Hesty, there are three trailers on this side of the building. I want you to take the Marines, drive the Humvees over, and set up shop in the middle trailer. Back up the Humvees and remote the radios into the trailer so we can have a CP inside with the radios. We are going to be here a day or two."

He paused for a moment with a look on his face that I didn't recognize. It was almost confusion but not quite.

"Sir?"

"Hesty, just pass on to Sgt Miller that that's what I want him to do. You just make sure the radios and antennas are all good. Oh, and make sure you set up with room for more. Salt Bravo will probably be joining us shortly."

"Yes, Sir." Now I understood. He had breached the chain of command by skipping Sgt Miller and going straight to me. It was poor form to leave

Sgt Miller out but I already knew that he relied on me to get things done and didn't have the same confidence in Sgt Miller.

Either way, we were happy to leave. It wasn't much fun staring at the beaten-down EPWs. I'd much rather be outside, messing with radios. I passed the message on to Sgt Miller and we did as the Major directed.

The trailers were three-room single wides. We backed the vehicles to the door in the middle. I started running remotes into the middle room and then set up antennas on the roof. From the roof I could see over the next warehouse and into an open area that looked to have a bunker and a few revetments dug.

By the time I finished with the radios and antennas, the rest of the guys had desks and tables moved into the middle room, making a nice CP area with cots set up in the two end rooms. One would be for the officers and Gunny, and the other for us. There was plenty of room to add a few more in each side.

It was late afternoon when we finished, with maybe an hour of light left. The lights in the trailer worked so we were feeling pretty good about it all.

Everything was turning dark orange from the sun sitting on the horizon and shining through the dark soot clouds when Salt Belly pulled up. I hung out the door of the trailer and waved them over. It was good to see those jokers.

We got them all settled in and directed their officers to where they could find Maj S. Suarez pulled out a camp stove and started heating up a large can of soup. It smelled really good and I hadn't realized how hungry I was. They were all gathered around the little stove and waved me over.

"Come get some hot soup!"

"Awesome! Thanks." I dug out my canteen cup and my trusty spoon that I kept tucked in the front of my flak vest.

"Here." Suarez was holding out the pot to pour some into my cup.

"Smells great!" I said. "What is it?"

"It's from my grandmother. It's something from Mexico."

When I hesitated a moment there was a collective chuckle.

"Just eat it – don't worry about it."

If they hadn't all been so vague and insistent, I wouldn't have thought anything about it. But there was something not quite right here. They were all eating it, though, so it couldn't hurt me. I just hoped it wasn't too spicy. I took a couple of spoonfuls, cooling them off a bit before I ate it. It actually was very good. It was a kind of brothy soup with some vegetables in it and some weird white stuff that was kind of chewy. It all tasted good, though.

"So what is it?" I said.

"You seriously don't know?" More chuckles.

"No," I said.

"It tripe! Cow stomach!"

"Really?" I said. "It's pretty good, kind of chewy."

"It's menudo, soup made with tripe. My grandmother sent me a whole case of the giant cans."

Hell, it was warm and tasted good so I didn't care. The Mexican Marines all thought it was pretty cool I was eating it with them and I was thankful they were sharing it with me. And I must say it was pretty cool to be eating tripe soup from someone's Mexican grandma at the airport in Kuwait City.

The officers came back after a bit. We sat in a circle and got a brief. The war was over. Kuwait had been liberated! Our job was basically done. It was possible there were still a few Iraqi stragglers around and probably some booby traps so we still had to be tactical and careful. We would probably stay there for a day or two while a few more teams joined up with us, then we would head back to Camp 5 in Saudi Arabia.

This was all great news but I admit I had mixed feelings. On one hand I was excited that we were done and going home, but on the other hand I felt like we should maybe continue into Iraq and dethrone Saddam. But there wasn't anything I could do about it, so I mentally returned to the present.

Since we had so many guys there and only one set of radios to watch, Gunny Falkner left me off radio watch for the night. Sweet! I cleaned my rifle, checked all the radios, and made sure the radio watch knew where the fresh batteries were. Around 2300, I stripped down to my skivvies, removed my boots and socks, and slid into my sleeping bag on a cot. It felt good to take off the nasty clothes I had been wearing for several days straight. I smelled really bad but I was so tired, I'd wash up in the morning. I fell asleep immediately and slept the sleep of the dead.

Part III

Commissioning and Flight School
(1993–2002)

Chapter 21

Married

I first met Lisa at a dive bar. She was five-foot-three and a well-toned 115 pounds. She rode a Harley, worked as a bartender, had tattoos, and smoked. And she had a biting sarcasm that often had me rolling. We started meeting at the pool hall regularly, then started going other places, too.

This was around August of 1993 – about two years after I had returned from Kuwait. Bill Clinton was in the White House and the Gulf War was quickly fading into the past. I was still in the reserves and back in school at Cal Poly, getting close to graduation.

I had felt a bit lost and directionless after I returned from Kuwait. Vietnam veterans had made sure we received a hero's welcome when we first landed, but no one else seemed to really get it. For a time I mostly just liked being by myself and did a lot of fishing, hiking, and mountain biking. But slowly I readjusted to civilian life and began to think about the future.

I always thought I'd go active duty when I finished school. And the best way to do that was as an officer. As I neared graduation, I had to decide between three opportunities. The first was a slot at Ranger school. The second was an upcoming operation to Thailand called Operation Cobra Gold. The third – and a potential life changer – was a slot at Marine Officer Candidate School (OCS) with a flight contract. The flight guarantee meant that I would have a slot at flight school as long as I stayed qualified. I had always wanted to fly, and the Marine Corps flew Bell Hueys just like in the old Vietnam movies. It was a dream shot to me.

In October, I accepted the orders to OCS and was scheduled to leave for Virginia on January 14, 1994. In December, I graduated with a GPA of 3.85, a far cry from the 1.95 I had in high school. I had finally figured out how to take school seriously. Everything was lining up nicely.

Lisa didn't understand the Marine Corps or what this all meant yet. I had taken her to the Marine Corps Ball so she knew the Marine Corps can throw a party. Other than that, all the Marine Corps meant to her was I packed all my green stuff in a bag and disappeared for a few days – or on occasion, for a month.

A few days after Christmas, Lisa said, "Don't expect me to just follow you wherever you go."

"We'll make new friends there," I said. "And there will be job opportunities there just like there are here."

"You mean you'll make friends. I'm not going to work at the PX or the Commissary with the Filipino Mafia."

It was often difficult for me to tell when she was playing bitchy and when she really meant it. I knew she had never really been away from home. I don't think she had ever been more than a mile from a 7-11.

"So what are you saying?" I said. "That you just want to stay here?"

"If I stay here, don't expect me to just sit around here waiting for you." Then it dawned on me. "You want to get married?"

"Well it would be different if we were married," she said. "But don't expect me to hang out with the stupid wives club."

So we started talking about getting married. Looking at it from a purely financial perspective, my pay would go up about $100 per month. Lisa would get health insurance and we'd get a housing allowance once I graduated OCS. So it made practical sense – or so my inexperienced mind thought.

We had a lot of fun together and seemed to enjoy many of the same things, so how bad could it be? I didn't believe in the idea of a soul mate or love at first sight. I knew marriage was a lot of work. It was just a matter of finding someone who was worth the work.

A few weeks before I left, I bought the best bottle of wine I could afford and brought it to Lisa's dad to ask his permission. He laughed – but it wasn't a negative laugh. He thought it was funny because in his mind, Lisa could do whatever she wanted. That, and he didn't like wine. He did respect what I was trying to do, though.

I started studying diamonds. I never realized how much there is to buying a diamond! I found a pretty good one at the exchange on base, which was a bonus because I didn't have to pay sales tax.

Next, I borrowed my friend's Jeep and developed a plan to take Lisa four-wheeling to a spot in the mountains that overlooked the entire LA basin. I figured we could watch the sunset, see the lights of the cities come twinkling on.

Lisa bitched and complained the entire way. "This is so stupid," she said. "Why are we driving on this little twisty, bumpy trail?"

"Just wait, you gotta see this place," I said.

"I gotta hold a death grip just to keep from falling out! We're gonna fall down this ravine and they will never find us."

"I've been up this road plenty of times – we'll be fine."

"My boobs are gonna bounce right off."

"Okay, I'll drive a little slower."

"We are already barely crawling."

Finally we got to the hilltop clearing. It was a beautiful afternoon and fairly clear. The Santa Ana winds had been blowing the previous week so the usual brown layer of smog was absent. We could see all the way out to Catalina Island.

I spread out the blanket, opened a bottle of wine, and poured two glasses. Lisa stood there with her hands on her hips.

"Here," I said. "Sit down, have a glass of wine."

"Why didn't we just go to the Treehouse or my bar?"

"We do that almost every night. I thought this would be a romantic change of pace."

I had hoped to wait until the sun was setting but I felt like I was on a sinking ship. I decided to just go for it. I pulled out the ring, got on one knee, and blurted out, "Lisa, will you marry me?"

"I knew you were going to do that!" she said. "You're just so predictable."

I was bummed. I didn't really know what to say. So I said, "So are we going to get married or what?"

"Let's go to the pool hall and play a few tables."

I was pissed off as I packed up the stuff. On the drive down, I told her I thought she was being cruel and that she should just tell me yes or no. She looked at me with a strange look and said, "You are being over-sensitive. Of course."

The next day we went to the Justice of the Peace and got married. It was like registering a vehicle. We took an oath and signed some papers. Then we drove out to the base and got Lisa a dependent's identification card. Our honeymoon was sitting on the bed watching TV and drinking beer. It seemed like it should feel different. We didn't tell anyone.

Two days later, I caught my flight to Virginia. OCS was twelve weeks long and many of the same techniques for surviving boot camp worked at OCS. The one major difference was there was little to no emphasis on following orders and a lot of emphasis on making decisions rapidly with incomplete information. The sergeant instructors would yell, "WHAT ARE YOU GONNA DO, CANDIDATE?" The officer instructors would then calmly explain that a 60 percent solution in time was better than a 90 percent solution too late.

The Virginia winter made me miserable. We had ice storms, marched on sheets of ice, and went to the field in the snow. I guess I've spent too much time in the desert but I'd much rather deal with the heat.

We graduated and were commissioned 2nd Lieutenants at the end of March. I graduated eighth in my class of 180. I was proud of that but it was mostly due to being a good runner, having previous experience, and being ready to work hard. But nobody cares where you graduate in your OCS class.

Lisa had come out the week before graduation and rented us a small apartment. My next school, TBS, was six months long at the same base. I had seen her for about twelve hours the weekend before graduation, but I was so exhausted I could barely keep my eyes open. And anyway all she wanted to do was go furniture shopping for the barren apartment.

A few days later, I started TBS. Even though we were commissioned officers, we were still herded around like cattle. TBS is designed to teach all Marine officers the very basics of every career field in the Marine Corps. We learned about administration, intelligence, artillery, armor, aviation, supply, and logistics. We also learned more about patrolling, urban warfare, unit movement, command, and control. There was a lot of classroom time but we spent a lot of time in the field, too. Days started early and ended late.

Lisa didn't appreciate my schedule. Most days I got home late and had to study and do uniform prep for the next day. Many times we would be out in the field for the whole week. By the time the weekend came around, I just wanted to sleep or had basic cleaning and maintenance to do.

Lisa was bored. She was in a new town and didn't know anyone. She didn't have a job and we didn't have much money. TBS was pretty competitive and I was continually stressed out about being ready for school and keeping up. Things weren't going very well between us. We argued a lot and she never had anything positive to say about anything.

The next school was going to be in beautiful Pensacola, Florida, and we would be there for about two years. We would have thirty days off between TBS and flight school so we planned to have a wedding in California, near where her parents lived. We fought about the wedding, too. Weddings are expensive and I was already worried about the amount of debt we had.

After ten weeks, Lisa moved back to her parents. She said it was to get ready for the wedding but I think it was to get away. School went much easier once she was gone. Instead of trying to balance my minimal amount of time between her and studying, I could just focus on school. It was a relief.

I did well at TBS and graduated nineteen out of 250. I was top of the class in physical fitness and missed a perfect score by one point. On our eight-mile endurance course run through the woods over obstacles with gear, I finished just six seconds slower than the perfect score. That has bugged me a bit ever since.

Job selection is based on class rank and what the Marine Corps needs. But since I already had a flight contract, I didn't have to select.

After the graduation ceremony, I literally walked to my car and drove to California. I changed out of my dress uniform while driving and made it all the way to the New Mexico/Arizona border before I had to pull over and sleep for a bit.

Back at Lisa's parents' house things were going better with Lisa until I found out she had gone to Lake Havasu with her ex-boyfriend for the Fourth of July weekend. She swore that nothing happened and she was just hanging out with friends, but it really pissed me off. I had to work hard to let that one go.

Things were a little stressful because the wedding was a week away. Lisa and her parents had done most of the planning and things were pretty well set up. I had arranged for the sword arch and ushers with my friends at 3rd ANGLICO.

The wedding was a package deal at the local Red Lion hotel. Everything was provided in one place. There weren't any of the crazy decisions about centerpieces or napkins. About the only thing we had to do was pick a meal from their set menu. Lisa's dad had put down $10,000 and we financed the rest. I was extremely grateful to Lisa's dad but a little sore about how much we had to finance. 2nd Lieutenant pay is better than Sergeant pay but I still hadn't made that much progress on all our debt and I would have to start paying on my student loans in another year. Lisa had student loans, too.

The wedding was a big party, though, and we had lots of fun. Between the Pomona Harley Owners Group and 3rd ANGLICO Marines, things got fairly wild.

It was good to see that my family, including some of my uncles and aunts, made it out too. My mother told me she was relieved that we were finally married and no longer living in sin. We hadn't told my parents that we were already married.

There were a ton of Lisa's family friends that I had to meet and they all started blurring together pretty quickly. But most of Lisa's expectations were met, which is what the wedding was really about.

A couple days later, we packed everything into a U-Haul and headed back across country to Pensacola. I was nervous about flight school already – excited but nervous. Things seemed to mellow out between me and Lisa – although she gave me shit the entire drive that this cross-country trip did not count as a honeymoon.

Chapter 22

Flight School

Like most schools in the military, flight school is broken into phases. The first six weeks is called Aviation Preflight Indoctrination, or API. It is mostly classroom work interspersed with lots of medical exams and a swim qualification at the end. We covered topics from aerodynamics to weather to airspace control. The amount of data that had to be memorized was intense. We called it drinking from the firehose.

I had to learn new ways to study. Up to that point I had mostly studied to learn concepts and then tried to apply those concepts to different situations. Flight school was pure rote memorization. The instructors didn't care if you understood the concept; they just wanted you to spout the correct bit of data back to them at the correct time. I had expected flight school to be more like college and less like other military schools. Every week there was a test and 80 percent was the minimum passing score. I studied a lot!

The medical exams weren't hard but they were exhausting, with endless questionnaires, constant blood and urine samples, and being poked and prodded. It felt like the doctors and surgeons were just looking for reasons to kick you out. But their job was to make sure you were medically suited to flying any Navy or Marine Corps aircraft.

The swim qualification was grueling, too. I had passed the Marine Corps water survival instructor test but this one was just as challenging, if not worse.

And then there were the dunkers. There are three different dunker tests, but the most famous is the helo dunker. It's a mockup of a large helicopter cabin suspended over a deep pool. It slides down two rails and slaps the top of the water, then it rotates 180 degrees and sinks into the pool. Everyone has to pass four rides. The first ride you simply stay put until all motion stops, then unlatch your seatbelt and swim up to the surface. The second ride is the same thing, but you have to wear blacked-out goggles. The third ride you can see again, but this time you have to find your way to the main door and exit there. Last but not least you have to find and exit the main cabin wearing blacked-out goggles. You are really only underwater for about twenty seconds, but while you are holding your breath, strapped into the seat upside down at the bottom of the pool, it feels like thirty minutes.

About 40 percent of each class drops out during this phase of flight school. If you get less than 80 percent on a test, you are dropped back to a later class to go through the academics of that section again. If you fail again, you are sent back and assigned a new job specialty in the Marine Corps. And if you fail something in the medical exams, you are gone, back to the Marine Corps for reassignment.

The next phase was Primary. We were assigned to a training squadron and finally got to start flying. We got to fly T-34Cs – a two-seat fully aerobatic turbo prop – for the next six months.

I didn't enjoy the first ten or fifteen flights because I was nervous and was rattled by the constant grilling from the instructors. At any time they could turn something off including the plane and we had to execute the correct emergency procedures while clearly and calmly describing what we were doing. The training worked, though. You learn the emergency procedures thoroughly so that at the inevitable point where you have an actual emergency, you often don't even think about it; you just execute.

At the end of the precision aerobatics stage there was a solo flight where we got to fly a T-34C alone. We were SUPPOSED to do loops and barrel rolls. I couldn't believe Uncle Sam gave me a turbine engine aircraft and told me to go have fun in it. There wasn't even an instructor in the back seat yelling at me! It was a beautiful day and I was ecstatic.

After Primary, we had to select one of three types of aircraft: jets, helicopters, or propellers. At that time, the Marine Corps had F/A-18s or Harriers for jets, C-130s for propellers, and Cobras, Hueys, Phrogs, and Sea Stallions for helos. I selected helos.

I have always been more interested in helos than other aircraft. Helos just seem more connected to the Marines – I liked the idea of bringing Marines into a landing zone and rescuing them from a hot zone. Going Mach 2 sounds like fun, but ninety knots at twenty feet is way more exciting. Proximity to terrain gives you a more significant sense of speed. Plus, jumping from a helo and fast-roping/rappelling from a helo had always been highlights of my training, so I never really considered any other aircraft.

As a helo guy I stayed at the same squadron flying the T-34C for another two months for the Intermediate phase of flight school. After Intermediates, helo guys transfer to a helo squadron for Advanced Phase. The helo squadrons fly the TH-57, which is a Bell Jet Ranger and pretty much the same thing as most of the news helicopters you see today. You go back to ground school for more aerodynamics, but this time it's about rotor wing aircraft or helos. There are some more aircraft systems, advanced weather and airspace classes, too. The aerodynamics and systems of a helo are a little more complicated.

The first thing you start working on is a hover. Holding a steady hover is a lot more challenging than I thought it would be. There are three basic controls, and each input has an effect on the other two. If you start sliding in one direction, you move the cyclic stick (the one between your knees) in the opposite direction a little bit. This changes the force of the main rotor to counteract the slide. By changing the force of the main rotor, you have lessened the power a little bit, which means you will start sinking. So you add power with the collective stick (the one on the left side of your left hip). This stops the sinking, but the torque has increased on the airframe, and now you have to push a little bit with the left pedal to counteract that torque and keep the aircraft from spinning. And of course if there is a little wind or the aircraft is heavy or lighter, it's all different. Once you get the feel, though, it becomes second nature. But that takes much of the Advanced Phase.

Once you are flying, a helo performs much like a fixed wing aircraft. Because of the increase in moving parts, there is more that can go wrong with a helo and there are a lot more emergency procedures to learn. Of course the big one is autorotations.

Autorotations are the helo version of gliding an airplane. You use the upward airflow of falling out of the sky to turn the rotors of a helo, enabling you to continue to fly the aircraft. As you near the ground, you use the built-up energy in the spinning rotors to slow the rate of descent and land the aircraft. Timing is everything. If you are too late, you smack the ground. If you are too early and you have used up all the built-up energy in the rotors and you start falling again with no control, and you smack the ground.

We practiced two types of autorotations. The first is full autos, where you turn the throttles to idle and "fly" the aircraft all the way to landing. They are practiced at an airfield with a level landing surface and there is Crash Fire Rescue on hand in case you mess up.

Power recovery autos can be practiced almost anywhere. Generally, the instructor simply turns the throttles to idle and says, "You have a simulated engine failure." That statement often gets abbreviated to simply "simulated," a word hated by aviators around the world.

The physical feeling that accompanies autorotations is unnerving. Your stomach hits your throat as you go from powered flight to falling. You go through the proper emergency procedures and direct the aircraft toward the closest level and clear landing spot. If you maneuver the aircraft to proper airspeed and nose attitude (pointed down more than usual), that gives you your minimum descent rate, which is often around 2,000-1,500 feet per minute. Once the instructor is satisfied that you are on parameters and have set up properly, they will give you back control of the throttle and you can bring power back onto the rotor and arrest your rate of descent. In populated areas, this happens above 1,000 feet. On military bases it might be at 150 feet. As a result, most helo pilots spend a lot of time watching for good places to land, even when the aircraft is running well.

The Advanced phase lasts about eight months. Again it depends on weather, aircraft availability, instructor availability, and how many students they are trying to pump through. From the time I checked in until the time I finished and got winged, it was a little over two years.

Meanwhile, Lisa had made some friends and had started a dental assistant program. She also got a part-time job bartending, so while I was at home stressing and studying, she was at the bar making a little money. There are some fantastic beaches in Pensacola and she usually liked going to the beach. I bought an old Glastron boat and got it running. We had some fun water skiing and just cruising around and exploring all the coastal waterways.

But we fought a lot, too, and when we fought, Lisa went all out. Oftentimes, I would just want to get away and cool off a bit and she hated that. On several occasions she literally ripped a shirt right off me trying to make me stay and argue. I tried to talk with her about it a few times when everything was calm, but that always just started another fight. At one point I asked her for a divorce because we spent more time fighting than anything else. She said, "No way! There is no way you are divorcing me!" I was perplexed. She said she didn't like being around me but she wouldn't think about divorce, either. Like many military guys, I hoped that maybe at the next job and the next place things would magically be better.

We started shopping for our first house and we went through several fights about where we should look and how much we could spend. In the end we agreed on a house and bought it. It was a big step in growing up, learning about mortgages, insurance, and taxes. On Saturday mornings, I would mow and edge my own lawn. I'd never really enjoyed mowing; it had always been a chore I was doing for someone else. But there was something satisfying now about mowing my own lawn and making it look good.

I'd also wanted a dog. Lisa agreed and we adopted a dog from the Humane Society. I named him Stuart. He was a blond lab/pit mix and about nine months old. Stuart became my best friend and I took him everywhere. There was a nice trail network through the woods close to the house. It was something that the three of us did together, and Lisa and I rarely fought about anything while walking.

Nearing "Winging" we all filled out a dream sheet. The dream sheet is broken down by aircraft models and where they are stationed. My top choices were Hueys East Coast and Hueys West Coast. While I liked California, I wanted to see some more of the country. Camp Lejeune had some cool stuff and a lower cost of living. I had talked to Lisa about it and she begrudgingly agreed that we should try the East Coast.

One day I got out of the shower and the stereo was turned up really loud. As I came out of the bathroom in a towel, I recognized the music. It was Wagner's "Ride of the Valkyries" – the theme song for Huey guys after the famous scene in *Apocalypse Now*. Lisa was standing in the middle of the living room grinning.

"What's going on?" I said.

"Captain Stoud called. He told me your selection."

"What?" I said. "Really?" I half suspected that she was messing with me.

"You got it! You are going to fly Hueys East Coast!"

Like a couple of kids we held hands and danced around the living room. It was one of the coolest things Lisa ever did for me. It was something I had dreamed about and worked hard for and I was getting exactly what I wanted. I was amped up and my wife was excited and dancing with me.

Chapter 23

Divorced

My assigned fleet squadron was in New River Air Station next to Camp Lejeune North Carolina. So that meant another cross country move. I packed all our house belongings in a Penske box truck and Lisa followed in our '94 Nissan pickup.

I had some fun stops planned along the way, but after a blow-out argument about a mountain biking stop, we just started driving. We made the trip in record time and pretty much argued every time we stopped. This horrible trip was all my fault. I was a stupid man.

We rented a furnished trailer in North Carolina while we started house shopping. Lisa hated the trailer and I heard about it almost every day. It was her lead-in line whenever she met someone: "And HE made me live in the dumpy stinky trailer in NORTH CAROLINA."

After three weeks, Lisa and I found a house that we both liked and Lisa lightened up on me about our living conditions. She enrolled in some classes at the local community college.

Our new house was just down the street from 1st Lt Kyle West, a friend from TBS and Flight School. We ended up spending a lot of time together. Lisa seemed to like him okay so we had him over to dinner frequently. And on weekends, we helped each other with house projects or went fishing together.

Everyone tells you that you will be studying the rest of your flying career and they are right. There is always more material to learn about the aircraft, more to learn about how the Marine Corps uses aviation, more to learn about threat aircraft and weapons systems, plus you always need study for your next qualification.

The next few months entailed getting to work at 0600 and getting home about 1900. Days at work were taken up by reading dry, strangely worded military publications, organizing documents that filled a fifteen by twenty-foot locked vault, and writing more procedures and dry publications.

I got to go fly about once per week. I loved it but the preparation was a lot of work. The debriefing after a flight was usually blunt, to say the least. If something went well, there wasn't a reason to talk about it. Most of the debriefs consisted of an instructor or senior pilot pointing out all the things you did wrong.

Flying around coastal North Carolina can be challenging. There is little terrain and the landscape is flat. We used rivers, roads, and water towers as landmarks to navigate.

Almost every flight was tactical. Flying low down the river, then popping over a tree line to land in a small clearing was exhilarating. We did a lot of section flying – which means two aircraft at the same time. We also started doing missions for the units on Camp Lejeune, with fast roping and rappelling from the helicopter, parachute jumps, and shooting for guys on the ground. I also started the NVG syllabus and got my night qual.

It was difficult to develop flying skills flying only once a week. But Marine aviation was in a transition in the mid-'90s – trying to do more with less money, which meant less flight time. All we could do was study a lot and be ready for our flights.

Lisa didn't understand any of this squadron stuff and didn't want to. She didn't understand why I came home from work at 1900 and then had to study or prepare for a flight. And on Saturdays I just wanted some decompression time. Occasionally we went water skiing and Kyle would come with us. She would tell me how bad I was at driving the boat. It pissed me off but Kyle thought it was funny.

In July my unit deployed to Twentynine Palms to participate in a CAX. Between moving ten aircraft cross country, two three-week exercises, and then bringing everything back to North Carolina, we were gone for ten weeks.

The flying in Twentynine Palms was awesome. It's basically one big range and we got to shoot all over the place. The insane heat and high altitudes made the flying pretty stressful, though. The UH-1N Huey is already underpowered. Some days, with the heat and altitude, the engines would only make 85 percent of normal power. And we were always flying around overloaded – either full of ammo or trying to fit one more grunt into the tight zone.

It takes more power to hover a helo than it does to fly along at sixty knots or faster. When you are in a hover, the rotor system is chopping up the same air over and over. When you have forward movement, the air is "cleaner" and requires less power to provide lift. There were times that we skipped down the runway a few times before we had enough forward airspeed to pull up and away and got steady flight. After ten minutes airborne, we would burn off about a hundred pounds of fuel so we would gain some lift back. Of course, if we shot some rockets we were doing even better. Oftentimes we returned to land with the Low Fuel light on.

At the end of the day, my flight suit would be half white from all the salt stains and I'd realize I hadn't taken a leak in six hours. I'd have a headache from being dehydrated and would check the schedule while guzzling a gallon of water. Then we'd start planning the flight for the next day.

We got back to Camp Lejeune in September. Not much had changed. I loved taking Stuart out fishing and had fun hanging out with Kyle but I didn't like having to deal with Lisa. It seemed like she was always complaining about something. She had finished the dental assistant program and was working as an assistant for a local dentist. I'm not sure how much she made because I never saw any of that money in our bank account.

Kyle and I got promoted to Captain the next month. It wasn't a big surprise but the pay raise was good. I had finally gotten Lisa's student loans and credit cards paid off and was starting on my own student loans. We had a beautiful house. I had just leased Lisa a brand new 4Runner, and we had a great boat.

Still, things weren't good enough for Lisa. And she never wanted to do anything with me. So why should we be married? When I tried to talk to her about it, she would scream and yell at me that I wasn't going to leave her. I didn't feel like I could talk to any of my family about it. Kyle was good friends with her so I couldn't talk to him about it, either. I didn't know what to do.

My parents came to visit shortly after I got back from another CAX in July. It had always been a bit tense between my mother and Lisa, but this time was even worse. One night when my parents offered to take us for dinner Lisa claimed it was because they hated her cooking and refused to go. I was trapped in the middle the whole visit.

Finally, when I was seeing my parents off at the airport, my mom asked me if I knew that Lisa and Kyle were having an affair. I was shocked to hear something like that from my Mom. And how would she know?

"No, Mom," I said. "Kyle is a good friend to both of us."

"He has a key to your house."

"I know, Mom, I gave it to him. I have a key to his house. We take care of each other's stuff while the other one is gone. It's no big deal."

I hadn't told my parents that I really wanted to separate from Lisa. Lately, I had been sleeping in the extra room at the house and Lisa and I were barely talking to each other. In my mind, we were already separated, just still living in the same house because we couldn't afford two houses.

A few weeks later, I got word that my unit was going to deploy to Norway for Combined Exercise Battle Griffin.

We loaded our aircraft, gear, and Marines on three C-5 Galaxies and headed to Norway in late January. It was cold! There was snow everywhere and the ground was frozen solid. Even inside the hangars, we had to stretch a huge tarp over the aircraft and crank up a couple of big heaters to get the aircraft up to a temperature so we could work on them.

After the aircraft were ready to fly, we spent six days doing a cold weather survival course out in the woods. That was fun but I was miserable in the cold. The flying there was awesome. The aircraft performed very well in the cold, dry air. The scenery was incredible with the frozen-over fjords and ridges of steep mountains.

The best pub in Stjordal was Bamses and it became our pub of preference. Every visit to Bamses was a successful mission. It didn't hurt that the local female population was stunning. True to the stereotype, they were all five-foot-ten, blond, and slender. It was kinda fun flirting with them but by midnight we were all headed back to the base.

We got home and it felt like we had been gone for a year. When we pulled in, all the families were there to welcome us home. Everyone except my family. Not that I was in a hurry to see Lisa, but I did need a ride home.

I went up to the duty desk and used the phone to call the house. Kyle answered. That was odd.

"Hey, man!" I said. "How's it going? Can you ask Lisa to come pick me up?"

"Just a sec," Kyle said. He put down the phone for a moment, then came back. "She says to just get a ride home with someone else."

"Oh, okay," I said. "Well, see ya in a while."

"Yeah, okay."

I got a buddy to drop me off at my house. Stuart went crazy when I walked in. Lisa was in the office on the computer. Kyle must have left.

Stuart and I went out on the back porch to have a dog bone and a beer. I had a knot in my stomach.

The next couple days, we pretty much avoided each other. Then, one night a few days later, I was studying in the office when Lisa came busting in, full of fury.

"Tiny's wife said you slept with a bunch of girls in Norway!"

"No, I didn't," I said. "And how would she know anyway?"

"Tiny told her!"

I know I wasn't acting exactly like a married guy should in Norway, but I wasn't sleeping around.

"I didn't sleep with anyone," I said. "That's just Tiny flailing about trying to get his wife off his ass."

"BULLSHIT!"

Almost without thinking I rolled into it. "You know what? You're right, I'm full of shit, I slept with probably fifteen girls in Norway. Every night."

"You asshole!"

"I'm so sick of your shit," I said. "I've asked you for a divorce for the last three years. I had enough so I went out and had an affair!"

"I knew it!" she screamed. "Get the fuck out of my house!"

I grabbed a few things and headed out the door.

I had the keys to my buddy Lucky's house, who was on deployment. Lucky had always told me, "If there's anything you need…" Over the next week, I got all my clothes, uniforms, and tools moved over. I started drafting a divorce agreement.

I assumed that we would just split everything down the middle, but Lisa got a lawyer and things got complicated, fast. I offered to buy Lisa out of the equity we had in the house and her share of the boat. She refused both.

I had paid off Lisa's school loans first because they were a crappy interest rate. I had deferred mine as long as I could. That was a mistake. Because that debt was incurred before the marriage, that didn't get split in the divorce.

I had registered both vehicles in Lisa's name because it was cheaper. She claimed that she owned them both. For the lease on the 4Runner, fine, it was a lease! But the Nissan truck was worth about $10,000 and I needed something for transportation. I was pretty stressed.

Through all this I was still flying. One night I was on the schedule for a three-hour night flight. I had gotten my low light qual but wasn't terribly comfortable. The NVGs we were flying with were significantly better than the old crappy ANVIS-5s I'd had in Desert Storm, but they still had their limitations.

We were taking off at 2100 and would finish at midnight. A couple of the good crew chiefs we were comfortable with would be supporting us in the back. The plan was to do a few laps around the pattern, landing at the field each time to warm up, then head out into the range area and do some landings in different landing zones.

The first hour or so went great. I'd fly a pattern to a landing and then give my buddy Mute controls and he'd do one. We switched back and forth, building our comfort level and skill.

When we got back to the airfield to do a few autorotations I swear it had gotten darker. Maybe I was just getting tired. But I had done a few autos with Mute so I wasn't too worried.

I set up for the first auto. I made my required radio call, abeam my intended point of landing at the required one thousand feet of altitude, rolled the throttles back to idle, and made the call inside the aircraft. We checked the gauges and reported instruments normal as I rolled into the steep 180-degree turn required. We were dropping out of the sky pretty fast, but that is normal in an autorotation. At 125 feet, I pulled back the nose to slow our forward airspeed and raised the collective a little bit to control the increase in rotor speed.

It all seemed pretty normal, but when I got to the next step, I couldn't bring the throttles back up. Everything seemed to go in slow motion. I tried moving the throttles down a little and then back up – no change. I had made a mistake in letting the rotor speed decay to about 95 percent. I knew we were going to crash.

I blurted, "Hang on, this is going to be a full one!" as I pushed the nose over to level the aircraft. A quick flick of the wrist with the stick and then back to center had us lined up for the grass instead of the runway. I pulled everything the collective would let me pull. We slapped the ground and bounced back up into the air and about fifty feet forward. Because I had used all the rotor speed to cushion our first landing, rotor speed was very low and the controls were now useless. I pulled the stick back into my gut as far as I could.

We ended up sitting in the grass. I could tell from how we were sitting with the belly on the ground that the skids had broken off. The engines were still turning over at idle speed and the rotors were flapping around like normal. I couldn't believe what had just happened.

I turned around. The crew chiefs in the back tend to get hurt more than the pilots – they have very simple canvas seats and lap belts compared to the pilot's full back seat and five-point harness. But everyone was okay. I flipped up my NVGs and Mute and I sat there looking at each other.

"I guess I should call tower and let them know."

"Yeah."

Minutes later the crash crew came running in and started climbing all over the aircraft. An ambulance showed up shortly after.

The next couple of hours – in fact, the next couple of days – were a hazy blur. The ambulance drove us to the hospital for a post-mishap physical exam. They took blood and urine samples, poked and prodded us, and declared us healthy. Next, they wanted a detailed account of everything we had done, eaten, or drunk in the last thirty-six hours. That was harder to write out than I thought it would be.

There would be two investigations. One would be the Marine Corps Mishap Investigation required, which can be punitive if the aircrew is at fault. The other would be the Safety Investigation.

In one of my conversations with the CO, he asked me if I had anything else traumatic going on in my life. I hadn't thought about it before he asked, but yes, I was going through a crappy divorce! I knew that some guys had been temporarily grounded during times like this.

The CO was furious. "Why the hell didn't you tell someone?" he said.

I was pissed because everyone knew. I had even been into his office to talk with him about on several occasions. I said, "But Sir, I did talk to you about it." He acknowledged briefly and changed the subject.

Meanwhile, Lisa and I had reached something of an agreement. We would sell the house and the boat and split the proceeds. I kept my tools, my bicycles, the computer, a dresser, a bed, and a desk. That was about it. Lisa defaulted on the 4Runner lease and drove the Nissan truck. I bought an old chevy S-10 for $600 out of the want ads.

I agreed to pay Lisa half of my paycheck after taxes for three years. It was pretty steep but my contract in the Marine Corps was up in three years and I didn't want to have to find a high-paying job right away because I owed alimony. At this point I had no idea where I would be in three years. She kept arguing for five years of alimony but finally agreed to the three.

The worst part was the custody battle over Stuart. But I didn't have any way to take care of him, so I let her take him.

The blood and urine tests came back negative. And they couldn't find any discrepancies in the throttles or engines. So that left pilot error.

The Mishap Investigation wrote it up as pilot error but not due to lack of quals, training, or abilities. More importantly, they said it was not negligent or intentional. Holding a little collective in and degrading rotor speed was a contributing factor. Landing on an uneven surface was a contributing factor.

The Safety Investigation made the recommendation that low-light autos only be executed with a Night Systems Instructor (NSI) on board. NSI is a fairly high qual usually reached with twice the flying hours I had.

I didn't agree so much with the Safety Investigation. I don't think the low light had that much to do with it. But they had to produce something, and this recommendation took it easy on me.

Finally, there was the damage assessment. Mishaps are divided into three categories: A, B, and C. A is the worst, with a total cost of $1,000,000, total loss of aircraft, or death or permanent disability of personnel involved. Class B is $200,000 to $1,000,000 or partial disability or hospitalization of five or more personnel. Class C is $10,000 to $200,000 or loss of five workdays. If you have a Class A mishap on your record, you are unofficially branded. COs are very reluctant to let you fly in their squadron. Even a Class B is a serious black mark. Class Cs are seen as a minor mistake.

Major "Balls" Shane, as the maintenance officer, had to submit a dollar figure report to repair the aircraft. I think there might have been some creative accounting there. I know the doppler antenna on the belly of the aircraft cost $125,000 by itself. I was lucky it didn't have a FLIR ball on it because those start at $250,000. In any case, Balls' total came in under $200,000, so it was classified as a Class C mishap.

It was a trying several weeks. Lisa lived in the house while it was on the market. When we got a reasonable offer, she had to move out.

Kyle called me that night. "Hey, would it be weird if Lisa stayed with me?"

"Uh, yeah," I said. "It would. But you know what, I don't really care."

"Hey, you were the one sleeping around on deployment."

"What?"

"You told me yourself the locals were very friendly."

"Yeah, I did say that I guess. That's not quite what I meant. But okay, whatever. Have fun."

In the long run I was getting what I had wanted – to be away from Lisa. Still, it felt like a sad country song to see my truck, my dog, and my ex-wife at my ex-best friend's house.

Chapter 24

Kosovo

It was over two months before I was cleared to fly again. The investigation took several weeks and then the Safety Board kept me off the flight schedule for a few more weeks because of the "turmoil" in my personal life. I never did hear or see evidence of any milestones or conditions that signaled I was ready to fly, but finally I got a call from one of the schedule writers notifying me that I would be on the flight schedule the next day. They gave me a couple easy flights to warm up, then it was quickly back into the heavy tactical flights and lots of test flights. It was great to be flying again and doing my part.

The squadron as a whole was putting a lot of work into getting the Marines, aircraft, and equipment ready for the chop down to the Marine Expeditionary Unit (MEU) squadron. (I don't know the history of the term "chop," but on a scheduled date you "chopped" down to the MEU, meaning you changed units, and now went to work for the MEU squadron.) Each Marine needed the correct qualifications and training. All the aircraft and equipment had to be ready to do an intense six-month work-up cycle followed by six months on deployment. There was no room for pawning off second-rate players or equipment. It made life busy and the days long, but it was great getting to fly so much.

The squadron we were joining was HMM-263, short for Helicopter Marine Medium squadron 263. They flew CH-46 Sea Knights, commonly referred to as Phrogs. The Phrog is another Vietnam-era helo, and most of them are as old as the Hueys we were flying. The Hueys I flew were UH-1Ns. It had a two-bladed main rotor but it had two engines, redundant hydraulic systems, and a longer cabin. The data plates on them had "born on" dates from 1973-1977, but they were all rebuilds – most had started life in the mid-1960s, and many of them had seen significant action in Vietnam, which you could see in their logbooks.

While HMM-263 was a Phrog squadron, as they became the MEU squadron they got reinforced with the three Hueys and six Cobras we brought, four CH-53s Super Stallions (referred to as Shitters) and four AV-8B Harriers. With those aircraft came all the pilots, mechanics, and admin personnel required to operate and maintain them. In addition, there were attachments from air defense units, airspace control units, and a few other folks that it takes to enable and maintain the Aviation Combat Element of the MEU for a year.

My career was back on track, my financial issues were managable, and I was gearing up for new adventures. Still, there was something missing. It had been a year since Lisa and I had divorced and friends were always trying to get me a date. I had gone out on a couple of set up-dates and none of them had gone well. Camp Lejeune is not a good spot to find a date. There are wives of Marines, daughters of Marines, and strippers. Sometimes, the women there fell into more than one of those categories. I wasn't interested in dating any of those. There were other women there but I never met them. Working long hours didn't help much either.

Among all the other characters at 263 was a female pilot. We were acquainted because we were in the same training squadron in flight school. I had talked to her a few times but didn't know her well. Now that we were in the same squadron again, I got to know her a bit better. Donna had a quick wit and dry sense of humor. Many of her jokes or snide comments went over the heads of the other guys. I thought she was hilarious (even though I probably only understood half of her jokes). She looked pretty good in a flight suit, too.

There was an obvious spark between us, and I was trying to build up the nerve to ask her out. I just never seemed to find the right time, and it felt corny to ask her to a movie and dinner. I didn't know what else to do on a date, though.

So it was Donna who made the first move. One night I found a message from her on my answering machine. She told me she was coming over Friday night so I better have something planned.

Donna didn't want to go out so I picked up Chinese and a rental movie. Actually, I picked up four movies. This was back in the days of VCRs and VHS tapes. Standing in the movie rental store, looking at the racks of VHS tapes, I had no idea what she had seen or what she liked. I got a romantic comedy, an action movie, a thriller, and a Monty Python. I figured that covered all the bases.

I knew better than to try to cook so I took the same approach at "Number One Chinese" and got a box of almost everything on the menu. Then I got a bottle of red wine and a bottle of white wine and figured I was set.

Turned out Donna liked red wine, liked all of the Chinese food, and we watched two of the movies. In classic fashion, at the start of the first movie, we were sitting on each end of the couch eating. Halfway through the second movie, we were cuddled up together in the middle of the couch. I definitely wanted another date!

Donna had a nine-month-old daughter and I was surprised that this didn't frighten me. Donna invited me over a few days later to meet her. Emily was the typical chubby baby. A little bit stubborn but a happy, fun child. It wasn't long before our regular Friday nights were eating pizza in the bathroom while we watched Emily taking her bath. After bath time, Emily went to bed and Donna and I would curl up on the couch and watch TV. These weren't the kind of dates I thought I'd be going on, but I enjoyed it and I loved being around Donna and Emily. Every once in a while, Donna would get a sitter and we'd go out to dinner.

Donna wasn't looking forward to the six-month deployment and was spending all the time she could with Emily. I understood and it really didn't bother me we didn't do much else together but hang out at her house.

We learned that our deployment would take us to the Balkans, which had been in turmoil since 1992. The Marines were first sent to Bosnia in 1993. In 1995, Air Force Captain Scott O'Grady's F-16 was famously shot down by a Serb Army surface-to-air missile and was rescued by the Marines from the 24th MEU. By 1998 Kosovo was becoming a hot spot, too, and we knew that we would be playing a role there.

As the countdown to deployment began, there was a lot of new stuff to learn because everybody had a different way of doing business. All those different units coming together and a lot of new personalities made things a bit hectic. There was some friction here and there, but for the most part everyone wanted to make it work.

We did a lot of one- or two-week small deployments. The ship we'd be deploying on would sail down from Virginia and the squadron would spend a week operating from the ship.

The day before we were scheduled to fly out to the ship, I arrived home to find Stuart tied up on the front porch. Lisa was still trying to screw me up. I was ecstatic to see him but panicked about what to do with him. I was leaving for six months the next afternoon. After an hour of frantic calls, I called Donna. She said her house sitter could take care of him at her house while we were away. What a relief!

After six months of our work-up period, we were finally ready to load up and cross the Atlantic. It was exciting and a bit of a relief. The home for a week, gone for a week schedule of workups was exhausting. We loaded up the aircraft and flew all twenty-four of them out to the ship. We were on our way!

The Atlantic crossing (TRANSLANT in Navy/Marine Corps lingo) takes ten to fifteen days. Between writing a flight schedule and flying, the usual day is twelve to fourteen hours. Then there are the watches and duties, so an eighteen-hour day isn't uncommon. There are no weekends on the ship. Every day is Monday. But it's not that big a deal when you really don't have anything else to do. I wasn't bored.

Flying "blue water" – meaning out of sight of land – was incredible. When you are thirty miles from the ship at two thousand feet, you can't see the ship or anything else. All you see is a flat, expansive ocean horizon. It can be unnerving.

During this whole time I barely saw Donna. The CO had a policy against inter-squadron dating. I was kind of ticked off about it but I understood his reasoning. Love in the workplace often leads to problems, particularly when the workplace is the profession of arms. Donna and I agreed that we would just be very casual about it and we'd pick up our relationship when we got home. We never went alone together anywhere and were strictly professional on the ship.

The squadron started getting more focused intel on the situation on the ground in Kosovo. Two major factions were in a retaliation war, with the Federal Republic of Yugoslavia and the Kosovo Liberation Army attacking each other. There had been several documented massacres, and there was reputed to be ethnic cleansing by both sides. The real victims were the local populace, who were often caught in the middle. Things had calmed down since the Kosovo Force (KFOR – a multinational stabilization force lead by NATO) had entered six months prior in June 1999. But there were still incidents where the KFOR were being militarily engaged. It was a confusing situation that required knowledge of history going back decades to really understand.

Our role was to provide air support to the different regionally based multinational brigades. Looking at the map, it reminded me of post-WWII Berlin, with the province divided into five sectors. The French ran the sector to the north, the Italians the west, the Germans to the south, and the US the east, while the Brits ran the central sector. Although these were the five major sectors, there were at least 30 different countries that contributed forces and there were US forces in almost every sector.

We based at an airfield in Macedonia near the major town of Skopje. Our daily missions would have us fly north out of Skopje to Camp Bondsteel in the US sector. We would refuel there and then proceed for our tasking wherever it was needed.

To get to Skopje, we flew from the ship in the Adriatic Sea over Albania into Macedonia. Albania wasn't exactly our best friend at the time. As we left the ship, we were carrying ordnance and live rounds for our personal weapons. The diplomatic flight clearances to traverse the different airspace were difficult to obtain.

We left a contingent of the squadron on the ship and the XO was in charge. When needed, they would fly to Naples for parts and then bring them "in-country" to us. Maintaining twenty-some Marine helicopters requires an almost daily inflow of parts.

It was still cold and the ground was covered in snow as we flew through towering mountains. It was beautiful but a bit nerve-racking. Our helos were loaded down and almost overweight. We flew only two hundred feet above the ground but the mountains were six thousand feet above sea level. The aircraft are a bit sluggish at that elevation.

We were all a bit nervous about the situation on the ground. The violence had abated significantly but the loyalties of numerous different factions made it difficult to understand who was against the US and NATO and who supported our participation. We all understood there were plenty of people who would love to capture a US pilot.

Flying in was uneventful, other than the rush of an occasional strong updraft or downdraft flying through the mountains. And landing at the huge airfield at Skopje was straightforward. We got the aircraft parked in their spots and headed into the big temporary hangar.

Our accommodations were in a tent city much like the ones I had stayed in during Desert Storm. It was made up of almost one hundred tents with gravel walkways in between. Each tent held thirty people. It was cold outside and there were patches of snow on the ground here and there, but mostly it was mud unless you were on the gravel pathways.

We soon fell into a daily routine. Since there were so many requests for armed escort, we flew the Cobras and Hueys a lot. I was flying every day and got to know the countryside very quickly.

The flying was beautiful. The landscape was ridgelines of tall mountains with fertile farming valleys in between. The farms were scenic, but many of them had missing sections of roof or walls from the violence of the previous few years. The valleys all seemed to have the dark blue ribbon of a river meandering through them. It was a long flight through a narrow mountain pass to get from Macedonia up into Kosovo. We used that pass as our checkpoint for getting the weapons ready. Although the entire area was designated a hazardous duty zone, Kosovo was the only place we expected any combat. We made sure everything was loaded and armed before we came out of the narrow pass into Kosovo and went into high alert once we crossed the border.

After a few days we got to fly up around Pristina. It is the capital and the biggest city of Kosovo. Founded thousands of years ago, its population was about 400,000 at the time. You could tell that it had been a beautiful city with lots of old stonework buildings. Now there was rubble in many of the streets and some of the buildings were half knocked down from the shelling. Looking at the outskirts of Pristina, I saw a few mortar craters and realized the farm ponds were mortar craters that had filled with rain and snow runoff.

We hadn't heard of any firefights for a few days. The Marines on the ground reported that they had received an occasional potshot directed at them but had never been really engaged. Intel reports indicated that the dissidents had a healthy respect for our aviation firepower and wouldn't try anything when they could hear helicopters.

Flying out towards the German sector one day, we received a call from a small recon unit for an emergency extraction. They had been concealed in an observation post and a farmer had stumbled on them. The farmer got some of his buddies, and an unfriendly crowd was forming near their position. Our rules of engagement were pretty specific. An unruly crowd was not justification for firing a weapon.

We flew direct to their position and circled it once before setting down. We could see the fifteen to twenty people a hundred meters to the west. They were waving angrily and you could tell they were shouting, although we couldn't hear anything. As soon as we set down, the Marines came running to load up. As they ran towards us, the crowd came running, too.

As they came, a few of them stooped to pick up rocks, which they threw at us. At that range, it wasn't any threat, but if they got close enough, a rock though the rotors or in an engine could cause some problems. We lifted as soon as the Marines were loaded.

We joked on the flight home that at least we could say the bad guys threw rocks at us. I couldn't believe all the reporting we had to go through when we debriefed the flight. Yes, it was an angry crowd, but maybe it was because we scared their sheep or something. The Intel guys are pretty thorough, though.

Six months is a long time to be gone and we were excited when it was finally time to start heading home. Donna was doing pretty well but it was hard on her being away from Emily for so long. While we were gone, Emily had started talking. It really hurt Donna to miss that milestone.

It took several days to sail back to Rota, Spain, to change over with the next MEU coming in. We finished turnover and the big washdown of everything on the ship (including the aircraft). Soon we were headed back across the Atlantic, less than two weeks from home. Two or three folks usually fly a commercial flight home from Rota to start getting things ready back at Camp Lejeune for the big return, and Donna was one of those who got to head back early. It was a bummer that I wouldn't get to see her for the next two weeks. The upside was there would be someone on Camp Lejeune to welcome me home.

On August 6, 2000, we did the big fly-in with twenty-four aircraft in formation, flying over the airfield packed with cheering families and loved ones. After parking all the aircraft and shutting them down simultaneously, we got into a large formation. As soon as the CO called out "Dismissed!" total chaos erupted. Three hundred Marines standing in formation broke into a run for the hangar. At the same time, the 450 or so family members who had been waiting at the hangar broke into a run to find their Marine that they hadn't seen in six months. It is always an emotional event.

At every previous homecoming event, I had been alone. I had never had anyone waiting to greet me. At every other homecoming, I had stood around while my buddies hugged and kissed their loved ones. I had never had the classic movie ending – the hero fights the big battle, flies home, and then his wife/girlfriend/family run to hug him as he gets off the plane. But here were Donna and Emily, waiting with all the other families running to hug me. It was a pretty significant moment for me.

Chapter 25

9/11

Donna called at 0850. I was groggy and disoriented. I had just gotten home from another deployment to CAX at 0400 that morning. Donna insisted I turn on the TV.

The World Trade Center was billowing smoke. It was hard to know what was happening. The talking heads were musing about a terrorist attack. I didn't believe it until the second plane struck the south tower in front of my eyes. Holy crap! What was going on?

I tried to call the squadron but all circuits were busy. I got dressed and headed to the base.

There was a long line of vehicles leading up to the gates, where they were turning people around. I waited until the MP finally got to my window. I held my military ID out the window.

"Hey, Lance Corporal, I just got back into town. I gotta get in and check in with my squadron."

"Sorry, Sir, base is locked down until further notice. I can't let anyone in or out."

"I understand, but I'm the assistant maintenance officer. I gotta get into my squadron."

"Yes, Sir, but I'm under strict direction to not let anyone under any circumstances in or out. I even had to turn a couple of squadron COs away. Please just head home and wait for further notification."

I went back home and sat on the couch, flipping between news channels. It was like a bad dream. The news about the Pentagon and Flight 93 came in, followed by horrific footage of the towers collapsing.

I tried calling into the squadron a few times and finally got through to a young Sergeant. He didn't have much information other than a message from the CO telling us to sit tight and check back the following morning.

Since I knew Donna would be stuck on base, I went to pick up Emily at daycare. Donna and I had been living together since Kosovo. Everything had been going great between us, and just a few weeks before I had formally proposed to Donna.

I had also been working to find a better balance between work and family. After talking it through with Donna, I had made the decision to transfer to a training command at Camp Pendleton. We were set to pack up our recently purchased RV and head west in just a few weeks.

Just as Emily and I got back home from daycare, Donna pulled into the drive behind us. We all hugged and kissed and went back inside, to wait to see what would happen next.

The next few days were surreal. The airspace was shut down while the FAA tried to figure out new security procedures. Everyone wanted to do something but we were told to just sit tight.

My decision to transfer to a training command at Camp Pendleton meant that I would not be involved in any planning or action taken against those responsible for the terrorist attacks. I would be on the sidelines while others developed plans and then deployed to carry out those plans. When the action came, I would not have any part in it.

My orders got delayed while the military commands wrestled with what was going to happen next. When my orders were finally re-authorized a week later, I finished checking out. Donna did the same and we started our drive west to San Diego.

Chapter 26

Married... With Children

We drove back across the country to Camp Pendleton in the RV. Both Emily and Stuart took well to the RV. We'd drive for eight hours and then stop to camp for the night.

I had driven cross country several times before, but this time was different. I was amazed at the outpouring of patriotism. There were US flags hanging from overpasses and just about everywhere else.

At one point, Donna and I talked about jobs and different places we could be assigned. I mentioned that I felt a little guilty going to a training squadron right when the Marine Corps was sure to be sending a lot of guys overseas. Donna's response was that if I had gone to another deploying command, she wouldn't have tried to move with me. That was a sobering thought.

We stopped briefly to visit my sister in Santa Cruz and then headed south. Vacation was over and it was time to get settled in at our new jobs.

We found a home for the fifth wheel in a nice park near La Jolla. Donna's job was close, about ten minutes. I had an hour drive up to Camp Pendleton.

Being back at Pendleton felt like coming home. I earned my instructor qualification quickly and was soon flying students. It was very different than flying in an operational squadron. You had to expect a student to try to kill you at any moment and be ready to catch an error or mistake before it became deadly. The training also seemed a little more serious because of the probability that the new guys would be flying with my friends at operational squadrons in a combat zone very soon. But the majority of the students were hungry to learn and wanted to do well. It also helped me get through the operational burnout that I had been feeling as I left HMLA 269.

Over in Afghanistan, our reinforced squadron of Hueys and Cobras seemed to be doing well. We knew more deployments to combat zones were brewing and most of us suspected it wasn't going to be a short conflict like Desert Storm.

Meanwhile, I got to go home to my family every night. I loved them and I loved not worrying about a separation. Emily had started calling me Daddy with no coaching or suggestion from Donna or me. That was momentous to me. Still, I worried I wasn't fulfilling my duty to the Marine Corps or the nation.

Donna and I were married at a ranch southeast of San Diego. Emily was Donna's bridesmaid, and Stuart was my best man – he even wore a tie.

For weeks I'd been focused on getting everything ready for the wedding and getting everything ready at work for me to be gone. But then standing there saying my vows to Donna it really hit me. I was looking at this beautiful woman, who was holding this beautiful little girl's hand. Stuart was sitting at my feet, and my family was all there watching. I started choking up and couldn't get through my vows.

Emily looked up at me. "What's wrong, Daddy? Why are you crying?"

I crouched down to try to explain to her that it was tears of joy. She seemed to understand and wiped my tears. I stood up and managed to finish stammering my way through my vow to Donna. Just as I finished, Stuart let out a huge sigh and slumped over to lay across my feet.

A month later Donna was pregnant – a little souvenir from our honeymoon. We were both excited. Donna was just eight months from the end of her obligation to the Corps. The pregnancy sealed the deal – she was getting out.

By October 2002, it became clear that we would be sending Marines into Iraq soon. The squadrons that were likely to deploy first were asking for pilots so they would be at full strength when they deployed. My CO had already transferred several guys from the training squadron to the operational squadrons.

I was working hard and I enjoyed my job as an instructor. But I was a war fighter. I wanted to get into the fight.

I knew Donna wouldn't like it so I didn't tell her about it. But I went to the CO's office and asked to be transferred to an operational squadron.

"Hesty, don't be an idiot."

"I'm ready. I sat out Afghanistan. Some of those guys just got home a couple months ago and they are going back out again."

"No, and here's why. One, you are about to have a baby. Two, I have other guys I can send. Three, I need you here to continue training new guys to send out. And four, this is not going to be short. There is going to be plenty to go around and you will have plenty of opportunity to play your part."

"Sir…"

"Hesty, you are the standardization instructor. So technically I'd have to ask Naval Training Command to transfer you anyway. I'm not going to do that. Keep doing what you are doing and be here for your wife and baby. Speaking of which, did you talk to your wife about this?"

"Um, no, Sir."

"Don't ever tell her you came down to ask me this."

"Sir."

I heard what he said and I respected his judgment. Still, I felt like I was being benched.

After the typical Christmas-New Year's slow down, the entire base went into high gear getting Marines ready to deploy. There were several large exercises, more convoys on the roads than usual, and lots of cargo trucks bringing stuff in. There was also more push than usual to get students moved through the pipeline and into the operational squadrons.

Units started shipping out to invade Iraq in March. The night before the invasion, a CH-46E from one of our squadrons crashed, killing four Marines that many of us knew, along with eight British Royal Marines.

Then the sandstorms hit. Flying in sandstorms sucks, and the photos we saw looked way worse than anything most of us had seen or experienced.

Within the first ten days, our squadrons had four major mishaps. Two of them resulted in the aircraft being totaled and the crews going to the hospital. One of the four resulted in three fatalities. All three were our friends and brothers. It struck everyone hard.

A few days later we had memorial services at the base chapel. We flew missing man formation flyovers for all the services. The training squadron instructors traditionally handle the missing man flyover for the memorials. It was an honor for me to participate but also a somber event.

The next week another Cobra went down, killing both pilots. The co-pilot had graduated from the training squadron several months prior. Both crew members were well known and well liked across all the squadrons. Both left behind wives, and Captain Ford left behind a two-year-old daughter. Again, we flew missing man formations for both memorial services.

Amidst the tragic loss of lives, there was the miracle of birth. Victor Walter Hesterman II was born April 17, a healthy eight pounds, ten ounces. It was amazing and moving to watch his birth and then hold this fragile little being. Nothing prepares you for holding a brand new baby who will rely on you for everything.

As we moved into the summer, I approached ten years of active duty time in the Marine Corps, so I was halfway to retirement. At the same time, my obligation was fulfilled and I could get out of the Marine Corps at the end of the tour if I wanted. Up to that point I had basically been going tour to tour without deciding if I wanted to go the full distance or get out and do something else. If I accepted another tour, it would likely be four years. It seemed silly to do fourteen years and then get out with just six years till retirement.

I was on the board for promotion to Major, and in September I would learn if I was selected or not. Promotion to Major also includes a significant pay raise. The Marine Corps has the science of retention nailed in this regard. Right when it is time to get out, there is always some reward dangled in front of you (assuming you haven't had a DUI or gotten someone killed). Promotion to Major almost guarantees that you will be allowed to continue to retirement.

Donna and I spent a lot of time talking about this. I also talked to the CO about it. The operations officer was a Major and a mentor to me, and he talked with me at length about it as well. And with the conflict going on, I felt some duty to continue.

Donna and I decided that if I was selected to Major, we would continue in the Marine Corps. And if I wasn't selected, we would look at getting out. Donna was officially out now and very relieved to have left the structured world of the Marine Corps behind.

In early September I got the email from the manpower office indicating that I would be promoted to Major. The job at the top of the list was air officer at 7th Marine Infantry Regiment, based out of Twentynine Palms, California. The Marine Corps sends pilots out with the grunt units to be liaisons for aviation matters. There are usually three in every battalion and then one at the regiment level. The job is a lot like some of the stuff I had done at ANGLICO back in the day. Whatever the unit needs aviation support for is coordinated by the air officers – anything from getting troops moved by helicopter to an F/A-18 laying a bomb on the right target. This would be a good career-building job, but it would be a lot of work and I wouldn't get to fly.

I soon learned that 7th Marines was deploying to Iraq in February. Although I had a new baby along with my wife and daughter at home, deploying to Iraq felt like the right thing to do. It seemed that everyone else had deployed to Afghanistan or Iraq and I would finally be playing my part. Plus, after a combat tour as an air officer I could probably ask for just about anything I wanted.

Donna wasn't too thrilled about it. She still didn't fully understand why I felt I needed to deploy and leave the family. But she agreed to the deployment, somewhat begrudgingly, only because she knew I would be miserable if I didn't go.

I didn't know exactly where 7th Marines would be but I knew it was near Ramadi. That week, Ramadi started making the news with eruptions of violence. I assured my family that I'd be in a headquarters somewhere and wouldn't be out on patrols or convoys. But I wasn't too sure myself.

Back at Camp Pendleton we had a promotion ceremony and I was promoted to Major along with a couple other friends. Donna was there with Vic on her hip. Emily pinned on my new rank insignia as part of the ceremony.

The next eight weeks were made up of traveling, classes, field exercises, and getting ready to move up to Twentynine Palms. I spent night hours looking at housing classifieds and realtor websites and applying for a mortgage. When I was home, we worked to get our belongings ready to move and trying to schedule movers. On weekends, we drove up to Twentynine Palms to look at houses. The housing market was still a bit inflated but rent was even worse, so we resolved to bite the bullet and buy.

One weekend in February, I drove up from Yuma and Donna brought the kids up from Camp Pendleton. We met up at the realtors' office and went to look at one last possibility. Emily was running around the empty house, opening every door and closet. We were talking to the realtor in the family room when Vic suddenly threw up all over Donna's arm and onto the carpet. The water service was turned off at the house so Donna and I cleaned the carpet the best we could with a bottle of water and an old T-shirt I had in the truck. While we were cleaning, Emily started screaming in the back bedroom. She had lost a tooth and it scared her. We joked that we should just buy the house. By the end of the day, the seller had accepted our offer. We moved a few weeks later, just one week before I had to check into 7th Marines.

Part IV

Iraq and Afghanistan (2002–2013)

Chapter 27

Iraq

On Monday I suited up in my Service Alpha uniform and drove to the base to get checked in. The regiment had been gone a month already. The Remain Behind Element (RBE) was mostly comprised of medical holds, Marines who were in trouble of some kind, and Marines who actually wanted to deploy but didn't have enough time on their contracts.

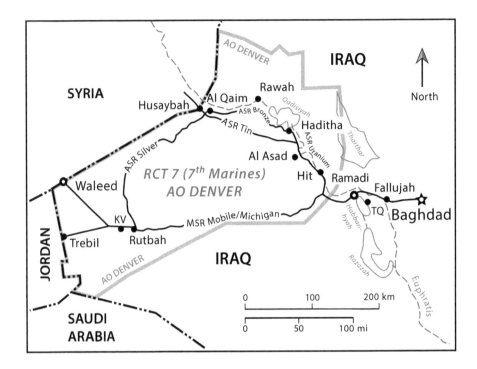

It quickly became clear that none of these Marines were superstars and that I was just a bother to them.

I managed to get a copy of the checklist and started working it myself. It took me three full days to click through all the PowerPoint briefs in the division database. This was one of those occasions where if I sat back and did as I was told, I probably would have been in Twentynine Palms another two months. I would have been home with my family for that time, and the deployment would have been that much shorter. No one would have questioned it but it wasn't the right thing to do. Not everyone understands or agrees with me about this, but I felt it was my obligation, my duty.

I drove to the armory and supply and convinced them to issue me the new gear and sign off the gear issue on my checksheet. Then I drove out to the rifle range and convinced them to give me ammo and let me shoot on a target on the far end of the range. The gas chamber was a little harder. I spent two days there waiting for another unit going through training before I found an empty spot.

Trying to get manifested on a Strategic Command (Strat Com) flight over to Iraq was another problem. The RBE hadn't even requested a seat for me. I learned that the 1st Tanks had a platoon shipping out the following weeks. A quick conversation with the officer in charge and I managed to finagle a seat with them the following week.

The last few days at home were tense. I've never figured out a way around that. We celebrated Vic's first birthday a week early since I would be gone on the actual day.

I left on a Saturday. As usual, we had to be at the base at three in the morning. While I was loading my seabags and rucksack into the van, Stuart jumped in and wouldn't get out. He knew something was up. Donna loaded the kids and we all drove down to drop me off.

I kissed them all goodbye in the parking lot and headed in to get my weapons and get manifested for the bus ride down to March Air Force Base. It's always tough to say goodbye like that and my strategy was to just make it quick and get it over with.

The flight over was the usual rigmarole of sitting in the departure airport for six hours before departure, followed by thirty-plus hours being on the same plane. We stopped in Bangor, Maine, for an hour or so while they refueled and restocked the plane. I walked the same ramp where I had almost broken into tears coming home from Desert Storm. The USO and a couple other organizations had representatives there and it was very supportive, with free calls home and cookies and orange juice. Again, the majority were Vietnam vets or the family of a Vietnam vet. Gotta love those folks and I can't say enough about what they do for our military members purely out of kindness and love.

The next leg was a long one. I was sitting next to a Lieutenant Colonel who was headed to work in the Plans section at 1st Marine Division headquarters. He talked about how incredible he was as a recruiting region commander and about his collection of tin Civil War soldiers. He had handpainted all the soldiers and set them up in historically accurate scenes from the Civil War. I respect studying history but he just came across as silly. Images flashed through my mind of the high-ranking officers at Division planning battles with toy soldiers on some big terrain model of Iraq. It didn't build my confidence.

I was nervous enough as it was. Here was Mr. Huey Pilot aviator going to join the infamous 7th Marines who had been in combat for two months. Grunts already hate aviators (until they need a lift or a bomb).

Plus, I hadn't seen any combat for over ten years, and many wouldn't consider Desert Storm combat compared to Afghanistan and Iraq. The best I could do was show up with my ears and eyes open and absorb as much as possible as quickly as possible.

The worst part was that no one could tell me exactly what an air officer did. Part of the job was to control aircraft. I had that covered. What about all the other parts? No one had answered that question for me.

We had another stop in Shannon, Ireland (yet another place I had visited on the way home from Desert Storm). We were now under the infamous General Order Number 1, which prohibited consumption of any alcohol. It also forbade porn on any media, impregnating or become pregnant, sexual acts, drugs, money, private firearms, etc.

From there it was on to the Kuwait City airport. That was kind of weird for me. Last time I had been to that airport, it had been in the middle of a battle. Now the US flew military members in and out on a daily basis and had been doing so for almost ten years.

We deboarded in the middle of the night onto a taxiway that seemed miles from any buildings. An Air Force sergeant with a tough book computer and a handheld scanner scanned all our IDs. While they were unloading the plane, I asked him a couple of questions.

"Hey, Sergeant, how long until we get a flight into Iraq?"

"Don't sweat it, Sir. As soon as this plane taxis out of the way, we are loading you all on a C-130 to take you up to Al Asad."

"Where do we get ammo?"

"You guys don't have any ammo?"

"Nope."

"Shit, they are supposed to have a unit rep out here that brings you all two mags worth."

"Is there someone you can check with to see if there is anyone coming?"

He pinched the handset on his shoulder and mumbled something into it. Unintelligible static came out of it. Evidently, he had understood the static.

"I'm it, Sir. As soon as this plane clears, I'm putting you on that 130 and you're off to Al Asad." He gestured to a C-130 sitting a respectful distance away with interior lights on.

"Well that sucks," I said. "I'm not too excited about flying over Iraq and into Al Asad with no ammo."

"I wouldn't go, Sir. I wouldn't do it."

To have an Air Force sergeant tell me that, I knew that something wasn't right.

I asked, "There an armory or something around where we can go check out at least some security rounds?"

He paused for a moment, obviously pondering something. "Tell you what, Sir, I have a bucket of five-five-six in my truck that just keeps getting bigger. Every time we send a unit out to go home, there is some fool that still has ammo that I have to confiscate. I can let you have that. That way I don't have to do the paperwork to turn it in."

Personally I would have mentioned that at the outset, but I wasn't going to complain now.

"Thanks, Sergeant. If you let me have it, I can promise that all those rounds will go back into Iraq."

He trotted off to his truck and came back with a five-gallon bucket filled to the brim with M-16 ammo. If I wasn't so anxious to get it equitably distributed, I would have laughed out loud.

That was my introduction to being an air officer. Over the next year, I would ask myself at least once a day, "Why is the air officer the one that has to figure this out?" The joke among air officers is that their duties get made up along the way. If it remotely has anything to do with aviation, aircraft, or even air, it becomes the air officer's responsibility. The classic joke example is when scuba tanks get delivered and no one knows what to do with them. What's in them? Air! Give em to the air officer! He'll figure it out.

It was still dark when our C-130 landed in Al Asad. The 1st Tanks crew was headed out later that day to another FOB so I was now on my own. I asked how to find the 7th Marines and was directed to a bus stop next to a row of port-a-shitters.

It was a five-minute ride to Camp Ripper (Ripper is the callsign of 7th Marines). I didn't see much other than dirt berms on either side of the road as we drove.

We pulled into an immense gravel parking lot next to a field with rows and rows of cans. "Cans" are housing units that are basically a shipping container with a door and an A/C unit. Across from the cans was a big plywood building with large tents attached to it, making an "H." The driver didn't know anything about Camp Ripper except that the "H" building was the chow hall. Glad he told me that because I would have headed in there thinking it was the headquarters.

I started over toward the low stucco buildings on the far side of the huge parking lot. The gravel in the parking was more like baseball-sized rocks. Walking was difficult and carrying 150 pounds in my seabag and ruck with weapons was downright challenging. The buildings were tan. Not a nice khaki tan but a dusty sandy color of tan. I would find out over the next few weeks that pretty much everything in Iraq was that color.

I finally found a building with a 7th Marines sign painted on plywood. There were about six of these buildings and they all looked the same except for these small signs.

I cleared my M-16 and 9mm pistol in the red barrel next to the front door and stepped inside. It was dark but I could see light coming from a doorway down the hall and hear the buzz of multiple radios. In a strange sense, the radio buzz was comforting. I dropped my bags by the door and followed the sound of the radios. I stepped through the doorway and around a partition wall and immediately knew I was in the Command Operations Center (COC).

The room was well lit and seemed deceivingly large considering the outside dimensions of the building. It was tiered with plywood platforms much like an auditorium, but instead of seats there were rows of desks. Each desk had multiple computers. There were four levels and each level had three desks large enough for two people to sit and work. The wall that all the desks faced had two large projection screens and a large map of the AO (area of operations). The map was at least ten feet tall. On either side was a fifty-inch flat screen. Just behind the front row of desks were two six-foot-tall stands holding the projectors portraying images on the two screens. The left screen was a scrolling log of entries, and the right screen was split in half. The top half was another scrolling log of entries, and the lower half was a live drone feed of some small town.

Most of the workstations were empty. The front center desk was occupied by two Marines, and the desk to their left had one Marine working on a computer. One other Marine was walking around and emptying the paper bags from the end of each desk into a larger bag labeled "BURN."

I stood there for a moment to make sure nothing serious was going on, then walked down toward the front row. As soon as I stepped onto the plywood steps, they all turned to look at me. The Marine in the center front was obviously in charge, and was a Chief Warrant Officer. The others were Corporals and Lance Corporals.

Chief Warrant Officers (CWO) and Warrant Officers in general are in between enlisted ranks and the officer ranks. Experience-wise, they are generally equivalent to at least a Major. As with any rank, there are good ones, bad ones, and indifferent ones, but on the whole, they are smart, efficient, and love Marines, but they don't put up with any of the Marines' bullshit. Most of them have been around long enough to dispense with any games and just get to business.

"Can I help you, Sir?"

"Please. I'm Major Hesterman, checking in to be the new air officer."

"Oh shit, Tom is going to be glad to see you."

Tom was Major Tom Freel, the current air officer who was supposed to be replaced before the regiment even deployed.

"Have a seat, Sir. We'll get you squared away right quick. Bet you need a coffee – you look a bit worn."

"Oh yes, please."

"Feeler will get it. Give your ID and orders to Smith here and he'll log you in and endorse your orders."

It's important to always get your orders endorsed. Basically, this entails filling in a little block at the bottom, and it is your proof of when you checked into a unit. Ten years later when you are trying to prove to the VA that you were somewhere or even proving to HQMC that you are eligible for retirement, it might be handy. Don't ask me how I know.

I handed my ID and orders to Lance Corporal Smith, who was the duty clerk sitting right next to the CWO. He opened a green logbook and started copying information down.

I said, "That gravel out there is kinda tough."

"Yeah, we've had a few turned ankles on that. The Colonel is all over the Four to get real gravel in here. The contractors just keep bringing in the same crap."

The Four refers to the S-4, Supply and Logistics, or in some cases the entire department.

I slumped into one of the camp chairs. It felt good to be sitting down. Feeler was back with a cup full of surprisingly good coffee. As I sipped on it, the Chief Warrant Officer continued.

"I'm Ray or Ski. Got a Polish name that everyone mispronounces anyway. Wanna get a quick sitrep?"

"I'm Hesty, and I'd love to get the skinny."

Ray first gave me a quick orientation on the map. He pointed out the locations of our four subordinate battalions. 3rd Battalion (3/7) was in Al Qaim near the Syrian border to the north. 3rd Battalion, 4th Marines (3/4), was in Haditha and Haqlaniyah. 2nd Battalion (2/7) was in Baghdadi just four miles east of us. LAR was out west at Korean Village with a platoon at Walid and Traybil. Those were the two border crossing points on the western edge of Iraq with Syria and Jordan respectively. Our entire AO was approximately the size of Wyoming, roughly 100,000 square miles.

Most of the regimental staff, including the Colonel, were down in the Fallujah area. I had heard about how the Blackwater contractors had been shot and hung on the bridge in Fallujah. During my travels the Marines had attacked into Fallujah, only to be recalled to sit on the outskirts of the city. 2/7, 3/4, and LAR all had large detachments there participating. Ray didn't know when they would be back. Maj Freel was with them. We had a "loaner" FAC from ANGLICO that was acting as the air officer here at Camp Ripper.

3/7 had Lima Company in Husaybah, which was on the border with Syria just west of Al Qaim. They had just finished a pretty big battle and had lost five Marines. That hit everyone pretty hard, particularly since the company commander, Capt Gannon, was one of the Marines killed. In the four or five days following, it had been fairly quiet.

Somewhere during the conversation, Lance Corporal Smith had handed me my orders and ID back. Ray recognized that my eyes were glazing over and in my current state I was not going to absorb any more.

"Feeler will show you where the Four is. They'll get you a can. Get a few hours of sleep, then come back and we'll get you around to get all checked in."

The Four was quiet except for their night watch, who was a Warrant Officer also. Bob asked me if I had called home yet, as they had a phone that could dial the States. Most of the phones here were tactical phones that only reached the local network set up by the US forces.

With the eleven-hour difference, it was the middle of the afternoon at home. I called and talked with Donna for bit. I let her know I was safe and getting all checked in. Then she rocked my world with the announcement she was pregnant. Holy crap! I didn't know what to say or think! I was beyond exhausted and wasn't thinking very clearly. But this was exciting! Then it dawned on me I wouldn't be home for the birth. We talked for a bit and I assured her I would call her in the next few days and we could talk more about it. My mind was totally reeling.

Bob could tell something was up when I hung up.

"Everything okay at home, Sir?"

"Well, yes, I just found out that my wife is pregnant!"

"Congrats!"

We chatted a bit more but I wasn't really engaged. Bob handed me a set of keys, warned me not to lose them, and drew me a map to find the can I was assigned to. He included where the shower and bathroom trailers were located on the map also. I put my flak vest and helmet back on, shouldered my gear, and trudged out into the night and the treacherous gravel.

I found my can and dropped my gear just inside the door. The can was eight by sixteen with a cot and a wall locker in it with a split unit AC hanging on one end. Two four-foot fluorescent lights brightly lit the barren room. I stripped to my skivvies and lay down on my sleeping bag on the cot with my helmet, flak vest, rifle, and pistol within reach on the floor. Then I passed out.

Chapter 28

Embracing the Suck

Showered and in fresh cammies, I headed into the COC around 8 a.m. I was still groggy but felt I better get checked in.

Since more than half the staff was down in Fallujah, I headed to the XO's office. The door was closed. Just as I was about to knock, I heard yelling from inside. Obviously the XO was busy so I stepped back from the door and waited. I couldn't hear the exact verbiage but someone was getting an ass chewing. There were even a couple of thumps as if a book was being slammed onto a desk. Suddenly the door flung open and an officer ducked out. "Good morning!" he said in a cheery, even tone. Then from behind the office door came: "Who's out there! What do you want?"

"Sir, Major Hesterman, incoming air officer."

"Ooh hoo. The new Air O! Come in."

As I stepped around the door into his office, I centered on his desk, standing at attention. The XO was skinny and looked tall, though it was hard to tell from the lounging position in the office chair behind his desk. Wispy dark hair – a little long for Marine regulations – framed his sharp features and truly a beak-like nose.

He said, "I hope you brought enough shit with you for the year!"

I had asked everyone from Division to "HIS" Marines in Twentynine Palms, and everyone had told me my tour would be six months. I had suspected that my tour might be a year from reading the deployment instructions, but now that I had arrived it was not terribly useful to have a cranky old man tell me I would be in Iraq for a year. I was angry but what came out of my mouth was, "Yes, Sir."

His tone softened a bit as he waved his hand at me and told me to stand at ease. He rambled on, talking at me for a while. What I gathered from his dissertation was that he didn't like aviators (not a big surprise) and he had done a tour with a squadron as an aerial observer back in the late '80s. It came across as "I was in a squadron so I know better than you."

I learned that the rest of the regiment would be back in a couple of days. They had a FAC borrowed from ANGLICO that had been acting as the Air O while Tom Freel had been down in Fallujah. I would take over from him today and then Tom and I would do official turnover when he got back.

Usually I give people the benefit of doubt, but walking away from the XO's office, all I could think of was Spicolli speaking to Mr. Hand in *Fast Times at Ridgemont High*. "You're a dick!" I took solace in the fact that a good XO plays the reciprocal of the CO. If a CO is the hammer, then the XO usually plays the good guy, and when a CO is the kind father figure, the XO plays the hammer for the organization. I hoped that the CO here would be easygoing.

Next I went to the S-1 (administration). The S-1 officer was another Warrant Officer, Rob – the one who had ducked out of the XO's office just thirty minutes prior. After he went through a list of things to make sure my pay was correct and my combat tax exclusion had started, I asked him about the XO.

"Yeah, that's my daily abuse," he said. "Every morning when I update him on admin stuff, he goes off. Today wasn't too bad. He didn't actually hit me with anything."

"Holy cow, that's insane."

"I'd rather deal with him than the Colonel, though."

"CO is worse?"

"Yup."

I had been chuckling about how everyone referred to the CO as the Colonel instead of by name or CO. I had never seen that before. But after hearing what Rob was saying about him, I was starting to worry a little.

I headed up to what would become my desk. I was still getting used to everything being made out of plywood. The tiered floor was plywood, the walls were plywood, the desks were plywood. The chairs were all camp chairs except the battle captain had a real office chair.

The computer was locked so I started looking through some of the notes on the desk. The Corporal and a Staff Sergeant sitting at the desk behind me introduced themselves and started giving me the scoop and gossip for all around the COC.

After a while the battle captain, a Major, hung up the phone he had been on and leaned over with an outstretched hand.

"Bill Vivus, welcome aboard. What kind of aircraft do you fly?"

"Andy Hesterman, callsign Hesty, I'm a Huey pilot."

"Sweet! Great platform – little bit underappreciated, though."

"Yeah, people always wanna make fun of the fat kid."

Then, much like Ray had done the night before, Bill gave me the scoop on the area of operations and what was happening. He also showed me official military chat rooms. On the secret servers were hundreds of chat rooms. Everyone had computers now. Even down to the platoon level there was internet connectivity, and most communications were done by chat, all roughly based on radio nets from back in my days as a radio operator. In addition, there was both a wire phone network and a voice over internet protocol phone network. There were three radios on my desk for talking to aircraft, but they weren't hooked up to anything.

After Bill had explained the chat rooms, the screen in the center of the wall made more sense. It was the 7th Marines chat room. I started to recognize some form of all the reports I had memorized back in my radioman days. No more having to copy messages down on little yellow pads and make three copies.

Next I was introduced to Ghost, the FAC borrowed from ANGLICO that had been acting as the Air O while Tom had been down in Fallujah.

Ghost showed me how the subordinate units submitted aviation requests on email, how he reviewed them and forwarded them up to the Air O at Division.

Around 1630 each day, the ATO (or air tasking order – basically a very hard to read flight schedule) came out for the next day. It was published by email but it was simply a scanned PDF of the same ol' ATO hard copy format I had been familiar with since Desert Storm. He showed me the contact list, our block of request numbers, and a couple other things and he was done.

"I'm gonna go hit the gym. Why don't we meet up at 1630 when the ATO comes out and we'll go over that and we should be good."

I had a million questions and was sure there were a million more that I didn't know to ask. The most pressing in my mind was how the four-day cycle of the ATO worked. There are a lot of steps that happen between getting a stack of requests and an ATO being published as a flight schedule. Requests were due by the evening three days before the day they were going to happen. The battalions were supposed to collect all their requests from subordinate companies, add in ones from the battalion, then prioritize them all. Same thing was supposed to happen at the regiment and division level. This continues until they get to MEF, who then sends them back down to the wing, who farms them out to all their subordinate squadrons for support. Oftentimes there are more requests than aircraft available so the lowest priority requests fall out. It was a long cycle and to the FAC down at a company, it seemed like a black hole. Oftentimes, he wouldn't find out if he was getting support until the day before an operation.

I started hitting Ghost up with some of my questions.

"How have you been handling requests that come in inside the three-day cycle?"

"Those are just immediates. I send them back and tell them to submit them direct to the DASC."

"What criteria do you use for prioritization?"

"I just send them up to Division and let them assign priority."

As we continued, I got the distinct feeling that Ghost wasn't really acting as an air officer but was a FAC just relaying information back and forth.

"What email address are they sending them to?"

"Freel just gave me his password so we are still using his."

At that point, it seemed I'd do better getting answers from Tom Freel or on my own. I agreed to meet him at 1630 but asked him to leave the computer logged in so I could surf around a bit. He headed out and I started surfing around the SECRET web.

The first thing I noticed was the desktop was completely covered with icons. The computer was running very slowly, too. I found the division's website and from there I was able to find the MEF's and the wing's websites. There wasn't much info there but I was able to add some names, emails, and phone numbers to the contact list on the desk and flipped through some of the PowerPoint mission briefs.

Bill sent his clerk over to help me navigate my way through some of the chat rooms. He showed me the master list where I could find all the chat rooms that existed. I logged into a few that were aviation related and started watching the dialogue taking place. I found the MEDEVAC chatroom that thankfully wasn't too busy, but I watched a couple of MEDEVAC evolutions happen. I was starting to get a feel for it.

The chat program was an off-the-shelf solution – it wasn't a specific military application. As I watched, I could see miscommunications happening everywhere. Some of the login names were positions (what we called billets) and others were names or abbreviations of rank and name. Basically, it was a total free-for-all.

Bill was on the phone when he turned to me and said, "It's for you."

"Who is it?"

"2/7's XO. He's pissed off they aren't getting much air support and wants to talk to the Air O."

Wow, not sure what I could do after being in this position for a few hours. I hesitantly took the phone

"Sir, this is Major Hesterman. I'm the incoming Air O."

"Hesty, is that you?"

I still was not sure who I was talking to. "Yes, this is Hesty."

"Holy shit, man, it's Henderson, Brian Henderson!"

Brian Henderson had been in my platoon way back in The Basic School. He was the one who had a lawyer contract and gave it up to be a grunt!

"Damn, brother! Haven't heard from you in ages! How's it going?"

"You know, just here 'embracing the suck' like always. When did you get here?"

"Just got in last night."

"Damn, well welcome to the suck! Here is the deal, though. My Air O is down in Fallujah with the CO and two of our companies. The FAC here hasn't got us any patrol or convoy escort for a week now. I dunno if he's fucking it up or are we just getting screwed, but this is unsat. We gotta get some air at least once in a while."

"Damn yeah – sounds like something's messed up. But I'll be honest with you – I don't really know how this is all working yet. But I'm working on it and we'll figure it out."

"Okay, good deal. Tell Bill I'm sorry I went off on him."

"Copy that. Take care, man. We'll talk later."

"Out."

I hung up and sat back down at the Air O desk. I relayed Henderson's apology to Bill. He nodded and commented that he had never seen Henderson spool down so fast.

The next few hours I looked through the emails and tried to understand the tracking methods Tom and Ghost had been using. The only thing I could find was that they never deleted an email. I knew I wouldn't be able to keep stuff straight that way so I made a quick spreadsheet that had all the vital info from a request across a row. Then I made a few headers so the rows would be broken into groups by the day. Just to try it out, I plugged in the info from the outgoing emails for the day, which only had four requests. Seemed like it would work. I was starting to feel like I was getting some organization.

At 1630 Ghost came back in and pulled up the ATO that had just been published. We scanned it and found three missions in support of our battalions.

"Three out of five! Schedule is published, our day is done! Time to hit chow."

"You don't let the battalions know what missions they got?"

"They get the ATO – they can figure it out."

"Okay, well I'm gonna hang out and surf around a bit more."

"Suit yourself. Good luck, man."

With that, Ghost was gone and headed back to ANGLICO. I had the reigns until Tom Freel got back.

Chapter 29

IEDs and VIPs

I quickly developed my own system for receiving, tracking, prioritizing, and submitting air requests. I became familiar with our AO on the map and the locations of the trouble spots. My spreadsheet for air requests was working pretty well. On any given day, I was dealing with four days' worth of requests: the requests being submitted to me, the requests I had submitted to Division, the requests that had been tasked to Wing, and the ones that were supposed to be flown that day.

The ATO was written by a program purchased by the Air Force called Theater Battle Management Core System (TBMCS). It was complex and inflexible. The Marines over at Wing hated it. I hated it. Even trying to read the ATO was a chore. But all our flying had to be submitted up to the Joint Force Air Component Commander (JFACC) in Qatar for integration with the theater flights. The JFACC wanted everything in TBMCS, so that's the way it was.

Just when I thought I had a grip on things, the rest of the Regiment returned. Tom lit up when he saw me. I guess it was because seeing me made it real. He was about to head home. His eighteen-month tour with six months deployed turned into two years and nine months deployed. That made me wonder about my tour. The next couple days, Tom split his time between sitting with me and getting his check out and preparations for travel completed. And then he was gone.

I soon met all the important characters around the regiment. The colonel was exactly like Ray had described him. He was gruff, impatient, and to the point. He seemed to be intelligent, though, which would go a long way. I met my immediate boss, the S-3, referred to as the OpSO. I also met the S-2 (Intel), S-4 (Logistics), and S-6 (Communications) officers who were all majors. They were all my peers and I became fast friends with them.

Now that the Colonel was back, the 0700 Ops/Intel meetings resumed. Designed to give the Colonel a snapshot update each morning from all his departments, it felt more like daily beratings in front of all your peers. We called it getting the face-shot. The Colonel would wait until you just got your PowerPoint slide up and started your spiel, and then he would launch into a tirade about how inferior and stupid you were. He'd quickly transition into a speech about how the Marines deserved better support. While his points were somewhat accurate, yelling at us didn't magically make more aircraft available or change the MEF's prioritization matrix. And it chapped my ass that I had to spend two hours gathering all the information to build the PowerPoint slides exactly like he wanted, with the colors he wanted and 7th Marines logo in the right spot, etc. etc. He never read what was on my slides anyway.

Of course, now that all the subordinate battalions were back and operating again, the number of requests coming in tripled. That was good in a way because it meant the regiment was out there patrolling and operating, but it also meant longer days for me.

Somewhere, high up in the bowels of headquarters, when the big heads were deciding what mixture of forces to bring to Iraq, they came up with a plan. What ended up happening was the Marine Corps brought a division worth of infantry along with the aviation assets that would normally support a regiment and a half. I'm sure it made sense in some matrix somewhere, but either the mission description wasn't accurate or someone miscalculated. Needless to say, we ended up being pretty short on aviation.

That meant we had to get pretty creative to get as much support as possible. It also meant that the Lieutenant Colonels had to be "re-educated" that they were no longer VIPs with aircraft at their immediate disposal. That was not always a pleasant interchange and resulted in plenty of one-way conversations.

One of the problems with being an air officer is you are basically a man without a home. Grunts hate aviators, and the colonel made it clear how he felt. They constantly complain about not getting enough air support. If you assigned each Lance Corporal their own aircraft and pilot, you'd still get complaints about not having enough air support. Then you go to a planning meeting at Wing with your "fellow" aviators and they hate on you for demanding so much support for the grunts.

That played a big part in the Angry Majors club. Some days it was called the Bitter Majors Club, but it was the S-2, S-4, S-6, and me. None of us were infantry officers and we were hated by those around us. That was my crew and we're all still best of buds to this day.

Usually an air officer travels pretty close to the commanding officer. Our Colonel liked to get out to see his battalions. He liked to drive. I'm not sure if it was impatience, refusal to follow someone else's schedule, or if he realized that when he used an aircraft, one of his battalions couldn't use it. Regardless, he was on the road a lot, and he took me with him several days a week.

It was hot, dusty, and uncomfortable riding in a Humvee, but it gave me a much better appreciation for the terrain and the challenges the battalions faced. It also gave me a chance to meet face to face occasionally with the battalion air officers I was trying to support.

The Humvees we rode in were the old soft-top models that had steel plating welded on for doors for some degree of protection from IEDs. UpArmor vehicles were coming in but were going to the battalions first, as they should. I had to do some rigging to get an antenna out the window for my radio. I hung my GPS on a string over the door so it wasn't blocked by the steel plating on the roof. Every now and then, I would hand over hand pull the string in to check our position or to mark something on it. It was pretty redneck but that is what I had to do to make it work.

The first time we were hit by an IED, it went off behind our vehicle but in front of the following vehicle. It didn't cause any serious damage but caused some serious ringing in my ears for several hours. I found myself doing the "IED lean" after that. If you lean towards the outside of the vehicle a bit, you can get your helmet to overlap the collar on your flak vest to maximize your protection. You keep just enough space to see between the brim of your helmet and the top of the door.

We had another IED strike between Haditha and Al Qaim. This one went off in front of our vehicle but behind the lead vehicle. I remember riding along and suddenly I couldn't see or hear and my chest and head hurt. The fine powdery sand instantly made a dense fog, and the sound of the detonation was so loud that it didn't register as sound. I was just left with a hissing in your ears and you couldn't hear anything else. My chest felt as if someone had just donkey kicked me right in the sternum.

We were lucky that it wasn't a coordinated attack and we didn't suffer any injuries. The front tires were blown out and the windshield cracked. We just limped it back to Haditha on the run-flats.

The hard part of being on the road was the stack of requests on my desk and in my email when I got back. Plenty of times it was an all-night event to catch up. Even when I wasn't on the road, I was often facing eighteen-hour days. The worst part was when I did get back to my can to get some sleep, I often couldn't sleep. I would lay there stressing about what all I had to get done.

There were two distinct types of support requests: tactical requests and what we called admin requests. The tactical request were fairly easy. They were usually in support of a particular operation or type of patrol. Usually it was Cobras and Hueys or F/A-18s or Harriers. Occasionally there was a tactical helicopter assault where the aircraft would insert the Marines to do a specific operation.

The laborious part was the admin requests. It is surprising how often people think they need to move around the battlefield. The hard part was sorting out what was really necessary and what was just a nice-to-have. Oftentimes I would have five or six people lined up at my desk waiting to ask me about how to get a flight to somewhere. It got to the point where the clerk would line them up outside the COC and they would have to come in one at a time. Some of them were legitimate and some were just people thinking they could go on a trip.

It took me a while to crack the code on all the requirements for detainees. A battalion could hold detainees for three days but then had to either let them go or get them to a regimental level detention facility. Seventy-two hours is less than the ATO cycle so we eventually just started requesting detainee flights every three days for each battalion. On the day of the movement, we would either cancel or adjust the numbers to match what the battalion actually had.

The regimental facility could hold the detainees for four days. At the end of that time, they had to be returned to where they came from or sent (with accompanying evidence) to Abu Garaib. To make things more complicated, different aircraft had different escort ratio requirements, and of course everyone wanted their escorts back after they delivered the detainees. On more than one occasion, my requests to return escorts ended up being sourced before the detainees and escorts actually flew to their destination. Eventually, I got a system worked out in conjunction with the Lieutenant who ran the detention facility and the legal officer.

When the detention facility Marines turned over, I had to start all over! I ended up writing several cheat sheets: "How to move detainees," "how to request a flight," "how to get around the battlefield," and similar.

Eventually, the S-6 suggested I put all this stuff on the website. Wow! I didn't know I had a website! He had one of his guys come over and show me how to use it and how to update it. Soon I found myself answering emails with links to all the info on the website. A few weeks later, I found that the Division and MEF websites instructions were simply links to my website.

VIPs were a constant pain in my butt. Everyone from congressmen and high ranking military to authors and reporters. When they came to our battlespace, it became my responsibility to get them to the places they wanted to go.

Their aides and assistants would tell me things like: "We need a Huey at 1430 to take Honorable Mr. So and So to Haditha and then back to Baghdad." Of course, the true root here was that the aide wanted a ride on a Huey. I had to go dig up how many security personnel and how many assistants (what we called "strap-hangers") would be accompanying. More always showed up than were estimated, so I had to come up with a "plus three" estimation. Keep in mind, in that environment, with a combat load, a Huey can carry three to four people.

Then there were escorts and backups. If there were twelve passengers required, that meant there needed to be another aircraft capable of carrying twelve flying along with them in case there was trouble. And you can't send an aircraft carrying a VIP around without some firepower, so there would be at least two escort aircraft flying along with them. So you end up with six Hueys and between two and four Cobras for the mission. Simply because one guy wants to go visit Haditha. And that was the majority of the Cobras and Hueys we could source in one day. This often meant little to no helicopter support for the warriors out there doing what we were sent here to do. It got under my skin a little.

In addition, we had the joy of a CNN team as imbeds. It was a team of three – a cameraman, an assistant, and Arwa Damon. They (she) wanted to go everywhere! I only had to deal with her requests for aviation, but I heard all about her demands for other things like internet bandwidth, communications stuff, combat gear, vehicles to get around on base, and the like from my brother Bitter Majors. The directive from the Colonel was "give her whatever she wants." I honestly don't know how good of a reporter she was, but she was a pain in our ass.

She was notorious for doing drive-bys. Once, at 0200, I was walking to the shower trailer wearing flipflops, shorts, and towel around my neck and carrying my hygiene kit. She appeared to be heading back from the female shower trailer.

"Hey, what are the details on my flight for tomorrow?"

"Uh…looking good. Don't think you will have any trouble."

"Good. What time are we leaving and what time are we coming back?"

"Sorry, can't remember. Check on the website, the copy of the schedule I posted in COC, or at my desk. I'll be at my desk by 7 in the morning."

"Hey, do you think you could mention to the Colonel that it is inappropriate for Marines to walk from their cans to the shower trailer just wearing a towel?"

Woah. Here she was wearing a white Under Armor shirt with no bra and some "adventure pants" so snug they might as well be leggings. I get it, it's hot, but come on.

I said, "I think it would mean more coming from you, ma'am."

About two weeks in, I realized that to really do this job right would require about thirty-eight hours per day. I had started begging for an assistant early on. BK the S-6 had sent me a radio operator. Generally, the air officer has a radio operator assigned anyway. He was a young Lance Corporal. He tried hard but he didn't have the experience or background knowledge to really help me much. He did answer the phone and handed out "how to" sheets to the constant walk-ins, which helped. It was the constant significant decisions that I really needed help with. They required background knowledge of aviation stuff and had to follow the regulations and prioritizations. I just couldn't trust him with all that. He was a good kid; just didn't have the background for it.

Finally, the division air officer called me to let me know he had another Major inbound to be my assistant. I was overjoyed! Pugsley showed up a week or so later. He was a Reserve Major and just happened to be another Huey pilot. I was surprised that I didn't know him. There were about seventy-five Huey pilots who were Majors and I had run across most of them by this point in my career. Either way, it was great to have him helping. It took a week or so to get him spooled up, but soon we had our shifts worked out and a pretty good division of labor going.

Pugsley was a strange cat. He was a nice guy and tried hard, but maybe he was just too nice. The other officers in the regiment didn't really like him. He was easy to make fun of. Each day, after we changed over and he left, I'd hear a couple of "You know what Pugsley did today?" stories. Nobody disliked him; he just didn't fit in very well. Either way, I was glad to have him aboard and he kept me from going insane.

It didn't take long listening in the COC to realize that all the IM Chat rooms had serious miscommunication issues. For the most part, IM Chat had replaced radios as the main means of communications between units and up and down the command structure. Since everyone seemed to know how to "chat," there weren't radio operators passing the messages. The problem was, you often didn't know who was on the computer typing – it could be a high-ranking officer or it might be a PFC on watch.

I had a few conversations with Bill and Ray and discovered they were just as frustrated as I was. One of the biggest issues was the one-word responses. Someone would enter a question, which would be followed by a few other entries. Then someone would enter "yes" or "roger" but it was unclear who made the entry and what they were responding to.

My solution was to apply simple radio communication techniques. First, you must always list the stations you are addressing. On the radio you never said "yes." You said "You, this is Me, affirmative." The equivalent in IM Chat was to type the name of the person you were answering and then your answer. It was laborious but effective. I added a few more simple communication techniques from my old radio days and wrote up a little cheat sheet. I didn't have authority over everyone in the rooms, but at least the guys under me would communicate precisely.

Both Ray and Bill loved the idea and thought it made complete sense. Most Marines recognized standard radio jargon anyway, even if they weren't a radio operator. A day later, the policy for using standard radio protocol in the IM Chat rooms became standard throughout the regiment and the subordinate battalions. This isn't to say we eliminated confusing chat, but it cut down miscommunications significantly.

In addition, our guys looked and sounded more professional in the chat rooms. A little peer pressure and some "monkey see, monkey do" and soon most of MEF, Division, and Wing were using standard radio protocol in all the chat rooms.

Chapter 30

Michael

I had been emailing with Donna almost daily and calling her every week or two. BK had a phone on his desk that allowed me to dial the MWR line in Camp Pendleton and get connected to our home phone free of charge.

Donna and the kids were doing well. They missed me and I them. Vic was walking and talking now. Everything was going as well as could be expected until I got an email from her in early August. The email was short and just asked me to call home as soon as I could. It was about 2000 when I checked that email so I ditched out of the COC and went to BK's office.

Donna answered and immediately I could tell something was wrong. She sounded as if she had been crying. She was into the third trimester now and she'd had a sonogram that day. They couldn't hear a heartbeat. After more tests, the doctors discovered that the baby had died.

I was in shock. My mind was spinning and I didn't know what to say or think. Over the last few months, I had gotten used to the fact that I would be coming home to a new baby. It felt like the baby was already at home waiting for me.

Physically Donna was fine, but because she was so advanced in her pregnancy, they were going to induce labor. I couldn't fathom what that would do to Donna but I knew it was going to be rough for her. She had gone to the Red Cross representative on base and sent a message requesting I be there. A Red Cross message is about the only way to bring a Marine home from a combat zone before his tour is up. This didn't exactly fit into the usual categories that get approved. It was still possible, though, and I was going to do everything I could to be there for my wife.

Donna had given me the Red Cross message number so I took that down to the Admin section and gave it to them to look up. Then I headed over to the XO's office. The CO was already gone for the day. The XO listened to my explanation and shook his head.

"Hesty, I don't think so. I can't approve that. I'll talk to the Colonel when he comes in, but don't get your hopes up. I don't think he will approve it, either."

"But, Sir…"

"I understand this is rough on your wife but it's not like she died or anything." With that he walked out.

I was on fire that night. I did everything I could to help Pugsley get through the next ten days if I wasn't there. We had a battalion that was turning over with a new battalion. That meant flying nine hundred Marines in and then flying nine hundred Marines out. I had already been working on the plan but now I had to race to get everything done. I wrote all the support requests. Then I made Pugsley a spreadsheet of the flow of Marines in and out so he could follow along and make sure everything was going correctly. I wrote out a daily ops guide to help him make sure he didn't forget anything on the day-to-day operations. I felt like I had a pretty good turnover for him when the day crew came walking in.

I went and checked in with the Admin section. The had received the Red Cross message and it had been approved pending the Colonel's or the XO's approval. I headed to The Colonel's office. He waved me in and listened to my situation.

"Do you think Pugsley can handle it?"

"Yes, Sir, I wouldn't ask if I didn't."

"Go. I'll give you the full ten days."

"Thank you, Sir."

I was out like a shot. Back to the COC to brief up Pugsley on everything, then back to my can. I shoved a couple pairs of skivvies, my hygiene kit, and a blanket in my go bag. Back to the COC to get a ride up to the airfield after a quick stop by the admin shop to pick up my travel authorization.

I had looked up the flights to Kuwait and there was a C-130 headed down with a couple pallets of cargo. I was pretty sure I could finagle my way onto that flight. When I got to the passenger terminal, the clerk at the big plywood desk took my information and told me to have a seat; he'd see what he could find.

"Hey Lance Corporal, how about I just go Space A on Heavy 68 at 1200?"

"I dunno, Sir. I don't think they can take any pax."

"Hey, can I just borrow your phone for a minute?"

"Sure."

I called over to the C-130 squadron.

"Heavy operations."

"Hey, Paki, this is Hesty. Listen, I'm headed out on emergency leave. Can I catch a ride south on Heavy 68 as Space A?"

"Sure, dude! Plenty of room. Why don't you just come over to the squadron and we'll load you here as flight crew."

Ninety minutes later I was bouncing down the runway in the back of a C-130. There were two pallets in the center under cargo nets and about twelve empty seats down each side of the plane. The crew chief and I were the only ones in the back of the plane.

Many hours and flights later, I boarded a flight with a short layover in Dallas. I was still in my crusty cammies. I wished I had taken the time to shower and put on fresh cammies before I left. I was feeling a bit embarrassed and wondered how many people could smell me. Fortunately, the flight wasn't too crowded. I had an aisle on one side and an open seat on the other.

The third seat to my right was occupied by a fit middle-age man, just starting to gray at the temples. He smiled at me and stretched out his hand. "Thank you for your sacrifice."

I shook his hand and mumbled, "Thank you."

I still haven't figured out how to respond when people say this kind of thing. Unlike a lot of service members who complain about empty thanks, I do appreciate it when people say, "Thank you for your service," or something along those lines. Honestly, though, I get a bit embarrassed and am never sure what to say. In this particular instance, I really wasn't in the mood to talk to anyone.

The man looked at my two sets of wings on my uniform.

"My name is James Wright. My son is a Marine – he is in Recon."

That name rung a bell but it wasn't clear just yet. I said, "Is he in Iraq?" and just as I said that, the name clicked.

"No, he is back in the States now."

Cpl James "Eddie" Wright, this man's son, was at Walter Reed or one of the follow-on hospitals recovering from having both his hands blown off. Some incredible surgeon saved his leg from having to be amputated. I had heard the story of the Recon patrol that was ambushed near Fallujah in April. The commander had been killed. In spite of his injuries, Cpl Wright had directed one of his Marines how to apply tourniquets to three of his limbs, then continued to direct vehicle movement and machine gun fire. It was an impressive story. A picture of Cpl Wright saluting with a bandaged arm and no hands had become famous in Marine circles.

We talked the rest of the flight. I wished him the best and a speedy recovery to his son. I didn't find out until a few years later that Mr. Wright was actually a Colonel in the Air Force. I am still in awe of the man's humility and sacrifice. Both the father and the son.

Typical military bureaucracy and delays kept me from flying directly to Palm Springs in a timely manner, so when I finally reached San Diego, I decided it would be easier to just rent a car and drive the rest of the way. I had called Donna at each stop. In Washington, she had told me that Dee Dee, her best friend since first grade, was arriving shortly. When I called from Dallas and San Diego, no one answered.

I drank a gallon of coffee and drove like a madman from San Diego to Twentynine Palms. It was early afternoon by the time I arrived at the house. Donna was laying on the couch with Stuart at her feet. It was a strange homecoming. I was ecstatic to see Donna and she me but the circumstances were somber. She lay back down on the sofa and told me she had just gotten home from the hospital an hour before. Dee Dee had the kids at the pool to give Donna some room.

We lay on the sofa together for a while, just holding each other. Donna finally looked at me with her wry expression. "It would be okay if you went and showered."

So I did. It felt really strange to be in a normal shower, in normal clothes, and in my own house.

I didn't know what to say or do for Donna. She would occasionally tell me some small detail of what had happened. For the most part we just held each other.

Dee Dee flew out the next day.

I played with the kids, took them to the pool, watched them make mudpies and blanket forts and all the stuff that two- and five-year-olds do. Stuart never left my side.

We had a small funeral two days later. Father David had been there for Donna as a spiritual advisor and confidant. At the gravesite, it was just us and Father David and his wife. He paused for a moment during the ceremony. Donna and I had talked about names but hadn't finalized yet. Michael had been a top consideration so it seemed right when Donna told Father David that his name was "Michael."

It was August and very hot in 29 Palms. I thought maybe Donna would like to get away so we talked about just jumping in the RV and heading somewhere for a couple days. We ended up heading to a nice RV park on the Colorado river near Lake Havasu. We just waded and played in the sand at the water's edge and took lots of naps for the next few days.

Donna was a trooper. She worked hard to support me having fun with the kids and to enjoy being home for a bit. I could tell though that she was grieving. We really didn't talk about it much. In hindsight, I probably should have asked her to tell me more about how she was feeling and about her experience.

Just when being home started to feel real and normal, it was time to go. I said goodbye to my family and headed back to Iraq.

Chapter 31

Hit

There had been talk of a large scale attack into Fallujah since I had arrived. The whole debacle over the Blackwater contractors and the Coalition attack that had been called back had left a bad taste in everyone's mouth. Since then, Fallujah had become a sanctuary for bad guys. They were doing whatever they wanted with no consequences from any of the Coalition forces.

We had drawn up rough plans for a Division attack (two regiments in the city and two battalions on the outskirts). Now we were getting indications that we might actually get approval from the Interim Iraqi government. The planning increased and we started creating more detailed plans. I spent a lot of time on the phone and emailing with the Division Air O and the other Regimental Air O. It was going to be a pretty crazy air plan of attack with over 18 Forward Air Controllers in an area of 15 square kilometers. We had to plan it out very accurately to keep aircraft from bumping into each other while they followed directions from 18 different guys on the ground. A compact urban fight like Fallujah is very difficult to support with aircraft that require a lot of space to maneuver and deliver weapons that have an Effective Casualty Radius (ECR) of 500 meters. Most of our aviation ordnance was considered "Danger Close" within 1000 meters of friendly troops.

I give credit to "Static," the Division Air O, for coming up with the plan we ended up adopting. In the old days, attack runs by aircraft were based on known checkpoints on the ground. Our doctrine really hadn't caught up with the technologies of GPS and precision guided weapons. What Static did was take our old generic TRAP (Tactical Recovery of Aircraft and Personnel) template and converted it to a Close Air Support template. We called it a "keyhole" template.

The center of the template was a GPS point in the center of Fallujah. There was a five mile ring and a ten mile ring around that point. Between the two rings, it was divided into quarters based on compass headings. This made it easy for an aircraft to put the centerpoint in the GPS and stay oriented and in the correct quadrant. The quadrants were then layered into altitude blocks that were separated by 1000 feet for safety. A Regimental Air O could assign a section of aircraft a quadrant and an altitude. Then the FACs in the city could talk them onto the target they wanted struck. The FAC would request approval for a strike at a particular time and the Regt Air O would get approval from the Division Air O. The Division Air O was responsible for the inner five mile ring. He would approve a three minute window for that FAC and aircraft to be in the inner ring to deliver ordnance. The aircraft would then have those three minutes to enter the inner five mile ring and drop their ordnance.

In the meantime, the Regt Air O would be checking the positions of all the close friendlies to make sure everything was a safe distance from other units. It was a little bit more complicated than usual, but it was the most responsive coverage we could come up with for the incredible density of troops and aircraft we were expecting. Now we just had to wait for Multi National Corps Iraq to work an approval date with the Interim Iraqi Government.

Pugsley's replacement showed up and we did a few days of turnover before Pugsley headed back to the States. I'm not sure how Pugsley worked such a short tour, but I was glad to have had him and was just as happy that a new assistant had arrived before Pugsley left. Seymour was a young Capt from the C-130 community. The strike aircraft stuff was pretty new to him but he was pretty quick to learn.

The town of Hit (pronounced Heet) had started acting up. An ancient town on the Euphrates river with records dating back to 1600 BC, it sits halfway between Camp Ripper and Ramadi and in the southern portion of our area of operations. The bad guys in Hit had started acting like the bad guys in Fallujah. They were running around in black pajamas with red headbands and all kinds of weapons, randomly terrorizing locals. The good thing was the boldness of bad guys made it easy to identify them. The bad thing was that Hit was a very dense six square kilometer area with an estimated 700,000 residents.

We started developing plans at 7th Marines for a three Battalion attack. It would be an urban block by block fight. As I watched the grunts plan out their attack, I futzed about how to do the air support plan. Then it occurred to me, this was the perfect time to use the Fallujah plan, just scaled down for three battalions. Two battalions would be inside the city with LAR (the 3rd battalion) on the outskirts. The template wasn't scaled down because the aircraft still needed the same amount of space to maneuver. The units involved would be scaled down, though. As the Regt Air O, I would own the inner circle and each battalion would have a quadrant in between five and ten miles where they could stack aircraft and keep them safe from running into other aircraft.

The aircrews and FACs were already familiar with the template from the Fallujah planning. I sat down with a few of the planners from Wing and we worked out routes to get into and out of the area. After that we added a few low altitude battle positions for the Cobras and Hueys we had a solid plan.

We had enough intel and reporting to justify a temporary amendment to the ROE (rules of engagement). Basically, the black pajamas, red headband and a weapon were considered an enemy combatant uniform. Psyops, Civil Affairs, and the HUMINT bubbas starting spreading the word in Hit that if you wore that and carried a weapon you would be shot. They used flyers, public radio announcements, tribal council meetings, and anything else they could think of to help spread the word.

We decided to split the regiment headquarters: half would stay in Camp Ripper and the other half would set up a temporary COC in the field to oversee the operations in Hit. Seymour had a pretty good grip on the day-to-day operations at Camp Ripper, so I would be going and Seymour was staying.

We geared up and loaded into Humvees in the middle of the night. Our convoy must have been a mile long. It was a slow drive down Route Uranium and out into the desert west of Hit. In the meantime, two battalions had moved to the north side of town and LAR had crossed the river to the north, heading toward their assembly area on the east side of the river.

There was a railroad track just to the west of Hit, elevated on a large berm. We set up our mobile COC just to the west of that berm. We had several large tents joined together and the vehicle radios remoted into the main tent. We finished getting everything set up and all the radio checks done just as it started to get light.

I enjoyed setting up the radios and making sure they were remoted correctly. It was very similar to the setup I had worked with back in my early days as a Lance Corporal. BK's radio Marines were happy to have some help, although they were suspicious of me at first. They weren't so sure that a Major would really know how to set up a radio.

I had four radios remoted to my table: two VHF radios for talking to the BN Air Os and two UHF radios for talking to the aircraft. I had my whiteboard and map setup hanging on the tent wall behind my table.

I knew I could go about thirty-six hours without any sleep before I started getting stupid and couldn't function. We had already been on the go for about twenty-four so I knew I should get a couple hours before the attack started. Since I wasn't going to have any aircraft on station for a couple hours yet, I told my clerk I was going to go rack out before this big operation kicked off. I told him exactly where I would be in case anything happened and someone needed me.

I slept for about three hours before my clerk came and got me. It was approaching noon and was getting too hot to sleep anyway.

The first section of aircraft would be arriving in about forty-five minutes. We were in radio silence mode before the attack so I couldn't check in with the BN Air Os for another thirty minutes. I got a cup of coffee and stood next to Ray's desk and the master map. The BNs were all in their assembly areas and ready to go into the attack. It was eerily quiet. As I looked around the tent, I saw that everyone was at their desks staring at maps or documents.

The next thirty minutes crept by. Finally, we were free to talk on the radios as the battalions started their movements into the city. We really didn't know for sure how this would go. I checked in with my Air Os and let them know a section of F-18s and a section of Cobras would be on station in fifteen minutes. Nobody had any strong feelings that they needed the aircraft yet so I gave the F-18s to Dirty with 3/7 and the Cobras to Fab at 3/4.

Nothing happened as they all rolled into town. It was a bit anticlimactic. There was a whole town ahead, though, and plenty of room and time for things to get crazy.

An hour into it, there were a couple of small engagements. We could hear the sound of the gunfire coming over the berm. None of the skirmishes had been big enough for anyone to use aircraft, but they were doing a great job with the "keyhole" template and the aircraft were providing great situational awareness to the Marines on the ground.

As the Marines moved south into the heart of the town, they were getting a little more action. 3/7 on the western side used a Maverick missile from an FA-18 and then a gun run. The template was working well and we hadn't had any issues. The relatively low number of engagements using aircraft made it all pretty simple so far.

Dirty was setting up another for another FA-18 mission when the Colonel grabbed me. "Do you need to be here for this?"

"No, Sir, Dirty has it all handled. I'm just monitoring to make sure everything goes right."

"Grab your radio and your binos, come on."

I followed the colonel out of the tent, strapping on my helmet and slinging my rifle. I wasn't sure what was going on. I checked my pocket radio, a PRC-117, and made sure I could hear Dirty talking to the aircraft. The Colonel was walking quickly with the Sergeant Major in tow. He was headed toward the berm between us and the city. I jogged a little quicker to catch up.

When we got to the berm I scrambled up and lay down across the tracks, looking into the city through my binos. I could hear the aircraft above us and was trying to pick out the checkpoints Dirty was describing to the pilot to verify the grid position he had sent. I thought I had the building picked out they were going to strike. I looked over to describe it to the Colonel when I realized both he and the Sergeant Major were standing on the top of the berm with their hands on their hips like they were watching a football game. I wasn't so sure about that. For some dumb reason, I stood up too. We were probably eight hundred meters from the edge of town. It wasn't a shot anyone could make with an AK-47, but if someone had a sniper rifle we would have been easy targets.

I heard the pilot call inbound, meaning he was heading toward the target. I clicked the handset and said, "Cleared into the keyhole." "Roger" was the response. Dirty gave him "Cleared hot." I relayed that to the Colonel. The aircraft was coming in from almost directly behind us and shooting in a west to east direction. That was good geometry to be attacking parallel to the front line of battalions.

"Missile away!" We could hear it from the aircraft. The intended target was a few blocks into town so we were easily 1,400 meters from the intended impact. That was well outside the ECR (effective casualty radius).

We heard the *whosh* of the missile. It impacted in the empty sand halfway between us and the town. That was only three hundred meters away! Too close!

The Colonel started yelling. "What the fuck! Those fucking aviators are trying to kill me! What the hell is going on! Hesty, I want to know what the hell happened, why the hell isn't he hitting the target."

He continued on but I was trying to hear the radio so I tuned him out. The pilot had called "bent missile" as soon as he recognized it wasn't tracking to target, but I couldn't hear the rest of the conversation because the Colonel was ranting. We had scrambled back down the western side of the berm toward the COC. I told Dirty he still had the keyhole as I was trotting back to the COC. He ended up running the aircraft again using a short burst of 20mm from the machine guns.

Generally, the Mavericks were good missiles and we rarely had any issues from them. Since the pilot had called "bent missile," they knew something wasn't right. Usually if the missile loses its laser spot, it de-arms and levels out. This one had definitely detonated and it hadn't leveled out. It was well short of target, not way long of target like when a missile levels out. I probably wasn't going to be able to find anything out about what had just happened until the pilots landed, but there was no reason to stand there and take abuse from the Colonel. I was nervous anyway about being away from the other radios and the COC. If something else came up I needed to be able to plot stuff on the map and have the use of all the radios.

I dropped my helmet and sat down at my desk. I got a call from "PITA" at LAR on the radio. They had a squad down by the one bridge crossing the river. They were taking pretty good machine gun fire from across the river, but since that was 3/4s area, they were having trouble returning fire. I got Ray on the situation and he assured me that 3/4 didn't have anyone within eight hundred meters of the enemy machine gun.

PITA explained that he wasn't with that squad and couldn't really control aircraft down there because he didn't know what they were looking at. I told him to have his squad leader from that southern squad come up on our FAC channel so I could talk to him.

I finally got the squad leader on the radio. He told me the machine gun was in the big blue mosque just south of the bridge on the western bank of the river. There were several mosques in town, but only one with a big blue dome roof. I looked at my satellite imagery of the town and saw exactly what the squad leader was describing.

The next section of aircraft checked in and I put them in the holding area on the east side of town. Then I explained the situation and had him start scanning the mosque area for machine gun fire. I leaned over to Ray and pointed on the map.

"I'm setting up to shoot a Maverick into this area. I need double confirmation that 3/4 is clear and doesn't have anyone in this area." I drew a circle with my finger in a five hundred-foot radius from where I thought the machine gun team was.

The FA-18 crew said they could see the muzzle flashes and confirmed what the squad leader had described. Then he gave me the code to his litening pod, which meant I could pull up his feed with my laptop hooked to a SHF receiver. I tuned it in and now I was looking at the same thing they were seeing in the cockpit.

With a few more back and forth conversations with the squad leader and the FA-18, I was confident we were all looking at the correct target. It really was the ledge on the roof of the mosque. I was hesitant because it was a mosque. All through ROE classes and pre-deployment training it was bludgeoned into our heads: "Don't shoot a mosque unless someone from the mosque is shooting at you." I confirmed again with the squad leader. It was effective fire and they could not move from their hole without being exposed to accurate machine gun fire.

I briefed up the FA-18 on the fire mission I wanted. Ray had given me the thumbs-up that 3/4 was clear and no one was danger close. I was really nervous but tried to sound totally confident as I explained to the FA-18 crew that yes, I understood it was a mosque but yes, I wanted them to put a Maverick into it. I obviously couldn't point a laser at the target so he was going to have to lase it himself to guide the missile. He moved the crosshairs of his litening pod onto what I described, and I confirmed on the feed that that was where I wanted the missile.

I checked one last time with the squad leader. "Are you still receiving fire from the mosque?"

"Yes, Sir! We gotta move. We gotta get out of here but they got us pinned!"

"Roger, stand by, TOT 18."

That meant time on target at eighteen minutes past the hour.

"Profane (FA-18 callsign) TOT of one eight."

"Copy one eight. Turning outbound so we are going to lose sight for a minute."

"Roger."

The ligtening pod hangs under the aircraft. It doesn't have a full 360 degrees of view. He was letting me know my feed would go black for a minute as he got into position to fire the missile.

"Okay, so we are gonna put this sucker right into that mosque."

"Yes, I'm buying your missile so it's my call."

The feed came back up and I could see that the crosshairs for the laser were still in the right spot.

"Turning inbound."

"Roger continue, still have troops receiving fire from the target."

"Roger."

I double-checked the geometry, looked at where the missile should go if it lost tracking. I glanced over at Ray one more time for that last check from 3/4.

"3/4 says light the bastards up."

I keyed into the handset.

"Profane, you are cleared hot."

"Roger, cleared hot. Maverick missile going into the blue mosque."

"A Firm."

"Missile away."

"Roger."

The heat from the missile blurred the video feed, but it looked like a good shot. The ten seconds or so that it took the missile to fly to the target seemed to take forever, particularly with what had happened with the last Maverick shot. But then the missile hit – exactly where intended. The video feed bloomed out a little from the brightness of the explosion. Just as the feed was coming back into focus it went black. The aircraft was turning away again.

The radio went crazy. Since the mosque was one of the bigger buildings in town, everyone could see it. The squad leader was back on the radio yammering at a million words per minute.

"Sweet shot! Those fuckers are pink mist! They are just gone! That was perfect!"

"Hesty, this is Profane. Good hits. Looks like half of the roof is gone. I can see flames coming out of the mosque."

Just as he was describing it, the video feed came back and I could see that half of the dome was missing. The wavering of the edges was an indication of flames coming from inside the mosque. Part of me wanted to stand up and whoop, while part of me was thinking I was going to go to jail. Instead, I just keyed the handset again.

"Nice work, Profane. Good hits. I'd say we've got three enemy dead and a machine gun destroyed."

I finally remembered to breathe and I looked around the tent. The Colonel was standing in the middle of the tent with his hands on his hips, watching me. He didn't say anything but gave me an almost imperceptible nod. To me that meant, "That'll do pig, that'll do." It also meant that should I take some heat for lighting up a mosque, I could expect some backing from the Colonel.

Everyone else in the COC was watching me, too. When I started looking around, they all turned back to their maps and radios. Ray shot me a tight-lipped smile and a thumbs-up.

There was a bit more to wrap up for the mission and then all seemed to be quiet. After fifteen minutes or so, the adrenaline had worn off and my neck started noodling. I checked in with all the boys on the radios and they were doing fine; no requests for aircraft. Ten minutes after that and I was having serious problems keeping my eyes open. I stood up from my chair and looked around the room. Ray and I were the only ones awake! These hardcore grunts were all sleeping on their desks!. The OpsO was slouched in his chair with his chin on his chest. Internally I was laughing. They all gave me crap for slinking off to sleep for a while when we first got set up, but now that we were well into the fight, who was awake?

The rest of "the battle for Hit" was pretty mellow. There were a couple more small engagements and we flew several sections of aircraft over the town until it got light the next morning.

After that, we packed up and drove home. The drive home was painfully slow but at least it was daylight. One of the vehicles got a flat. Rather than risk having a convoy sitting stationary on the road for a few hours, we drove home at 25 mph because one vehicle was on its runflat rim.

We had only been gone about seventy-two hours, but rolling back into Camp Ripper was like coming home after a long trip. And we knew that planning and preparation for Fallujah was about to get crazy.

Chapter 32

Fallujah

In Fallujah we were tasked with clearing fifteen square kilometers of tightly packed buildings, with an estimated four thousand bad guys. It would be the first large-scale urban battle fought by the Marine Corps since the Battle of Hué way back in 1968 – the year I was born. We all knew Fallujah would be a history-making battle.

In preparation, Psychological Operations (PsyOps) and Civil Affairs started leaflet drops and radio broadcasts to warn the locals. Meanwhile, we began the logistical nightmare of moving the regimental headquarters down to Camp Baharia, which was just a mile or two outside the city of Fallujah. Once established, we would assume control of First Battalion, Eighth Marines (1/8), First Battalion Third Marines (1/3), and the Army's Second Battalion, Second Infantry Division (2/2). I would be the Air O for three of the six battalions fighting in Fallujah, and PEZ, my equivalent over at 1st Marines, would support the other three battalions. Over the next several weeks, the two of us would control hundreds of aircraft supporting almost four thousand Marines on the ground.

Camp Baharia was 170 kilometers from Al Assad, on fairly good roads. But with a military convoy of about forty-five vehicles, the threat of enemy attack, and a good possibility of IEDs, we planned for a six-hour drive. A few hours in, my driver flipped his night vision goggles down with the infrared search light on, effectively blinding himself while we were going 45 mph. He swerved into the median and missed a large concrete barrier by inches. Then, a short while later, a "friendly" outpost opened fire on us. Fortunately they were poor shots and didn't hit anyone. Otherwise the drive down was fairly uneventful.

We pulled into Camp Baharia in the wee hours of the morning. The camp was surrounded by a ten-foot-high cinderblock wall, making a half-mile square block. The northwest corner of Camp Fallujah's barrier wall was just a hundred meters to the southeast. The two camps were a hundred meters apart at the diagonal. We spent several hours unloading all the vehicles into the same type of sixteen- by thirty-five-foot General Purpose (GP) tents I had stayed in around the world. It was late October and it was turning cold. I was glad I had brought some of my cold-weather gear.

The next day we got the COC set up. I had two computers on my desk and a small hutch built out of plywood to hold three radios. On the wall behind me I hung a few small maps and a small whiteboard with a depiction of the airspace management keyhole.

BK and I took a break later that day to walk around the camp. Years ago it had been a Ba'ath Party vacation resort. There was a man-made lake in the center with a small island and a scenic arching bridge, along with the remains of a tiny amusement park. Everything was rusted and rundown and riddled with bullet holes.

The next few days I worked with the S-2 and the Fires Officer building target packages. There were over 150 targets we wanted to strike before any Marines stepped foot into the city. Some of these targets were suspected defensive IEDs, some were enemy ammo stockpiles. Suspected command-and-control locations, machine gun emplacements, and simple barriers were on the list too. Each target package included six or seven pages of descriptions, justifications, supporting intel and imagery, weaponeering of the ordnance desired, and the desired end result.

Meanwhile, the entire staff was working on the Confirmation Brief, which we were to present to the Multi-National Corps Iraq (MNCI), the Interm Iraqi Government (IIG), the US government reps, and of course Division and MEF. I would be briefing the aviation plan and actions. The day after the brief we scheduled a Rehearsal of Concept exercise. We called this a ROC walk – on a large-scale terrain model, we would walk through all the different phases of the plan.

The Colonel was completely stressing everyone out, telling us how approval for the operation depended on how well we briefed. All the generals would be there, along with representatives from IIG and MNCI. And we were told to expect General Casey, the commander of Coalition forces in Iraq.

Luckily, we now had a new XO who was approachable and reasonable. He let it be known that if we (the staff) had issues understanding or filling the Colonel's demands, to come see him first and he would help us out. That made it feel like teamwork instead of an adversarial command.

Our target packages had started coming back down the command chain. They were all conditionally approved. The condition was that we couldn't strike any target until it showed hostile act or hostile intent. But how do buildings, dirt berms, or sandbag bunkers show HA/HI? Simple – they don't. So you can't shoot them.

The Colonel was furious and we all took an ass-chewing. His final comment was: "Resubmit ALL of them." So we did, all two hundred of them.

Lucky for us, Division and MEF were familiar with the Colonel and we didn't receive any heat for our resubmissions. Still, they came back with the same answer: we needed HA/HI in order to strike.

The only thing we could do at that point was request as many hours of drone time as possible and watch all the points of interest 24/7. The S-2 and I both made these requests through our respective channels and then sat in the COC watching UAV images and directing them to our approved targets.

Seymour and I had been taking twelve-hour shifts. I couldn't hide at night anymore – I was always getting paged – so I went noon to midnight while Seymour took the reciprocal. While Seymour was in the COC, I spent most of the time working on planning, target packages, and other stuff, so I was still getting only three or four hours of sleep per night.

A few days later, the endless hours of watching UAV feeds finally paid off. It was just after dark and I was watching a target house in south Fallujah. Intel reported it was a command and control center for the bad guys in the southern portion of the city, which we had code-named Queens. I had watched several small groups of three or four wander the area, then enter the target house. Occasionally a group of two would come back out and walk down the street, visit a few other buildings, then return to the target house. But with the black and white display and resolution from eight thousand feet, we couldn't tell if it was the same bad guys each time. Still, we were pretty sure there were fifteen to twenty guys in the target house.

The S-2 was sitting next to me and we were discussing what we might find as HA/HI. Then all of a sudden he jumped up and walked out. I didn't know if he had gone to take a leak or had just gotten bored. But a few minutes later, he returned with his imagery analyst and the SJA (staff judge advocate, a Marine lawyer) in tow.

It had become standard practice over the past few months to have the SJA in the COC when we were getting ready to strike something. It wasn't a perfect system, but it gave us a quick sanity check from a legal/ROE perspective before we pulled the trigger. I think the SJA enjoyed the break from his other duties. He was a fellow Major and we all called him "Judge." A thumbs-up from Judge followed by a "Cleared hot" into the radio were usually the last things said before an explosion appeared on the screen.

Well educated and well spoken, the imagery analyst was a senior Sergeant who was very skilled at deciphering the pixilated images displayed on our screens. We had watched UAV feeds for hours together and developed a good rapport. He slid into the seat next to me and I described what I had been watching. The S-2 and the SJA stood behind us. I typed a message into the chatroom we were using for UAV control and the camera slewed up the street to show five guys walking towards the target house.

With a completely level voice and no hint of excitement, the imagery analyst said, "That's easy, Sir, we've got 'em."

"How so?"

"Hostile Act. They are all carrying weapons." He leaned forward. "Look, they are only swinging one arm, then when one of them turns… there, see? You can see the butt of the weapon between his arm and torso."

I turned around. "Judge?"

Judge took a minute before replying. "Well, by the new ROE, carrying a weapon in Fallujah satisfies Hostile Act. I can see exactly what you are saying, Sergeant – they do all appear to be carrying weapons. I'd say you've got it. Justified strike."

"And if they walk into the house with those weapons, do we have a justified strike on the house?"

"Well…"

I said, "We have an approved target package on that building. The only condition is Hostile Act."

"In that case you are golden."

My head was whirling. Plans and branches of plans were beginning to take shape. "Okay, boys, let's do this right. I'm thinking they are moving weapons into the target house. Not sure, though. So how 'bout we watch a little longer and see. Let them get a few more into the house. Meanwhile, I'm gonna scrape up an aircraft from somewhere." Using a common abbreviation for the S-2's official title, I said, "2?"

"Hell yeah! Sergeant, you brief up the battle captain. I'm gonna go find the Colonel and fill him in. Hesty, find us some Air!"

I got on the horn to Division. This was not the usual situation for an immediate request and I wasn't 100 percent sure how to proceed. I didn't have a Troops in Contact situation so it didn't really justify going straight to the TACC. It was a fleeting opportunity, though, and we had to act fast. Division Air O would point me in the right direction. I kept one eye on the screen as I talked with Division.

The five bad guys had entered the target house. The adrenaline was kicking in as I told the Division Air O what was going on. I could hear the excitement rising in his voice as he told me he'd have me an AC-130 in a few minutes. Turns out 1st Marines had an AC-130 working for them just to the west of the city. It seemed like as soon as I hung up the phone with Division it rang again with the 1st Marines Air O calling me.

"Hesty, this is PEZ. Division told me to send you my AC-130. What you got?"

"Yeah, I got some guys carrying weapons into one of our target houses."

"You can see that they are carrying weapons?"

"I got an imagery analyst sitting here with me. He's the one that broke it out. Looks like they are stocking them up in this house."

"Sweet, man! Blow the whole stinking block! AC-130 coming to ya, man. What's the contact?"

"Ripper 32 on Cherry 89."

Ripper 32 was my official callsign at the regiment, and Cherry 89 was the code for one of my Tactical Air Direction frequencies.

During the conversation, two bad guys came out of the target house and were walking up the street again. The Sergeant patted my shoulder and pointed at the screen when it happened. I tapped into the chatroom for the UAV crew to keep the camera following them.

My radio buzzed with the AC-130 checking in.

"Ripper 32, Basher 52 with you at 10K, block Alpha, got 3+30."

This meant he was overhead the city at ten thousand feet and had three and a half hours before he had to leave to get fuel. The transmission continued describing the weapons he had on board. Halfway through the conversation I had to plug my open ear because the Colonel came blustering into the COC. He was talking loudly, which made it difficult to hear the radio handset. Fortunately, the S-2 and the Judge intercepted him so I could continue. He looked right at me, saw my finger in my right ear, and lowered his voice a bit.

I twisted the handset down away from my mouth. "Sir, AC-130 just came on station."

"Outstanding. Put it up on speaker."

I turned on the radio speaker. It seemed silly to me because he wasn't going to understand what Basher was saying and it just raised the possibility that he might interrupt me to ask me what Basher had just said.

I continued with Basher. I gave him the track and altitude of the UAV, then the ten-digit grid to locate the target house. I described the block the house was on, then the house itself. This was a challenging evolution because the houses often had less than two meters between them and sometimes appeared as one building. Fortunately, the lot next to the target house was empty. This made it a little easier to make sure he was looking at the same target.

Meanwhile, the two bad guys who had been visiting the neighbors were coming back toward the target house with three more of their buddies in tow.

"Sergeant J, looks to me like they are carrying weapons again."

"Well, Sir, those three definitely. The one on the south maybe. The other one doesn't have a weapon."

At any other time this would not have been enough, but the mission ROE for the Fallujah operation was a little different. We were confident that in Fallujah, at night, after a month of warnings, an innocent civilian would not be walking the streets with armed bad guys.

The colonel broke in: "Hesty, once they get into the house, drop it."

"Yes, Sir!"

Ray, the battle captain, broke in. "Sir, it's the MEF battle captain. They are watching the UAV feed and want to know if we are going to strike."

Classic. The problem with the UAVs was that others' units could tap in and watch your feed. I worried the added layer of micro-management was going to ruin our opportunity. I knew that Division and 1st Marines were already watching, probably had it displayed on their COC screens. Now MEF was in on it.

The S-2 asked Ray to make a sigact (significant activity) entry into the MEF chatroom. This would let everybody in the chain of command know that we had Hostile Act and it was at our approved target #39. Maybe they would stop interrupting us with questions.

Meanwhile, Basher tapped the target building with his infrared pointer. I could see the beam in the UAV feed so we both knew we were talking about the correct house. I talked him onto the five bad guys walking in the street and told him I wanted one 105mm round in the middle of the roof once they entered the building. I knew the 40mm wouldn't be enough, but I was a little concerned about the damage a 105mm round might do to the surrounding buildings. The 40mm would be more likely to detonate on the roof and blow sideways, raining roof bricks all across the block, but it wouldn't do much damage to the occupants in the house. The 105 round would penetrate the roof and detonate on the floor. My educated guess was that the walls of the house and the walls surrounding the house would minimize the damage to the surrounding buildings.

The bad guys had stopped in the street and seemed to be having a conversation. Maybe they were passing around a cigarette. I felt like I had everything set but worried that any second, something was going to ruin our plan. I went back through the official Call For Fire (CFF) I had given the Basher crew. This was my first time calling live fire from an AC-130. It is something every Air O, FAC, and JTAC dreams of. Marines rarely get to use the AC-130 – it is usually reserved for Special Operations.

After what seemed an eternity, the bad guys resumed their stroll back toward the target house and entered the house. Immediately, I cleared Basher to engage with one 105 round.

I could hear the round being fired from the aircraft. A small black hole, probably two feet in diameter, appeared in the roof near the northeast corner. Simultaneously, a puff came out of each side of the building. It was impossible to tell if it was smoke, debris, or just heat when looking at the UAV's infrared camera feed. A split second later, we felt and heard the whomp of the round impact. It wasn't on the radio; it was real life.

The damage was less than I had expected. The impact wasn't exactly where I wanted, either, but this was a 105mm artillery round fired from a moving aircraft, not a laser-guided missile. The error was perfect; the actual impact was on the roof of the target, farthest from any adjacent buildings.

Basher came back on the radio. "Rounds complete."

"Roger, Basher, good hits. Stand by for reattack." I was waiting for the Colonel to tell me to hit it again. I didn't think it was needed but didn't feel like the destruction we had just seen on the screen was going to be enough for him.

After a few minutes had passed four bad guys came out the front door headed up the street. They weren't running but they weren't walking, either. My guess is they were stunned and I know they had a headache.

I told Basher to keep his optics on the "Tangos" headed up the street. I was glancing between the screen and the Colonel when he looked me in the eye, quite forcefully, and said, "Take them."

"Basher, keep your effects in the street, squirters headed north, clear to engage with 20 millimeter."

"Stand by, Ripper, adjusting orbit." He was adjusting his orbit so that rounds short or long of the target would be in the street instead of nearby houses. "Engaging."

I could hear the Gatling gun going off in the night sky above us. It was the classic "BBRRRRTT" sound. After a slight delay, the impacts were plainly visible on the screen. It was clearly effective rounds, leaving clouds of smoke or dust behind, in front of and right on top of the bad guys. As the clouds settled, we could see their bodies lying in the street, not moving. When the impacts showed on the screen, I couldn't help but give a little fist pump on my desk. There were a few "yeahs," "ohs," and "damns" around the COC. It was a bit like crowd reactions at a fireworks show.

"Basher! Good hits, BDA (Battle Damage Assessment), of four enemy KIA! Nice shots."

Seconds later, though, I was shocked to see figures running out of nearby buildings toward the bodies in the street and toward the target house. What was going on? I expected them to grab the bodies and carry them off, but instead they ran off, leaving the bodies in the street.

Sergeant J exclaimed, "They're getting the weapons!"

Eight to ten figures had run into the target house.

I typed furiously for the UAV crew to stay focused on the target house.

"Basher, stand by for re-attack on the target house." It seemed like ants crawling everywhere. "Judge, am I good for a re-attack? Sir?"

I didn't hear what Judge said but saw him nodding his head as the Colonel drowned him out, saying, "Hit 'em again!"

Basher put another 105 round through the roof of the target house. This hit was closer to the center of the roof. The results were the same as before, another two-foot hole in the roof and the puff out each side, with the over-pressure pushing smoke, heat, and debris out the windows and doors. The explosion was cleanly contained inside the building.

The streets were empty save the four bodies. Nothing changed for the next ten minutes. The Colonel wandered away giving me a nod as he left. Another "That'll do, pig."

My computer dinged at me. It was a message from Division: "Good job, Hesty, nice shot." The adrenaline and the extra observers in the COC wandered away. After another ten minutes, I thanked Basher for the work and sent him back to 1st Marines. I had just fired 7th Marines' first rounds into Fallujah and it was a success. I was very relieved – it felt like the whole world had been watching. It also felt like we were finally making a little progress.

I made a mental note of a new TTP (Tactics, Tips, and Procedures) from that night: always have a re-attack ready. It had paid off and now there would be at least eight fewer bad guys shooting at our Marines when they marched into the city.

For the next thirty-six hours, we took turns staring at UAV feeds hoping to find another hostile act so we could take out another target, but it never happened.

Part of our "Preparation of the Battlefield" was conducting feints on different sides of the city. This had several purposes: it kept the enemy guessing which way the big assault would come, it enabled us to learn more about enemy defenses, and it also generated more intel on their communications networks and activities.

1/8's Air O ran two sections of F/A-18s, a section of helos, and a Harrier during one of their feints. It was mostly gun runs and a few mavericks, but they dropped a GBU 38 on a building at the edge of the city. The GBU 38 is a GPS-guided, five-hundred pound bomb. It is capable of impacting within one meter of the ten-digit grid. So it should impact inside a six-foot radius of the intended point. This drop was off by about fifteen feet. That's not too bad, but further off than it should have been. It ended up impacting on the backside of the building, blowing it off, which had the desired effect. The error prompted the S-2 and me to do some research.

We sat down with our maps, overhead imagery, and a special program we called "piss-off" for deriving accurate ten-digit grids from stereo optical imagery on a laptop. The maps and map data we had for Fallujah were different than the stuff we had for everywhere else in Iraq. Turns out the elevations in the map data were incorrect. The elevation data was taken in 1927 whereas the horizontal data was from the 1980s. It was combined together to create the data on our maps. For GPS-guided munitions, having the incorrect elevation created a bit of error. Missiles and laser-guided munitions wouldn't have this issue.

Picture a non-powered bomb falling off an aircraft at 25,000 feet. The fins on the bomb steer it as the lateral energy dissipates and the vertical energy increases. The result is an arc that starts out mostly horizontal and then becomes almost vertical at the end. If the GPS thinks the ground (and the point of impact) is at a different height than it really is, it will impact at the wrong point. My genius buddy the S-2 came up with a correction. When deriving the ten-digit grid, use the azimuth of the path of the bomb and take the ten-digit grid six feet on that azimuth from the intended point of impact.

It made sense to me. This was not at all a doctrinal adjustment. This was a field adjustment to make what we had work for us. With the close fight in the urban environment and the density of friendlies, getting a bomb into the right spot was very important. Now I just had to find a way to test it before it became critical.

It was the first week of November and we had been at Camp Baharia for three weeks. D-2, meaning two days before D day, the IIG officially approved the operation, with one change. Up to that point the operation had been called Operation Phantom Fury. Now it was called Al Fajr (New Dawn). The Iraqi government wanted the operation to have an Iraqi name to show the Iraqi people why "we" were fighting this epic fight.

During the night of November 7, Marines, sailors, soldiers, and Iraqi soldiers moved from their respective camps by convoy to the assembly areas north of the city. It was only a six-mile movement, but this was a reinforced division's worth of troops moving into attack positions, so it took eight hours. When the huge column stopped at the northwest corner of the city, everyone was in their correct positions to turn left and be in place for the attack into the city.

In the meantime, LAR and Iraqi 36 commandos moved onto the peninsula west of the city and took control of the hospital and other key buildings. Small Craft Company was patrolling the river with their fast attack boats. The Army's Blackjack Brigade had secured the eastern and southern sides of the city. It was kind of cool having the Blackjack Brigade cover our eastern flank. They were one of the few Army units that had fought with the Marines against the Japanese in the Pacific island campaigns of World War II.

I sat in the COC and directed UAVs to watch the edge of the city. There really wasn't much else I could do to support. We watched the city intensely for signs of Hostile Act/Hostile Intent but hadn't found anything yet. On the western side of the city, in the 1st Marines sectors, they had some skirmishes and were exchanging fire with the bad guys, but so far there was no activity in our sector.

In the early morning hours just before light, the D-9 armored bulldozers started building ramps and busting down the railroad berm, making a notch in front of 1/3 and 1/8 so that vehicles could get through. Force Recon and their pathfinders had spent the night sneaking around and marking out lanes for the battalions to follow through the trash and obstacles as they went into the attack. Now they were set up in sniper positions as overwatch in the vicinity of the railroad berm. A few of them were already in the outer blocks of the city. One team had had a skirmish getting into position, but fortunately their Air O was with them so all I had to do was ensure he got the aircraft he requested and follow along with his missions. They had a couple of gun runs and shot a maverick missile, then things seemed to calm down.

As the sun came up, so did the anxiety level. The battalions had been sitting in their assembly areas for several hours. They were densely packed and would be sitting there for a few more hours until the actual attack began. Our frontage seemed to be fairly quiet so far, but we knew that at any moment all hell would break loose. The sky was loaded with aircraft and the Air Os down at the battalions and companies were having them scour their own frontage.

At this point my plan was to provide overwatch but push control of the aircraft down to the boys in the breech. I would back them up on their missions by following along and making sure they weren't shooting at any friendlies as we moved into the city.

Sometime that afternoon, each of our battalions fired line charges from their breech sites on the berm. The line charge is like a thick rope of explosives. A rocket pulls the rope off the deployment vehicle. Once it is on the ground, it is detonated to clear a path safe of mines and IEDs. The line charges going off made booms we could hear and feel from the COC. A few of them had significant secondary explosions, indicating mines or IEDs had been detonated along the path. Before the dust settled, there were Marines pouring through the breeches and through the last hundred meters of open ground and into the city. There were Marines on foot, tanks, amtracs, Humvee gun trucks, and all manner of vehicles moving into the city.

I was watching a Scan Eagle UAV feed. It was tough to know where to look. I could only observe a few blocks at a time. Each battalion had multiple aircraft under their control but no one was making any calls for ordnance yet. The COC was crowded. Everyone wanted to know what was going on. Fortunately, they were fairly quiet so I could hear and talk on the radios as I shuffled aircraft around to the battalion Air Os.

Over the one-mile frontage of the regiment (three battalions), the front edge was fairly jagged as different blocks had different degrees of resistance. The individual company units were doing an amazing job keeping the frontage fairly even.

Aircraft checked out and new aircraft checked in. I kept shuttling them down to the Air Os. They'd had a few engagements so far but all of them had run like clockwork from a geometry-of-fires perspective. The Air Os were keeping their situation awareness very accurate and I hadn't heard a single thing that made me doubt any of the controls. Even the Air Force JTACs with 2/2 in the east were sending some aircraft ordnance downrange and keeping it controlled without unnecessary risks.

1/8 called and asked me for a little help. I had been watching them run a section of Cobras firing a Maverick missile at a minaret. Their Air O briefed me up on the situation. After taking sniper fire from a minaret at a mosque about four blocks into the city, they had fired several SMAWs (shoulder-launched rocket) into the small balcony near the top of the minaret. But the sniper fire had continued. The Cobra they just ran had put a TOW missile into the minaret just below the balcony. Still they had sniper fire coming from the minaret. They wanted me to pull a ten-digit grid for them, hit it with a five hundred-pound bomb, and try to knock down entire minaret. Roger that! I asked them to give me at least a three hundred-meter radius with any friendlies closer than five-hundred meters behind a significant wall. I was a bit nervous about trying this correction so close to our guys. This was definitely a danger close mission.

I called Division and asked for a fixed wing with a GBU-38. The aircraft had been flying with a mix of GBU 12s (laser-guided five hundred-pound bombs) and GBU 38s (GPS-guided bombs). There was enough dust and smoke in the air now that we were starting to get nervous about using laser guides. The huge tangle of powerlines everywhere in the city was a possible issue for lasers as well. Division replied that he had a single Harrier with a GBU 38. He only had about twenty minutes left on station before he'd have to turn around for fuel. Perfect.

I worked up the ten-digit grid on piss-off to place the bomb right at the base of the minaret and made the correction. Swifty 71 checked in with me with the standard brief. I gave him a quick explanation of the situation and a nine-line brief for his attack. He plugged in the ten-digit grid and had his sensors on the target minaret in moments. I explained that I needed him to follow the attack azimuth within five degrees. Usually you give the aircraft as much latitude as possible for their attack run. In this case, I wanted to parallel the side of the mosque that the minaret was attached to. If the bomb was long or short, it still wouldn't hit the mosque. Of course I also needed my correction to work, and to properly test it, we needed the bomb on the correct azimuth. Hitting long of the target wasn't a problem – that was definitely bad guy territory. I was worried about hitting short and endangering friendlies.

I double checked with 1/8 and they had everyone five hundred meters from the target. I did a quick mental math drill and came up with a TOT of 26 (meaning the bomb would impact the target at twenty-six minutes after the hour), which was about five minutes away. It turned out that 1st Marines had a TOT already approved for 27 working on the west side, which moved us to 30. Our standard of deconfliction was three minutes. This way we were sure that the previous aircraft would have exited the inner ring of the keyhole.

"Swifty 71, Ripper 32, earliest TOT I can get approved is 30. Can you work with that?"

"Affirm, Hesty."

"TOT set at 30. Just to confirm, this is Danger Close and we accept it."

"Swifty."

It cracked me up when guys switched up my callsigns but I didn't really care. All it meant was I knew the guy and when you are laying large ordnance very close to good guys, that is usually was a good thing.

I knew 1/8 was on the radio listening but I double-checked with him on the back radio to make sure he got everything. This was actually working backwards from normal SOP. Usually the battalion Air O worked the air and the Regimental Air O listened in. Here I was running the Air and 1/8 was listening in just to make sure it all went the way he wanted. Then again, I had a lot of resources at my fingertips that 1/8 didn't have, I wasn't getting shot at, I wasn't running around, I wasn't outside in the freezing rain. Hell, I even had a cup of coffee on my desk.

I looked up across the COC and gave everyone a heads-up that I was running a mission for 1/8 and TOT was 30. Most everyone already knew that because they were listening to me talking on the radio.

"Swifty 71 inbound."

"Swifty, Ripper 32, cleared hot."

"Swifty is wings level."

"Cleared hot." I didn't need to clear him hot again but wanted to make sure there was no confusion.

The Harrier transmitted a little beep when the bomb released. "Bomb away."

I echoed to the COC and to 1/8 on the radio: "Put your heads down, bomb away." I heard the roar of the jet overhead as he accelerated up and away and back into his holding area.

About twelve seconds later, right as my watch ticked over to "30," the screen bloomed out white. A second later, we could hear the whomp of the impact. The radio crackled from 1/8 at the same time the image recovered on the screen. I could hear whooping and hollering in the background on the radio. There were hushed "Yeah! Oooh! Hell yeahs" trickling around the COC as the image of the stump of a minaret came into view.

"Shack! Beautiful, direct hit, impacted the minaret about ten feet off the ground, it disintegrated!"

Swifty was now out of fuel and ordnance. He needed to return to base (RTB).

"Swifty, direct hit, that was a perfect shack! Don't know how many snipers were in there but that is at least one enemy KIA. You are cleared to switch and RTB, thanks for the work!"

"Anytime, Hesty. I'll be back. Find me some more fuckos to schwack."

I tapped into the chatroom with Division: "Mission complete, Swifty 71 switching, RTB."

I checked back in with 1/8 and they were good for the moment. I told them I had Basher (the AC-130) checking in in a few minutes and I would send them over. 1/3 still had a section of F/A-18s they were working. 2/2 hadn't asked for anything and I knew those Air Force JTACs would bitch like hell if they needed something, so for the moment I was set.

I leaned over to the S-2 and we discussed the field correction. We did some geometry figuring and decided we needed to add a little more. We were really close but the impact was ten feet higher than desired. Based on the steep trajectory of a bomb, the last several feet it was probably an 8:1 slope. The adjustment was between one and two feet. We decided we'd go with adding one more foot.

As my nine Air Os in the field had breaks in their action, I briefed them all up on what we had worked out and how it had worked with me controlling the air for a battalion. Their biggest challenge was they only had visibility of where their own company was located, and there were about fourteen companies working our sector. But I had a wall-sized map right in front of me that was getting updated every few minutes and I could get the battle captain to rapidly confirm positions. I was offering friendly clearance confirmations, pulling corrected ten-digit grids, or even running the show. All they had to do was tell me what they needed.

I learned that when 1/8 cleared the mosque next to the minaret we had knocked over, they had found a huge cache of weapons. That made me feel better.

1/8 worked Basher for the next couple of hours. Even if I didn't have the radio on, I would have known they had Basher firing. I could hear the BRRRRRTT and the whomp whomp of Basher shooting.

1/3 was having trouble with a single-story building about four blocks south. We went through the same drill. I directed an F/A-18 to drop a GBU 38 in the center of the roof. It almost went down a chimney. When the bomb detonated, the walls fell outward and the intact roof simply dropped to the ground. It was perfect; very little debris flew out of the house. There was a plume of dust and smoke out each window and doorway, but the adjacent houses looked like they didn't have any damage. It was like we just folded up the house.

I asked the crew what fusing they had set on the bomb and they told me a twenty-five-millisecond delay. I now had my preferred engagement system down. The short delay allowed the bomb to penetrate the roof and detonate on the floor. The overpressure pushed the walls out and the roof fell in, crushing anything that was inside the building. The grid correction also seemed to be working perfectly. That bomb was dropped within two hundred meters of friendly troops, and they were ecstatic. Deaf, but ecstatic.

I ran a few more missions that night for 1/3. It was the wee hours of the morning now. The battalions had made huge gains. We had expected them to take two days to get where they were now. There had been some hard fighting and there were plenty of casualties getting evacuated, but they were doing great. The COC had cleared out except for the watch-standers.

The last mission I ran for 1/3 was a two-story building. I asked for a thirty-five-millisecond delay fuse, hoping it would penetrate through the roof and the first floor before detonating. We didn't get the clean roof drop like on the previous couple of missions. Also, the building may have had more reinforcement than the previous buildings. It half collapsed. As I watched the building crumble, I remembered the first mission where the bad guys came running back into the building. I immediately requested the next available TOT, which was three minutes. I asked Profane (FA-18s) to set up for the new TOT for re-attack. The second aircraft was ready and rogered up. As we watched, black figures started to come out of the woodwork and run into the building. I double-checked with 1/3 that it wasn't friendlies and explained that I wanted an immediate re-attack. They stayed in their hunkered-down positions and we dropped a second bomb on the house after about fifteen more bad guys had run in. The entire building collapsed on itself this time and there wasn't much chance anything survived in the building.

I asked Seymour to pass what we had learned on to the Air Os, then went off to grab a few hours of sleep. With all the aircraft we had flowing that day into night, there had been aircraft ordnance dropping almost every five minutes. That was some good support for the Marines on the ground duking it out face-to-face with the bad guys. I drifted off to sleep to the sounds of Basher's guns, occasional artillery fire, and fixed wing dropping five hundred-pounders.

The next few days followed the same template: oversee several air missions and run a few air missions. While it doesn't sound like much, it was pretty fast-paced. Even when I wasn't monitoring a mission or running a mission, there were plenty of firefights going on. I was constantly in alert stage red, always tracking and always prepared.

It took about three days for the bad guys to try something different. They got tired of getting beat up badly at night and switched to a daytime activity pattern. This was exactly the opposite of how everything else had gone for the past eight months. Previously, the daytime had been quiet and the enemy activity picked up around sunset. Now, they would pick up the fight about ten in the morning and bed down for the night by sunset. I think this switch was the result of the effectiveness of the AC-130.

1/8 was setting up for a renewed push the next morning. In the COC, I could see the Marines stacking on the north side of an east-west running, ten-foot-tall cinder block wall. The wall was at least eight blocks long and on the north side of a fairly sizable street. From the positions of the Marines bunched up with their backs to the wall, I estimated they were adjacent to one of the large steel doors that were typical of Fallujah architecture. As the UAV continued in its orbit, I got a view of the southern side of the wall and saw there were dozens of insurgents stacked up there! Literally six inches from the Marines on the north side of the wall!

While waving and pointing to the screen of the UAV feed, I shouted into the radio to the Air Os to hold the Marines in position – that there were bad guys on the south side of the wall! As soon as Bill caught what I was on about, he was on the Ops radio passing the same warning to the company commanders.

The bad guys had set up a perfect trap. The Marines would come pouring through the gates of the wall, facing south and oriented toward the first row of buildings. Their backs would be to the dozens of bad guys waiting behind them against the wall.

The Marines stopped moving on the screen so it seemed a crisis had been averted. Now it was time to seize the opportunity. Simultaneously, I asked the Air Os and Bill if we could get the Marines off the wall and back into the next row of buildings to the north. Then I would run a section of F/A-18s down the street, blazing 20mm through the row of bad guys waiting against the wall. To get the effects of the 20mm onto the bad guys at the base of the wall, the aircraft would have to fire from the south. That meant any stray rounds, fragmentations, and debris would be headed north right into friendlies.

I was amazed at how quickly word got passed, and the Marines melted northward into the protection of the first block of buildings. It didn't take long to get a section of F/A-18s briefed on the situation. This was quite a bit different from any of the other missions we had run in the past three days, so I spent a little more time describing the situation and desired results. The pilots agreed with the plan and had the wall in view in their sensors. A double-check from the Marines that everyone was clear and I got a time on target approval from Division. The F/A-18s were cleared hot and made their guns runs. Just thirty seconds apart, the two aircraft chewed up the base of the wall and the north side of the street with thousands of 20mm rounds.

The destruction was incredible. This was different than dropping a building or knocking over a minaret. I could see the effects of large-caliber machine gun rounds hitting human bodies. There were bodies and pieces of bodies strewn up and down the street and some actually splattered on the southern side of the wall. This felt way more personal than any of the previous missions. I had to remind myself that these men had been preparing to rip into our Marines just minutes earlier. They had been preparing to rip into our Marines just minutes earlier.

As soon as I called rounds complete, the Marines restacked on the northern side of the wall and then breached the doors moments later. The first few Marines immediately turned left and right to cover the groups of bad guys strewn in the street. The second groups flooded across the street and into cover along the first block.

Later that same day, I heard that a friend of mine from 1/8 had been severely wounded while trying to drag a wounded Marine out of the street. He was the Gunnery Sergeant I had worked closely with months earlier doing the helibourne vehicle checkpoints back in Al Assad. One of the combat correspondents covering 1/8 had captured the incident in a series of photos that soon became famous. The Marine died but the Gunnery Sergeant was expected to survive.

The next day was November 10, a huge day in the life of any Marine. It was the Marine Corps' birthday and always a celebration. Even in the middle of a battle, Marines will take a few moments out of the day, read the commandant's message, General Lejune's message, and tell each other Happy Birthday. Even the Army PsyOps guys got in on the action, blasting "The Marines' Hymn" through their loudspeakers. The intel chatter indicated that it drove the bad guys nuts, and better yet, the Marines loved it.

The Colonel had been going into the city to visit the battalion's headquarters. After about two weeks, things had slowed down a little, and I got invited along. It was a great opportunity to meet the Air Os face-to-face and see how things really were going. Since the battalions had advanced south of the major east-west highway, it was an easy drive in from Camp Baharia. I rode in the back of an Amtrak with my head and rifle barely sticking out the troop port on top.

The city looked like it had been at war for years. Every building had bullet holes if not tank round holes or worse. Every block had a building that had been reduced to rubble. The bird's nest of powerlines across the rooftops and power poles looked like enough wires to run four or five cities. We even drove by the blue mosque and I got a close-up view of the minaret damage.

The smell in the city was devastating. There was open sewage flowing in the street and garbage everywhere, but even through that, you could smell death. Rotting corpses were mixed in with the rubble and laying in some of the streets. The efforts to clean up had really just begun on the very north end of the city and hadn't gotten this far south yet. The Iraqi Red Crescent (sort of like our Red Cross) had been removing bodies and burying them in accordance with Islamic Law. The bad part was they refused to do anything with the foreign fighters. They were only taking care of the bodies of locals.

The fighting and clearing in Fallujah continued over the next week. There were a few more missions to drop buildings and several more missions to knock over minarets. Fallujah was known as the City of Mosques, with approximately 133 mosques in fifteen square kilometers. More than ten of them were now missing minarets as a result of me directing aircraft ordnance. I knew that 1st Marines had knocked down a few too. Every single one was a legitimate military target, but I was concerned about the possibility of an Al Jazeera campaign about Americans emasculating Islam. The bad guys had a way with turning lies into truth, and I could envision them going crazy about the destruction of the mosques. Fortunately, it didn't happen and there never was any flap over it.

At one point I was chatting with one of our interpreters. "George" wasn't from Fallujah but he came from nearby. He laughed when I expressed concern. He told me about the smugglers' routes that led from the Mediterranean Sea to Baghdad from ancient times until now. He told me that smugglers had put Fallujah on the map, which was why the town was different from the others in Iraq. According to George, the vast majority of the mosques had been built in the 1980s. They weren't the historic monuments and cultural centers that we believed them to be. Under Saddam Hussein, if you built a mosque, you were exempt from government taxes for ten years. George laughed as he told me that all the successful smugglers built mosques to keep the government out of their money business.

His story made me feel a bit better. In addition, we had found that more than half of the mosques in Fallujah had weapons stockpiles and fighters hidden inside. That voided their religious exemption and made them all valid military targets.

By mid-December, everyone had transitioned to clearing operations. The entire town had been swept. Now the Marines had to go building by building, room by room, and check under every mattress, blanket, carpet, etc. There were still bad guys hiding in the city and still firefights every day. On the whole, though, there was much less violence. The Civil Affairs Group, Naval Construction Battalions, and similar agencies were in the city. They were distributing food and water to the estimated one thousand residents who had stayed. They were draining sewage and flooded streets, fixing water mains and sewage lines.

The AC-130 had stopped flying for us every night, and the frequency of our own aircraft had slowed significantly. There were still multiple UAVs and at least two sections of aircraft up over the city at any given time, but the majority were looking at rooftops and down back alleys for Marines as they cleared individual buildings. From an Air O or flight crew's perspective, it was almost boring.

We had been there for two and a half months, and for the last few weeks there were no aviation engagements. Marines were still patrolling but firefights dropped to almost nothing. We ran straight through Christmas and New Year's without even knowing they had occurred.

January's focus was on the first Iraqi elections to happen in decades. The plan was for the Iraqis to do everything and for the US forces to simply provide security. The idea was that if a US service member never touched a ballot it would eliminate any possible interpretation that we had influenced the elections. In reality, US forces had to jump through multiple hoops to make the elections happen.

On the whole, the elections were considered a success, although many Sunnis boycotted them, so that put a damper on the results. The one story that sticks with me is from the Marines who were in charge of security at a polling station just down the road from us. They noticed a man toward the back of the security check line who exhibited many of the indicators of a suicide bomber – wearing too much clothing for weather that day, acting nervous, and constantly scanning the crowd.

Using an interpreter, the Marines called the man out of the line and pointed him off to the side. He started to charge the Marines, yelling "Allah Akbar." When they raised their weapons to fire, he turned to run away. The Marines started to pursue. Fortunately, they didn't get close before the man tripped and detonated himself. Amazingly he survived, and the Marines started first aid and requested a MEDEVAC. Apparently, the man lived and was eventually sent to Abu Ghraib.

One second this guy is trying to kill people with a suicide vest, the next second Marines are trying to save his life. That's Iraq for you in a nutshell.

By the end of February, we were back in Al Assad. We had turned over our battlespace in Fallujah and re-assumed our original battlespace in the northwest. I was back to being a travel agent, but with even less aircraft availability while they fixed everything that had been pushed to the limits in Fallujah.

All told, we dropped eighty-seven 500 pound bombs, four 2000 pound bombs, sixteen missiles, eight gun runs, seventeen rocket runs, ten gun runs from helos, and forty-four missions from the AC-130 with various mixes of their weapons. Every single mission was danger close. That was a lot of aviation ordnance. And not a single incident of fratricide. I am proud of that.

The Multi-National Corps Iraq figures stated that four thousand bad guys were in the city before the fight. Twelve hundred enemy were killed and one thousand were captured. Our losses were sixty-three troops killed in action, 535 wounded. Of the wounded, more than half returned to duty. But what struck home the most was 7th Marines: thirty-one killed in action and 220 wounded in action. One of the JTACs with 2/2 was killed. Those were our guys, the ones we knew personally.

Chapter 33

Redeployment

Our return home was penciled in for mid-April, so it was time to start working on our redeployment. "Redeployment" is a term I never really liked but it is used extensively. Deployment obviously means movement to theater. To me, redeployment should mean returning to theater after having been somewhere else, like home. But the official use of the term is "return from deployment." Redeployment means going home.

Most of the Regimental Headquarters had been in Iraq since February, going on fourteen months deployed. I was approaching the twelve-month mark. So it was exciting to finally see a light at the end of the tunnel.

I tried not to allow myself to think about going home. The deployment calendars, countdown timers, and all that stuff just reminded me how much I was missing. So I used the box trick and put that thought in a box and tucked it in the back of my mind. But once our return home became imminent, I couldn't help but be excited.

I needed to figure out what command I was going to next. If I were to follow the party line, I would just get back to a squadron. But if I went back to a squadron, they would send me to the next squadron deploying, and if that happened, I would likely be back in Iraq within six months. If Wing didn't send me to a squadron, I would be seen as an "extra body" and they would send me to fill an IA (individual augment) billet. Who was asking for IAs? Units about to deploy. Which also meant I could expect to be back in Iraq in about six months.

Since there weren't any squadrons in Twentynine Palms, there weren't many jobs for aviators there. Manpower management emailed to let me know they wanted me to stay at 7th Marines for another year. I knew Donna would be less than thrilled to hear that.

Congress had just confirmed limits to the amount of time service members could be deployed. If a service member was going to be deployed longer than 365 days, the Command had to issue a statement about why that service member was critical to success. I knew Commands wouldn't want to do that. In addition, a service member was required to have "dwell" time equal to their deployment time before they could be deployed again. If you deployed for six months, you had to have six months at home before you could be deployed again. This was all encouraging. Since I was finishing a twelve-month deployment, it should be twelve months before I had to deploy again.

About the same time, the Colonel received confirmation that he was going to take over the Tactical Training Exercise Control Group. TTECG is the organization that oversees the large-scale CAX exercises in Twentynine Palms. They do everything from teaching classes to serving as field referees for the three-week-long Combined Arms Exercises (CAX) that ran throughout the year.

The Colonel was redesigning the CAX program to be more applicable to Iraq Operations. Since I had more time and experience as an Air Officer in Iraq than anyone else in the Marine Corps, he wanted me to come be his Air Officer field referee when he took over. I was flattered that the Colonel had noted my experience and asked me to do it, but still, I wanted to see what else Manpower had for me and talk to Donna about it.

My head was whirling. The Colonel was a powerful man and was going places in the Marine Corps. Having him as an ally was a good thing. However, it was exhausting to work for him. I didn't know if turning him down would piss him off and work against me. Normally I tried to ignore Marine Corps politics – it was one part of being an officer that I really didn't enjoy. But sometimes you can't avoid it.

Then again, I already had some good material to use at TTECG. Static had asked me to write a few short papers on the tactics and techniques I had used so he could share them with other Air Officers. And I had almost written a book preparing the turnover binder. The idea was to have a document that anyone else could read and then take over your job with minimal interruptions in operations. In addition, I had also co-authored a few articles for the *Marine Corps Gazette*. The S-2, Fires Officer and I had been directed by the Colonel to write and submit them. The articles were about Marine Corps doctrine and what worked and what didn't work in Fallujah. We also proposed changes to doctrine, equipment, and training. Our first drafts were usually pretty good, but by the time we edited them to say what the Colonel wanted them to say, they would be crap. Writing an article to say what someone else wants it to say is a painful process I hope to never repeat.

Donna wasn't too thrilled about the idea of me going to TTECG. I wasn't really sure why. I think it was continuing to work for the Colonel and being in the field every other week.

We started our turn over with 2nd Marines. They were from the East Coast. Not that it matters, but they did have a little different approach to things. I was a bit surprised at how confident (arrogant?) my personal relief was, and how he thought he could just waltz in and do the job. Usually it is a ten- to fourteen-day process. The first half consists of the outgoing guy doing the job while the incoming guy observes. Then at the halfway mark the incoming guy does the job while the outgoing guy observes and helps. I spent more time with his assistant than with my relief. He wanted to take over after two days. That was okay with me, though. It gave me time to write and submit the Command Chronology (history report) for 7th Marines for the last six months.

Finally, the day arrived and we were in our cleanest uniforms, waiting at the airfield for our C-130 flights to Kuwait. Our flight to Kuwait, day layover there, and subsequent contract air flights back to Southern California went as expected. At March AFB, the armory vans met us and we turned in all our weapons. I felt naked walking around without any weapons. It was a good naked, though.

We boarded buses and headed up to Twentynine Palms. The hour-long drive seemed to take forever. As we entered the town of Twentynine Palms, the sidewalks were crowded with people waving flags and shouting "welcome home." I was feeling very proud and thankful to be back on US soil.

On base, they had the large football field covered with tents, inflatable games for the kids, and a huge BBQ. The loudspeaker was blasting rock music but was interrupted by the announcer as we pulled in.

"Ladies and gentlemen! 7th Marines!!! Welcome home, gentlemen!"

The three white buses disgorged their contents of ninety Marines, and we all ran into the crowd of wives and girlfriends dressed in their best. Some of the ladies' "best" may have been a bit more appropriate for a cocktail party, but they wanted to look good for their husbands and boyfriends they hadn't seen in many months. There was hugging and kissing, crying and laughing.

I already had a tear in the corner of my eye when I finally spotted Donna, Emily, and Vic. Donna was holding Vic, who was now two years old. Emily was holding Donna's hand but came running toward me as soon as she recognized me. I scooped her up and then squeezed the three of them together and buried my face in Donna's hair against her neck. I could feel the tears rolling down my cheek.

"I'm home, Schatzi."

Chapter 34

Dwell Time

We got a "96," which meant four days off until I had to go back to work. I slept a lot and lay on the couch a lot, snuggling with the kids, Stuart, and of course Donna. Many men don't admit it but the lack of affectionate contact on a deployment is hard. The hand holding, caressing each other, deep hugs, nuzzling my wife's neck – I miss that on deployment. Of course I miss the truly intimate acts, but the simple little ones you don't think about, those are key, too. I made up for lost time.

I also spent a lot of time wrestling with the kids, going to tea parties, and all kinds of kid fun. Vic was walking and talking now. I had missed both of those developments. Emily was a precocious six-year-old and wow could she tell a story! I ate it all up. We had a late birthday party for Vic since it had just been a week prior. Four days flew by and it was back to work.

We had four battalions to take care of and one of them was about to deploy. The personnel count of the regiment dropped almost in half. Many of the personnel we had in theater were individual augments to make the regiment into a regimental combat team. In addition, all the Marines that had a transfer day or end of orders that occurred during the deployment were now transferring out. I became the assistant operations officer. Most of my buddies had left. BK and the S-4 had both transferred to new commands. Now it was just me and the S-2 left in the Bitter Majors Club.

I started catechism to be chrismated into the Orthodox Church. Donna and I had been going to an Orthodox Church for the last several years. She had officially converted and was chrismated (similar to an adult baptism) while we were living in Camp Pendleton. When Vic was born, we had both Emily and Vic baptized. I had grown up Lutheran. My parents and brother were still Lutheran. Both my sisters had converted to Orthodoxy years earlier. That's how Donna and I learned about the Orthodox Church.

I don't really consider myself religious. That term has many meanings to many people. You can also always find someone more or less religious so I'm not comfortable describing the scale. I prefer the term faithful. I have faith in God. Some are better at setting an example of how to be faithful, and some are worse, but I strive to improve, learn, and do better. Ultimately, in my opinion, it's not about what you present, it's about what you do, in your exact position. It's about what is in your heart and mind.

Starting catechism was the first step in learning more. Father David was the priest at the church we went to in the short period before I deployed. He had been very helpful for Donna while I had been gone and now he was very helpful in setting up classes and meetings that worked around my schedule. The more I met with him and listened to him, the more respect I had for him. I enjoyed our meetings and discussing the differences from things I had learned in the Lutheran church.

The regiment had a change-of-command ceremony coming up for the Colonel, and rumors were flying about the new CO coming in. His last name seemed familiar to me, and it all made sense when someone pointed out that his father had been the chairman of the Joint Chiefs. This could go a couple of ways. I've known many legacy Marines who didn't want anyone to know who their father or grandfather was. One of my buddies in flight school was a General's kid and I didn't know it until years later. He definitely made his own legacy in the Marine Corps. Occasionally, though, a legacy would walk around like their poop didn't stink.

Meanwhile, I talked to the Colonel and agreed to go over to TTECG, but told him I was having trouble with Manpower. They had flat out told me I wasn't going. He told me not to worry about it. Once the change of command happened and he took over, he'd get orders cut for me and he'd let me know.

I focused mostly on manning and training for the air officers at the battalions. Most of my time was spent in the office on the phone, on the computer, coordinating, cajoling, begging, directing, and occasionally writing. Every three weeks or so I'd set up a shoot and we'd spend a few days in the field. The best training for JTACs and air officers was practice. Battalions could do it on their own but it was more productive to have several battalions involved and I could do that at regiment. I loved going to the field and it gave me a chance to talk face to face with the new guys, have them practice with our new gear, and spread around lessons we'd learned from the last deployment. As a regiment, I had a little more pull to get the aircraft support. It tends to build on itself. The more squadrons you get to participate, the more want to come. I even got some Air Force and Navy squadrons flying in to shoot. Then I was able to offer some training back to the squadrons by letting them do a few artillery controls or airborne controls.

We got through the change of command and the new CO was in charge. It wasn't a drastic change but there were definitely some differences in leadership style. The new CO was direct but he wasn't as brash as the Colonel.

We all had interviews with the new CO. Most of my interview with him consisted of him telling me he wanted me to be his drug czar. He wanted me to be his urinalysis officer. No one liked being the crotch watcher, piss officer, or any of the other names we had for it. Yes, it was an important program but there was nothing interesting about it and it took a lot of time. It was particularly time-consuming when no one had been running a program for a while and you had to start from scratch, which was the case here. Oh well.

Twentynine Palms is a small town and only exists because of the base – it is very much a military town. But I soon noticed that whenever I left Twentynine Palms, no one else seemed to realize we were at war. When I was in Yucca Valley, Palm Springs, or even down in San Diego, it was business as usual.

Part of me liked it. In my mind, that's why you have a military caste. Whether they are a low caste or an elite caste, their job is to be the warriors, to fight the wars and protect the rest from all the horrible things that a war causes. To truly understand me, you have to have done and seen all the things that I have. I don't want that for my family, my brothers and sisters, definitely not for my children. That's my job, to carry that burden so others don't have to.

But there was another part of me that hated it. I wanted to scream at some of the fat, lazy civilians, stuffing their faces with Cinnabons at the mall: "Do you realize what Americans are facing right now in Iraq and Afghanistan?" "They are your countrymen, fighting and dying for our country's interests right now, at this very moment!" But people didn't seem to know and they didn't seem to care. Sure, I get the "Thank you for your service" and a 10 percent discount at Denny's, but what does that really mean? Usually the "Thank you for your service" is from another vet, often a Vietnam Vet who never got a single "Thank you." Those I believe. But Denny's? That's an advertising ploy so they can say they are veteran friendly.

Then there is the question I always get: "What do you think of the war?" I'm not going to tell you. As a military member, it's not my job to question the orders. My job is to execute them. As long as they are lawful orders, I will execute them to the best of my ability. That is a huge part of making a military successful. I am going to believe that this mission is worth the risk. I have to believe that the analysis was done and the correct answer was chosen. If I don't believe in the mission, I will fail. I have to believe in the mission. Just about every boot camp or basic training in the world teaches that. As you get older, wiser, and more experienced, you realize how much truth there is to this. At my level, I do not have the information, knowledge, or background to understand all the politics, finances, and national security issues that shape the decision.

"C'mon, though, you've been over there. Surely you've seen some stuff or know some stuff?"

No, actually, I don't have any inside information that would tell me if our presence in Iraq is critical to America's national security. I have seen some stuff; I do know some stuff. I know how difficult the mission is. I know that atrocities happen. I know how things are going in the area I was in. Al Anbar is drastically different from the rest of Iraq. I know that not all the media reports are accurate. But you knew that already, right?

This is not to say I'm not an American citizen. I vote, I pay taxes. I have some say in the government through our democratic system. I would like a more transparent government. I would like lower taxes. I would prefer that we weren't at war. But don't ask me what I think of the war as a Marine, as a service member.

We had a small family ceremony when my commanding officer at 7th Marine Regiment awarded me a Bronze Star for actions in Iraq. Donna had been doing some stuff in the Reserves and came in uniform. My three-year-old son came from daycare. He was wearing a kid version of our uniform I had gotten him because he wanted to "look like Daddy."

The CO made a comment about my Marine family and how my son would grow up to be a great Marine. I had to bite my tongue not to reply in a smart-ass manner. The CO meant it as a compliment, and yes, if my son, or my daughter, decides to serve, I will be the proudest Marine father. However, I do not hope that my children join the Marine Corps. I pray he and his sister find other ways to serve our nation. It was important to me to join and I am very proud of my service. I would do it again in a heartbeat. But I don't want my babies working like dogs and facing the risks like I did. It's a double standard, but I'm a dad and that's how I feel.

I was still readjusting to being home. Still dealing with losing a couple friends. Still dealing with missing a year of my wife and kids' lives. Still dealing with the lost pregnancies.

I couldn't find the answers to these personal conflicts. They are difficult issues and I had enough to work on. So I copped out. My defense was to stay on base, stay at home, stay secluded. Fortunately, my family likes being at home, going to the bowling alley on base or hiking in the hills. For the moment, my cop out didn't cause any family issues.

I was busy. Days were long but I got to go home to my family almost every night. A few weekends we took the motorhome and boat out to Lake Havasu or the river. Those were my favorite times. I was blessed to have a family that loves to be on the water as much as I do. Joshua Tree National Park was just a few miles away and we spent plenty of time there, hiking or just playing on boulders. We'd pile both kids on our little 50cc scooter and drive around between the Joshua trees and yucca plants in the empty lots across the street. One of my favorite moments was sitting on the porch swing in the early morning before it got hot, just sipping a coffee while watching the kids make mud pies in the dirt.

It was the early summer when we learned that the regiment was headed back to Iraq immediately after Christmas. The required dwell time had been waived because the Marine Corps didn't have enough regiments to support all the current operations. I couldn't decide if it was good news or bad news but we would be going right back to Al Assad and the same area of operations (AO) that we had had on the last deployment.

I spoke to Father David about it. He talked to the bishop and got approval to do a condensed catechism for me. I would be chrismated on Christmas instead of the usual Pascha (Easter) chrismation. Usually catechism lasts about a year.

The Colonel was over at TTECG now and he asked me to come by. I had been hoping to get an update from him. Having an estimated date would affect how I was doing some things at 7th Marines. I checked in with his adjutant. The Colonel called me in and told me to sit down.

"You know the regiment is going back to Al Assad, right?"

"Yes, Sir."

"With everyone having checked out, there aren't many left from the last deployment."

"Yes, Sir."

"In fact, from the officers, it's just you, the 2, and Captain Brandt. But Captain Brandt is going down to one of the battalions to be a company commander so that will leave just you and the 2. You need to stay in the regiment. They have no leadership experience left. You need to stay there and bring all that corporate knowledge you've gained."

With that my fate was sealed. Eight months after a year deployment, I'd be headed back for another year in Iraq. If I wasn't a little bitter already, I was now. And I was not looking forward to telling Donna. Part of me felt like it was my duty, but part of me felt pissed that out of the entire Marine Corps, they couldn't find another Major to do this job.

I was stuck. It was also a bit of a blow career-wise. By the time I got back, I would have been a Major for three years. Most of that time would be at an infantry regiment. A Major is expected to have filled certain billets by the time he is eligible for Lieutenant Colonel. Generally this is about year four of being a Major. They are different expectations for different jobs. As an aviator, you are expected to have at least been a department head in a squadron, if not an operations officer or an XO. In addition, I was going to be unqualified to fly because all my currency and qualifications would expire having not flown for more than eighteen months. That meant I'd be going back to the training squadron for four to six months for refresher training before I could get back to a squadron. I had a feeling this was a bad deal. Of course, the senior officers around the regiment had no idea about career path requirements for aviators. I talked to a few mentors from my squadron days and they all told me to just get back to a squadron as fast as I could. I felt a little bit screwed.

What I didn't admit to anyone was that I didn't really care about wearing the rank of Lieutenant Colonel. I was actually pretty happy as a Major. The pay increase to Lieutenant Colonel is dramatic, though. When it comes time to retire, the difference between being a Major and a Lieutenant Colonel is about $500 a month – for the rest of your life.

The next few months sped by. More and more "pre-deployment training" had been mandated. We were doing Humvee roll-over drills, spraying all our deployment uniforms with prometheryn, endless classes on culture, ROE, diseases, history, and more. It was all good training but it took time away from getting everyone good at their jobs.

We started to get an influx of new personnel at the same time. Division assured me that everyone had learned from the last deployment, and I would get an assistant air officer before we left. Of course, they asked me to pick someone from one of our battalions but that was a joke – the battalions needed air officers as badly as we did.

Christmas was coming and it was going to be rolled in with our pre-deployment leave periods. I got lucky and got the two-week period including Christmas. Donna agreed that we should invite my family down and host Christmas at our house.

It was a crazy but awesome Christmas. My brother with his wife and four kids came down in their RV and parked it in the driveway. My parents came and stayed in our RV parked on the side of the house. My eldest sister and her husband and five kids drove down. My other sister, her husband, and their one-year-old daughter came, too. We made up beds everywhere. All the kids piled in the living room on the sectional sofa and on sleeping pads on the floor – there were people sleeping everywhere. It was crowded but a lot of fun. Everyone was very gracious and got along famously. We ate in shifts because we didn't have enough plates and flatware for that many people.

Donna made special arrangements with a local restaurant. We all broke the fast and had a huge Christmas feast together at the Frontier Diner. It was a little different, but that's kinda how my family is. We watched the kids open presents and built a few rockets to fire off in the empty lots on our street. There may have been a few cocktails in there, too. I have a great family picture from this: everyone is smiling and laughing, even Stuart, and there is Dad, midstride, trying unsuccessfully to get back in place before the camera timer went off.

After Christmas break, it was full tilt, getting ready to deploy. Skinny (who no kidding was thin as a rail) checked in to be my assistant air officer. He was a young helicopter pilot with a dry wit. We chunked him through as much of the pre-deployment training as possible. He had a lot of information to absorb about being an air officer, but I wasn't too worried about it. He was quick to catch on and a smart guy to begin with.

Mid-January came rapidly and we were back on an airliner headed for Kuwait.

Chapter 35

Iraq Part II: Groundhog Day

Turnover with 2nd Marines was quite simple. We basically just got updated on the new personalities and relevant changes in ROE and SOPs. It was the classic "brief me on the exceptions" kind of deal.

Of course, 2nd Marines gave me and the S-2 a ton of grief. Things like:

"Hey, didn't you guys just leave?"

"What, didn't do well enough the first time? Gotta come back and try again?"

"Are you lost? You were supposed to go home nine months ago!"

"Mama didn't like having you home so she sent you back?"

It was funny the first eight or nine times. Then it was just old, repetitive, and stupid. So we had to throw some back at them.

"Yeah, they sent us back to clean up the mess you guys made."

"Laugh it up, fuzzball! In ten months, you'll be in my shoes!"

"I guess you guys couldn't handle it so they sent us back in."

"Don't worry, I took care of your wife while you were gone."

When we turned over to 2nd Marines eight months before, I had been undecided if their Air O was just confident or arrogant. During this turnover, I decided it was arrogance. He had reduced the workload of the Air O, which was a good thing. The bad part was that now all that work fell on the battalion Air Os. Technically, that was "legal," but I had a different approach. I attempted to help out the battalion Air Os whenever possible. They were the ones living out in the dirt.

The real kicker was the new Air O had destroyed the air officer Humvee. I loved that vehicle. BK as the S-6 had his guys configure it with just the right radios. It wasn't exactly how the USMC thought it should be, but it had everything I needed and nothing I didn't. Since it was a custom configuration, you couldn't just get another one. I didn't know the exact details of how it got destroyed, but he thought it was funny and wore it as a badge of pride.

"Yeah, I drove that thing into the dirt!"

"You don't have a license! Officers aren't even supposed to be driving tactical vehicles."

"Hey, gotta do what ya gotta do. That thing wasn't even up armored anyway."

His attitude highlighted a shift in mentality from the "old school" to the "new school." It reflected the influx of what we called GWOT money. GWOT was the Global War on Terror. Everyone had a much bigger budget now. I still held to the old-school mentality drummed into me during the early days, which was: take care of your equipment because if you break it, that's it, you don't get another. The new mentality was: if I break it, they'll just give me a newer better one. I still believed that the money would stop at some point and that this new mentality would bite us in the ass.

One of the things I did appreciate from 2nd Marines was that they had built an office trailer just outside the COC. Skinny and I now had our own place to work besides our desk in the COC. It also had secret and unclassified computers hooked up to the appropriate networks. So while one of us was on watch in the COC, the other could work on other jobs and projects out in the trailer. That office improved our quality of life tremendously.

In addition, there had been some major improvements in the local situation. As much as it sounds like I'm talking trash, 2nd Marines had done a lot of good work. You could now walk down the streets with little worry in many of the towns we would have either avoided or entered fully armored. Husaybah along the Syrian border was most noteworthy.

For the most part, though, the entire deployment was Groundhog Day. Life was a little better and I got a little more sleep than the previous deployment. But the majority of the challenges and efforts were the same.

Three months before we arrived there had been an incident in Haditha where Marines from 3/1 had killed twenty-four civilians, including several children. By January 2006 an investigation was in full swing and I had to deal with constant requests to fly investigators to and from Haditha.

The story, as I understood it at the time, was that a patrol from 3/1 had been hit by a coordinated ambush in Haditha. One of their vehicles hit an

IED and they came under small arms fire as they were trying to recover Marines from the damaged vehicle. One Marine was killed.

The normal reaction to a coordinated ambush is to assault through the enemy. First, that gets you out of the ambush kill zone, and second, it puts the most pressure on the attacking force. Most of the time the bad guys retreat and the Marines attempt to catch them and the IED triggerman if they can. Oftentimes this means clearing houses and other buildings looking for the gunmen and the triggerman.

Allegedly, the patrol leader, a Sergeant, led his men through several buildings, clearing with flashbangs and grenades, and they ended up shooting numerous innocent civilians along the way.

It was often hard to know the real story. The bad guys had gotten very good at getting inaccurate press releases out and published, and there had been many incidents where insurgents claimed the US bombed schools or hospitals. Sometimes they even used pictures of dead bodies that weren't related to the incident, and often claimed that slain fighters were innocent bystanders.

Additionally, 3/1 had been in Fallujah in November 2004, just a year prior. They had lost twenty-four Marines in Fallujah. They had returned home for only a few months before being sent back to Iraq and being assigned to Haditha. The tactical situation was much different in Haditha. Clearing a room or building in Fallujah was done with grenades and flashbangs. That technique was not appropriate for Haditha, where the number of uninvolved civilians was much higher and the threat level was lower. It was easy to surmise that the fired-up Marines may have acted too aggressively for the situation. Having one of your buddies killed right next to you could easily inflame the situation. It was a sad situation all the way around.

Meanwhile, the Wing has started a system called The Ring Route, which consisted of scheduled flights that flew the basic ring of the FOBs in our area. On even dates it would go clockwise and on odd dates counterclockwise. This helped scheduling immensely. You could now plan meetings and have a reasonable expectation that people could make it to your FOB for the meeting. It also cut down significantly on the lower priority requests Skinny and I had to process. The Wing hated when we called it a bus route, but as much as we disliked it, the truth was we were working logistics and transportation now. It was frustrating and demotivating at times. There was very little tactical use of aviation. No more bomb dropping or heliborne assaults.

On a larger scale, the primary focus of operations had shifted to building Iraqi forces and larger-scale infrastructure projects. The higher number of Iraqi soldiers meant I had to spend a lot of time dealing with flying them around. The Iraqi forces were referred to as Jundi. Technically Jundi means soldier, but police and National Guard often got lumped in this category as well. I lost track of how many different forces and types of forces we were building.

All Iraqi forces worked a three-week schedule. In other words, they would work for three weeks and then return home for a week of leave. In addition, to protect the Iraqi soldiers and their families, they were never employed in their home area. The result was that every week we were tasked with moving 25 percent of the Iraqi forces. Most of it was by air. That was an abusive schedule to work and maintain. It got better over time as things got standardized, but it was rough in the beginning.

One week I was working a large movement of one hundred Jundi from Al Qaim to Baghdad. We flew them by helicopter from Al Qaim to Al Assad, then moved them to C-130s for the flight into Baghdad. Concerned that some of them would miss the flights or get on the wrong aircraft, I went up to the airfield to assist the Marines who were there.

So far we had gotten about fifty of them in by helo and they were all waiting in one of the plywood buildings. The first C-130 was ready so I went to get them. I asked one of the English-speaking Iraqi officers to get them into a single-file line headed out the door. Then I could lead them out the door to the taxiway and the waiting C-130.

The Iraqi officer started yelling and beating them with his stick. It was somewhere between a swagger stick and a cane. I was shocked. It was a scene I'll never forget. They were scrambling around randomly like they didn't understand the directions while he screamed and beat them on the head with his cane. This wasn't friendly pushing them into line; this was nailing them on the head and shoulders with a full swing.

The Staff Sergeant helping me just stood there with his mouth open. It took me a second to snap to but then I rushed over.

"HEY, HEY, don't beat them! Just ask them to get in line! This isn't a big deal!"

"They are Jundi."

"Yeah, yeah, okay, but we don't have to beat them."

"You must beat the Jundi. It is the only thing the Jundi understand."

I was reeling. Reeling and angry. I know the feeling of being frustrated with junior troops but this was out of hand. I asked the officer to go to the front desk and check off the names on the manifest. Meanwhile, the Staff Sergeant used a little pointy talky and got them in line. I led them out the door while the Staff Sergeant followed up from the rear to make sure no one wandered off.

This display illustrated to me the conflict between how much we should let them do things their way and how much we should force them to do things our way. It got a lot more complicated when *their* way violated our policies or laws. There have been papers, studies, and books written about how different the Western way of thinking is from the Eastern, Islamic-based mentality. I didn't have the answers. But I had to roll with Western thinking on this one.

It also demonstrated how the locals seemed to only respect the most ruthless person or party around. No wonder the Iraqis were often indifferent to our suggestions, since we were working hard NOT to appear violent.

Another big infrastructure project was the Haditha Dam. This had been a big push since 2003. Over the last year, contractors had repaired one of the old generators and installed the first of two planned new generators, so finally the dam was producing enough electricity now to power all of Baghdad. Now the big push was the distribution system – the powerlines – which were needed from Haditha along the Euphrates River to Ramadi. From Ramadi the existing grid was sufficient.

2nd Marines had overseen the civil engineering project to build those powerlines. But as soon as a section was constructed, thieves, nomads, and other nefarious characters in the desert would pull down the towers and turn the copper and steel in for scrap metal. We would spend millions of dollars building powerlines in an austere environment and they would tear them down to turn in the metal as scrap for pennies on the dollar.

We continued the push to get the powerlines up but now had Marines and aircraft dedicated to patrolling them. It was frustrating. We were trying to help these people and they just destroyed everything we did.

A few weeks into the deployment a buddy back home had sent me a copy of a Marine Corps message soliciting applications for the next year's Marine officer instructors. Marine officer instructors (MOIs) are instructors/staff at the seventy or so NROTC units around the country. It is a three-year tour. Each year, twenty-five or so need to be replaced. I knew this could be a great opportunity.

The best part is that instructors are selected by a competitive board. That means manpower would have very little say about my getting orders to one of the NROTC units. It was a little bit like going over their heads, but in a legal way. The other cool thing was I would spend three years at a college. I wouldn't be on a base, and I wouldn't be deploying. I liked the idea of teaching and molding young minds.

I emailed Donna to ask her what she thought. I got a one-word email back: "YES!" Now all I had to do was put together a competitive application package.

I spent many late nights writing my military resume and the board essay and framing several letters of recommendation. I also asked the training sergeant to run me on a physical fitness test so that I would have a current score. Finally I got the package submitted. Now all I had to do was wait.

The CO and I had to fly down to MEF for a meeting. While we were waiting for the flight, he asked me what I was doing next (he had endorsed my MOI application). I think he was actually trying to do the career development thing he was supposed to do with his officers. The notable part of the conversation was when I told him I wasn't competitive for Lieutenant Colonel and would be on the board the next year. He said, "Don't worry about it. Look at me, I haven't done any of the things I was supposed to for a career path and I'm doing fine."

Two thoughts popped in my head: 1) Yeah, but your dad was chairman of the Joint Chiefs, and 2) I can tell you don't know anything about aviation career paths. It made me chuckle. Honestly, his father probably had very little effect on his career, but it seemed funny for him to say that.

I wasn't working nearly as hard as I had on the last deployment, but it was still long days and lots of work. Lots of planning things that changed and then required replanning.

The one thing about deployments is the simplicity. All you have to do when you are deployed is work. No kids soccer games, no rushing out of work by 5 p.m. to pick up the kids before daycare closed. You set all your bills up on autopay. That is not to say you don't think or worry about things at home, but in general, you have only one focus.

But some days the Groundhog Day aspect got old. Doing pretty much the same thing day in and day out is tiresome. Particularly when it's fixing other people's mistakes, and the same mistakes, day after day after day.

In early April I learned that I been selected for the MOI program at Auburn NROTC in Alabama! I was ecstatic, and Donna was beside herself. She was tired of living by herself with the kids. This would keep me home for the next three years and bring me home from Iraq in time to start the new school year in August.

My replacement arrived and we spent ten days working together. Then he took the reins and I was headed home. My BOG (boots on the ground) for that tour was 178 days – just shy of six months, and a drastic difference from the planned 365.

Leaving Iraq, I didn't know if I'd be back. The country and conflict had left a bitter taste in my mouth. I was immensely proud of what we had done and accomplished. I was proud of the tactical achievements. I was also proud of all the rebuilding, and all the civil projects we either accomplished or protected. But there was no easy solution for Iraq. Ultimately, I believed that we needed to pull out. But I knew the situation would backslide when we did. I firmly believed the biggest, baddest bully would fill the vacuum the moment we left. That character, whoever it might be, would end up controlling all the Iraqi security forces and the millions of dollars' worth of equipment we had provided. Hussein had been a tyrant, but he had kept the region stabilized.

On a smaller scale, though, I was leaving 7th Marines. As much as I bitched and whined, I loved 7th Marines and was proud to have been a member.

Chapter 36

Auburn

Auburn NROTC is a Navy command. I would be one of just two Marines out of a staff of twelve. I was a little nervous about rolling into a new command and having to learn all the Navy ways of doing business. Donna and I joked about how it would be a little more laid back.

Turns out, the staff there was terrific. As the MOI, I functioned as the OpsO for the unit. There were about 150 students in the unit. Only a small fraction were active-duty Marines or Navy and the rest were just average college students who were interested in becoming Navy or Marine officers. Quite a bit different than handling a platoon of battle-hardened Marines in Iraq or a shop full of dedicated Marine aircraft mechanics. Not better or worse, just different.

The learning curve was steep but I jumped in and enjoyed it. I taught two classes as an associate professor for the university: Evolution of Warfare and Amphibious Warfare, which were both required courses for all the NROTC students.

They were long days. Marine Physical Training (PT) started at 5:30 a.m. Then I taught the university classes throughout the day, with subjects ranging from marksmanship to leadership techniques to personal finances. In the evenings it was drill team practice from 6 to 8 p.m.

I loved it that nothing was CRITICAL. No one was going to die if someone missed PT or didn't make the class on Marine Corps organization. The students were all hungry to learn about life in the service. They brought an infectious energy that helped me move past some of the bitterness and frustration I felt after nineteen months in Iraq.

But the best part of the job was being able to go home to my family every night. There were also occasions I got to bring one or both of the kids to work with me. Emily was with me one day when I was teaching rope-climbing techniques. She watched quietly throughout the exercise, and then, when there was a rest break, she asked me if she could try. I was nervous about letting my eight-year-old climb up a twenty-foot rope.

But I let her have a go. She scampered right up to the top, slapped the crossbar, and came straight back down.

I proudly put my arm around her. "OUTSTANDING, sweetie!" I turned to the rest of them. "See? It's not that hard! My eight-year-old can do it!"

"Yeah, but Sir…she's YOUR daughter."

Meanwhile, Donna had been accepted to the university and had started working on a master's in wildlife biology. She was able to use the benefits I got as an associate professor as well as some of her GI Bill, and she also received some additional scholarships due to her good grades. I don't think her master's cost us a dollar. She was very busy: the graduate level courses she took were demanding, and she also taught some undergrad courses as a professor's assistant.

Once per week Donna and I would get a babysitter and go have a fancy dress-up dinner. On one of our dates, we were discussing how much we enjoyed Auburn. Donna surprised me when she said, "Yeah, if you'd done another entire year in Iraq, you may have come home to an empty house." I've never pushed her on how much she really meant that. I took the point to heart, though. She didn't like it when I deployed.

I was also able to coach Vic's first soccer team. That was a huge high point. He was five now and loved playing soccer. I had played as a kid and still loved the sport. It started out just helping the coach, shagging balls, and moving cones. After a couple weeks, I was asked to join as an official coach. It's tough for one man to control ten energetic five-year-olds – even for a Marine Corps officer. Coaching at that level is less about the intricacies of soccer tactics and more about just keeping them headed the right way. It was a blast and I was able to coach for two seasons.

The Lieutenant Colonel board rejected me for promotion. That stung. Effectively, the Marine Corps was telling me "you aren't good enough." After all the effort, all the blood, sweat, and tears I had shed, I didn't make the cut. The practical side meant I would have to retire in the next six years. I had to do another three years to be eligible to retire, but I couldn't stay past 2014. It stung because I cared and I had always been loyal to the Marine Corps.

Donna, my loving wife, didn't care. She'd had a different experience in her eight years of Marine service and didn't have the same loyalties to the Corps as I did. She'd had some difficult experiences as a woman. She was looking forward to leaving the Marine Corps behind and being able to run our own lives. I liked the idea of running my own life, too, but the idea of leaving the Marine Corps was a bit intimidating. I had been a Marine my entire adult life. It was all I knew. But I had at least another three years to figure out the next stage.

The three years of good family time were drawing to a close. In the spring of 2009, my choices for my next tour were limited. The Marine Corps, and the entire DOD, was still heavily involved in both Iraq and Afghanistan. Chances were I was going to get orders back to a unit deploying to one or the other. Part of me felt guilt, like I'd been hiding from deploying. But part of me wanted to try and hide for another three years. I had reached the point where I had been home for as many kids birthdays as I had missed. It may seem like a simple thing, but that was important to me.

The two options I had were Marine Aircraft Group (MAG) 29 in North Carolina or MAG 39 in San Diego. Donna said she would rather go back to San Diego than Camp Lejeune so that's what I signed up for. I hoped that if I could get to a squadron, I could get some flying time in and maybe, just maybe, look competitive for my last opportunity to apply for the Lieutenant Colonel board. The problem with my situation was that I hadn't flown since 2003, that last glorious flight I had in Gitmo, Cuba. I was six years out of the cockpit and a lot had changed.

When a pilot is out of the cockpit for over eighteen months, they go back to the training squadron for four to five months of refresher training. The UH-1N, my aircraft, had been phased out and now the Marine Corps was flying the UH-1Y. It was still basically a Huey, still performed the same missions, but it had different flight characteristics and limitations. Instead of "refresher" training, I needed "conversion" training. And that takes a little longer.

I called the personnel officer, a Lieutenant Colonel, at MAG 39 and explained my situation. I told him I needed to get back to a squadron. He agreed, but told me the MAG was swamped with requirements to send officers to fill temporary billets. It made sense from a manpower management perspective but totally screwed me. So I was going to deploy (in a non-flying) job so I could get back to flying in a squadron. So there was no way to get back flying before the next Lieutenant Colonel board.

A few days later, MAG 39 called me back with the bad news. They had been tapped to provide several officers to I MEF for their upcoming deployment to Afghanistan (AFG). The personnel officer had looked through the records of all incoming officers to identify any Air O experience to send to MEF. So I would be transferring to MEF as soon as I arrived and could expect a one-year deployment to AFG. At least we knew what to expect when we got there.

Donna started looking for wildlife biologist jobs in the Camp Pendelton area but there wasn't much available. Luckily, the Wildlife department of Auburn had a pretty good network for helping new graduates find jobs in the field and she was able to get an FDA wildlife job at Point Magu, a small Naval air station just north of Malibu (about a three-hour drive from Camp Pendleton). Since I would be deployed for the year anyway, she thought that sounded pretty good. She accepted the offer. My orders were for August but she needed to start at the end of May. She packed up the car and headed west. She rented a small duplex in nearby Thousand Oaks and started her new job.

The kids and I stayed in Auburn to finish out the school year. It was a bit hectic being the single dad. The kids got a little bit tired of my limited dinner-making abilities but they were good sports about it.

Soon it was time to head west to join Donna. I had sold our motorhome and bought a cheap travel trailer. My plan was to live in the travel trailer while in Camp Pendleton, then put it in storage while I was in AFG. Donna flew back out to make the trip with us. We hooked up the travel trailer to my truck and the family headed back west.

Chapter 37

Terminal Major

I had spent seven of the last twenty years in Camp Pendleton, so coming back was a little like coming home. Lots of things were familiar, but lots had changed, too. For example, the flight line had always included five skid squadrons made up of Hueys and Cobras, with a big sign that said "Welcome to Skid Row." Now there were several CH-46 squadrons on the flight line as well. It was kinda weird seeing all the '46s parked out there with the skids.

After I checked in it was the usual series of reunions of running into friends I hadn't seen in a long time. The manpower manager had turned over so the Lieutenant Colonel I had been talking to wasn't there anymore. I had a brief glimmer of hope that maybe my status had changed, but the new guy, another Lieutenant Colonel, had the same story for me: yes, I was to head over to I MEF, and yes, I could expect a year tour in AFG. And he seemed to agree my only hope of Lieutenant Colonel was to get to a squadron and get flying again: "The board is going to see an aviator that hasn't flown as a Major. They are going to think you are hiding from flying. You gotta do an IA billet and we need to send some solid guys down to I MEF to give the Air Shop some depth. You are perfect for it." I think this was the moment that I fully accepted my fate and decided I would attempt to embrace it.

I'd had several discussions with other friends about being passed over for Lieutenant Colonel. Many of them had noted that the most effective and happy Majors were often terminal. "Terminal" means terminal rank with no chance for advancement. Being terminal can be a big relief. If you are terminal, you no longer have to worry about political games or towing the party line. You can just do your job the way you think it should be done. As long as you don't do something really stupid, like get a DUI or have an inappropriate sexual relationship, you won't get fired. That has a freeing effect.

I spent the rest of the week doing the usual check-in stuff. There were a lot of redundancies but it was no big deal. I was getting paid a good salary to drive around, wait in lines, and put my information into green logbooks.

I wasn't really responsible for anything or to anyone yet so I ditched out at 3 p.m. on Friday. It was only 150 miles from Camp Pendleton to Thousand Oaks, but the drive took me straight through all of LA. Even getting an early start, it was a parking lot the entire way. I got in about 9:30 p.m. and the kids told me all about their week. Then we played about an hour of Mario Kart and shuffled the kids off to bed. I was happy they seemed to be transitioning to the new town, new schools, and new areas pretty well. We had a great weekend, going to the pool and the park and riding bikes and skateboards up and down the street. I put together a new shelving unit and fixed a few things around the house. Sunday afternoon came all too soon and I was headed back to Camp Pendleton.

If our pre-deployment requirements had seemed ridiculous before for my second tour in Iraq, it was truly out of hand now. For example, the biggest cause of battle deaths were IED wounds, so we had almost a week of IED training. And since most of those IEDs hit convoys, we had three days of convoy training.

In addition, there had been several incidents of US service members violating law of war, rules of engagement, or other limitations. Everyone has heard about the atrocities in Abu Ghraib. There was also the Haditha incident, and another incident of a Marine urinating on a dead insurgent. It seemed like one of these stories hit the news every week. Policymakers decided we weren't giving our service members enough training on law of war, rules of engagement, and such, so it became a weeklong series of classes.

It had also been noted that deployed US forces as a whole had had a high number of non-battle deaths related to vehicle rollovers. Some of them involved roof-mounted gunners; others involved drownings when a vehicle went off the road into a canal. So policymakers now demanded that all US personnel get vehicle rollover training before deploying. Of course, there was also a company that quickly built vehicle rollover simulators and was happy to contract with the government for the training.

The contracting bothered me. Most of these training evolutions were conducted by contractors or contract companies. And while many of these instructors had done a tour in Iraq or AFG as a young soldier or Marine, just having a background or some experience does not necessarily make a good instructor. I know those companies were making some large profits and I wasn't too impressed with their product.

Ultimately, all of these training requirements had the safety and security of our service members in mind. The end result was over three months' worth of training to be completed before deploying. This took away from us being able to brush up on operational training and get into tip-top proficiency.

This was a big transition time for the Marine Corps. As long as I had been in the Corps, there had been between 172,000 and 175,000 active-duty Marines. Now, to support the constant deployment cycle and the requirements of fighting two wars, Congress had approved the Marines to swell to 212,000. Standards were lower and Marines were often rushed through training. We started to have less quality overall and more issues with younger enlisted Marines and officers.

Still, with "The Long War," only about 20 percent of the Marine Corps were deployed at any one time. And less than half of Marines had deployed at all. In effect, the same Marines had been deploying over and over for the last six years. I had witnessed this firsthand during my time in Iraq, where I had seen plenty of my friends show up twice on six-month deployments. I met guys who had two or three deployments to Iraq and one or two to AFG. The six-on, six-off or year-on, year off-cycle wasn't uncommon. Now back at Camp Pendleton, I couldn't believe the number of Marines coming to join I MEF FWD that had never deployed. Maybe all that pre-deployment training was a good idea after all.

Just before Christmas, we got the word that our January departure to AFG had been delayed until early March. I wasn't real thrilled about it. It meant that my current situation of only seeing the family on weekends was extended. By this point, we were all itching to get the deployment started.

We finally deployed on March 5. In typical Marine Corps style, we showed up at 3 a.m. and dropped all our gear, two seabags, and a rucksack in the stacks. Then we waited in line for the armory to open. Of course, someone forgot to tell the armory what time to be there.

We finally got our weapons and had one last roster call before boarding the buses. As we boarded the bus, we each got handed two one-gallon ziplock bags. One was busting at the seams with medications and the other was full of bolts and weighed five pounds. Turns out the contractor had sent our beds to the correct address in AFG but the hardware to assemble them had arrived at I MEF FWD in California. It might have been useful to get the five-pound bag of bolts *before* we put our seabags on the pallets. Oh well. I just shoved the bolts and anti-malaria pills into my pockets. With that, we were off on the usual five-day process of flying to a war zone.

Chapter 38

Afghanistan

The mission in AFG was almost a carbon copy of the mission in Iraq. Simplified, it was to suppress the violence enough to allow the Afghan military forces to develop to a point where they could take over. At the same time, we were attempting to foster the growth of the economy and to allow some type of representative government to become self-sustaining.

One big difference from Iraq was the poppy issue. Estimates ranged wildly, but somewhere between 50 and 80 percent of the world's heroin comes from Afghanistan. And approximately 75 percent of Afghanistan's heroin is produced in the Helmand province, where we were stationed. The early mission in AFG included eradicating poppy fields. Millions, possibly billions, of dollars had been spent trying to replace the poppy

fields with another crop. For the most part these efforts fell flat on their face. The special hybrid wheat that was developed for the region was planted by hundreds of farmers. Most of them plowed the free wheat seed under and replanted poppies when the warlords threatened to kill their families if they didn't.

By the time I MEF deployed, most of the enthusiasm for our mission had waned. I didn't have the wisdom or the background to come up with any better ideas. But it didn't matter. I was going to be the assistant air officer and run the shop of five officers and two enlisted Marines the best I could.

Per usual, we arrived in Afghanistan in the middle of the night. Camp Leatherneck was a large Forward Operating Base (FOB). It was almost

1,600 acres. Camp Bastion was the British main FOB in Helmand and immediately adjacent to Leatherneck.

We all piled off the buses into a sand and gravel parking lot. Spaced out before us was row upon row of white metal billeting cans. The cans were just like the ones we had used in Iraq, except these had concrete pads poured under them and concrete walkways between the rows.

A seven-ton flatbed truck pulled up behind the row of mini buses, and Marines started dropping the seabags off the truck onto the ground. That's exactly why you pack carefully. It's worse than the airlines.

I found my can and was happy the key worked to unlock the door. The can was brand new and the split unit A/C had just been installed. The snipits of wire and the empty box were still laying next to it. And right in the middle of the floor was a pile of steel bars and angle iron. Yup, that was the bunk bed. And I had a five-pound bag of bolts in my pocket to put it together.

We spent the next few days turning over and getting settled in. I was starting to really understand the size of I MEF. The outgoing crew was a beefed-up MEU. Normally a MEU is about three thousand personnel. They had been reinforced to almost 10,000 personnel. A MEB (Marine Expeditionary Brigade) is about 12,000 personnel. The Ground Combat Element of an MEB is a reinforced infantry regiment. Basically the the same thing as 7th Marines in Iraq.

By contrast, I MEF brought almost 18,000 personnel into AFG. We were getting additional troops from the UK, Georgia (not the state but the country adjacent to Russia), Bahrain, Estonia, Denmark, Lithuania, Tongo, and a couple others. The total strength was over 30,000. Then there were Afghans also.

There was another alphabet soup of Afghan forces: ANCOP, ANA, ABP, ANSF, ANP, ALP, etc. This was Afghan National Civil Order Police, National Army, Border Police, National Security Forces, National Police, Local Police. Their numbers were growing by the day. I learned that Afghanis is a currency (and sometimes a cookie). People from Afghanistan are Afghans.

The area of operations was almost 30,000 square miles. It encompassed the Helmand province and portions of the Kandahar, Nimruz, and Farah provinces. The terrain of southwest AFG is much like Iraq – dry, sandy desert. It is a little bit higher elevation so it gets colder in the winter. The area of operations included the Helmand River, which flows through the eastern side of the province. Of course, 90 percent of the population lives in that green belt. The vast majority of the Combat Outposts (COPs) and Forward Operating Bases (FOBs) were along that green belt. These included places like Musa Qala, Garmsir, Sangin, Marjah, and Lashkar Gah. The Kajaki Dam is also in this province. It was strikingly similar to the Haditha Dam in Iraq. It also creates the largest reservoir in AFG.

Fortunately, the rapid growth had been expected and the supply channels were prepared. We ordered several tables, computers, and whiteboards. We soon had our workspace set up with eight-foot folding tables and multiple computer workstations on each.

This all fell under NATO with the forces here specifically being called ISAF for International Security Assistance Force. Because of the layers, we ended up having four different networks and each network required its own distinct computer. We had the standard unclassified network, which is the same internet everyone has access to. Then we had our usual US SECRET network. Because we don't share all of our secrets with everyone in NATO, we also had a NATO SECRET network. There were countries sending troops to support ISAF that weren't members of NATO so we also had to have an ISAF SECRET network. And we had to keep flip-down covers on all the computers in case we had a guest in the office who wasn't authorized to view a certain level of information. Receiving information on one network but needing to share it with someone on another network presented problems. It was a royal pain in the ass.

Three Brits came to join my Air Office crew. Two were female officers, both Flight Lieutenants, the equivalent of a Marine Capt. The third was harder to equate in terms of rank. He preferred to be called Sergeant Major, but got the treatment of a Warrant Officer. Jace was all business when appropriate, but he had a hilarious and very British sense of humor, too.

Cpl Geyer was happy to have a little more female presence in office and Jace and I hit it off right away. In addition to his sense of humor, he had been a champion rally car co-driver and driver (rare to succeed in both seats) and an accomplished musician. He had two sons, approximately the same age as my two kids. We had a lot in common.

They all fell into their roles smoothly and it was an easy transition. The rest of the FECC (Fires and Effects Coordination Center) got some

UK reinforcements as well. Turns out, we were integrating the British Command with ours and it was now a combined command.

I divided up our responsibilities, then spread the collateral duties out as evenly as I could. It all started with a great relationship with my boss. Drowsy basically took all the high-end staff meetings. That was almost a full-time job, and I was so happy to be free of that. There were still plenty of planning meetings and integration meetings to attend at my level, though.

I focused on setting policy and managing the office. The vast majority of my time was dealing with the 150 assault support requests (ASRs) we received daily. I had to screen, correct, and then prioritize them before sending them off to Wing for tasking. It was laborious going through every single request, then putting them all in prioritization order. On the average day, I was in the workspace from 7 a.m. to 11 p.m. Most of that time was spent reviewing and prioritizing ASRs and answering all manner of questions. The phones were almost constantly ringing.

The two Marines I had, Cpl Geyer and Sgt Belkin, worked as office assistants. They worked on a twelve-on, twelve-off cycle. They answered the phones, screened visitors, and helped me with the first several layers of ASR screening. They would go through them first and check for date, time, passenger, and destination errors. While we were handling all the subordinate unit requests, we also wrote all the requests for the I MEF staff. This turned out to be a huge chunk of time. The Marines helped out immensely with that. I would have gone insane if I didn't have those two helping share the load.

The day-to-day grind was very similar to my time in Iraq. The difference was that I rarely left the base. I was also working at a level two commands higher than the regiment. That meant I had almost no interaction with the Marines outside the wire doing the mission. Generally, I talked to planners and unit representatives who were also living the FOB life. I also had very little interface with any Afghans. I met a few interpreters and a few Afghan Army officers but that was it.

The first three weeks or so, we had a lot of requests not getting supported. There were simply more requests than aircraft to support them. Every day was a shotgun blast of requests to all the different FOBs in all different directions. It was frustrating for the requestors and frustrating for me. It made it difficult to plan a meeting or a pick-up. I spent a lot of time staring at the map trying to come up with a better way.

I talked to my buddy Shaggy over at Wing about it. Shaggy was the one I sent all the approved requests to, and he assigned the tasking to the squadrons. I told him we needed to do something like the Ring Routes we had in Iraq.

"The General told me straight out we aren't going to do a ring route. We are not a bus service."

"Doesn't he realize how much efficiency we could gain?"

"Well, I'm pretty sure he does but this is kind of a political thing."

I festered on it for a few days. Then I realized I didn't need Wing to make a route. I could do it! If I only sent Shaggy requests for a certain number of FOBs for a particular day, he would support them the best he could. If it looked a little like a ring route, so what? He could tell his General it was just what MEF tasked him to do.

I could stipulate to all the requesters to only submit requests for certain FOBs on certain days. I was the MEF assistant Air O. Drowsy would back me up. Now I just had to come up with a system that was simple and made sense.

I noticed that about half of the places we flew to were north of Camp Leatherneck and half were south. Bingo! We'd just go north on one day and south the next! If someone needed to go to a meeting at Camp Dwyer, they would fly down on the south day, have the meeting on the north day, then return on the following south day. It was simple, easy to remember, and would get us about halfway there.

I started writing the Fragmentary Order (FragO). I named it NOSE, plain as the nose on your face. North Odd, South Even. The NOSE program was born.

During the first few days with the NOSE program, there were a fair amount of ASRs that didn't match and went the wrong way. I wrote a standard email and sent it back to the originators reiterating the basis of the NOSE program. Requestors or originators, the people who were actually writing the ASRs and submitting them, ranged from Lance Corporals to Colonels. I had to be a little bit careful with my responses. I couldn't insult the colonels and I had to go step by step for some of the junior Lance Corporals.

After a few days, it seemed to snap right in. Shaggy was loving it. His guys working the routing every day had half the work. The real benefit was the efficiency gained. Our number of unsupported ASRs went down at least 30 percent. At this staff level, statistics and statistical analysis was a big part of our day. That not only made Wing look good but also helped the people who needed to fly around or send materials by air.

Jace decided that it was his job to keep an eye on me. He did a pretty square job of it, too. Every now and then, he would grab me, saying "C'mon." He'd have the truck already checked out and would take me over to the little coffee shop on the UK part of the base. It was a great breather, and nice to get out of the stressful office for a few minutes. We'd sit for 10-15 minutes, drinking a good coffee and chat about this and that, or nothing at all.

I had suspected that my job in Afghanistan was going to be sitting in front of a computer all day. Now it was confirmed. So I ordered a nice office chair from Amazon. It was breathable mesh with good lumbar support to counter my back pain. Years of carrying a heavy pack, parachute jumps, and the horrible position of flying a Huey had all added up. I also ordered an egg crate mattress topper. I used to love going to the field, sleeping wherever I could find a level spot, and living the "snake eater" life. But I was starting to feel too old for that hardcore Marine stuff. I'd already had two knee surgeries and my knees were always stiff. Particularly in the mornings.

I was in heaven when the chair finally arrived. It was obviously different than the other crappy office chairs we had been supplied with. I knew it was $140 I couldn't get back but figured it was worth it for a year of seating comfort and back support.

It became the office joke that no one was allowed to sit in my chair. Of course, I also suffered a bit from some jokes like people hiding it a few times, saying Colonel So-and-So came in and said he needed it. But it was worth the money and the jokes.

We referred to KIA personnel as Fallen Angels. The flights that move them are called Angel Flights. The organization that collects them, cleans them up, and prepares them for flights back to the States is called Mortuary Affairs. They do an incredible job for our Fallen Angels. Sometimes they don't have much to work with, unfortunately, and they are always on a short timeline.

The standard is to have the deceased back to Mortuary Affairs in twenty-four hours and on a flight back to the States in forty-eight hours. We usually had them back to Mortuary Affairs in twelve and on a flight home in twenty-four. The priority on an Angel Flight was only superseded by Troops in Contact (TIC), or a Medevac flight. Plenty of times I had significant VIP flights that volunteered to either delay or bring the Angel back with them. This was true of both civilian/governmental VIPs and military VIPs. I've been on several flights with Fallen Angels and it is an intense experience. Nothing about the flight really goes any different other than the Angel is loaded last and unloaded first, but sitting in an aircraft next to a body bag or a silver aluminum box is sobering and emotional.

Camp Leatherneck is one of four or five major airfields that had international flights, so the majority of our troops who were killed flew into Camp Leatherneck. We would have an Angel Ceremony to meet every Angel Flight. An email would go out to everyone on the camp, and everyone who wasn't actively engaged in something was supposed to go. Of course, some made more of an effort than others. I went to about fifty ceremonies during the thirteen months I was there, but that probably accounted for only 30 percent during that timeframe.

The actual ceremony is simple: two lines of people march out to the back of the aircraft after it stops, the aircraft opens the tail ramp, and everyone faces inboard and salutes as the escorts carry or wheel the Angel from the aircraft between the two lines of people and into the Mortuary Affairs hangar. After the doors close, everyone faces back the way they came and marches off. It is all executed with tight, controlled military precision in the rain, blowing sand, freezing cold, or stifling heat. I had a lump in my throat at every single ceremony.

Sometimes you knew the name of the individual and sometimes you didn't. In November 2010, we had a ceremony for 1stLt Robert Kelly. As Lt Gen Kelly (Robert's father) stated many times, Robert's death was no more or no less tragic than the thousands of other deaths, but his Angel ceremony stays with me a little stronger than the others. As a father, I can't fathom how difficult that must have been.

Jace decided that going for a coffee once a week wasn't a good enough break. He soon instituted 'tea time' for our office. Someone found a little table that fit up under our work tables. I brought in a shemagh to use as a tablecloth. Someone made a "Meeting in Progress" sign to hang on the door. Cpl Geyer would go around and turn off all the phone ringers.

It soon became a daily ritual. Jace would start brewing at 3:45, and when the clock hit 4, the sign went on the door, the phones got turned off, and the table would get dragged into the center of the room. We'd all turn our chairs around to face the table in the center of the room and Jace would pour us each a cup of tea. Someone always had biscuits, cookies or some treat to share with everyone. For twenty minutes we wouldn't talk about work. We'd share a pot of tea and some treats and talk about the new iPhone or movies or cars or whatever. It was fantastic.

Occasionally we would get interrupted by someone ignoring the sign and busting in the door. Invariably, once they saw us gathered in the center of the room, they'd apologize and retreat. It was awesome.

It soon became a thing to get invited to Air Shop tea. On Tuesdays we'd invite the Col. He seemed to enjoy it. We invited Drowsy frequently but he usually said, "You guys enjoy your thing, I'm not going to come ruin it."

Everyone wrote home and requested special treats to share at tea. We got to try all kinds of British biscuits. I still don't fully understand the difference between a biscuit and a cookie, even after it was explained to me several times.

JR, my good friend from Auburn, sent me a huge box of Moon Pies. I explained to all the Brits what a Moon Pie was and showed them how tasty they are if you microwave them for 10-15 seconds.

Tea became the highlight of our day. Everyone planned around it so nothing would interfere. Once the tea was gone, usually about 4:20, we'd slide the table back into its hidey-hole, take down the sign and turn the phones back on. Everyone would snap right back to work, feeling ready to attack our challenges with renewed vigor. I swear our efficiency doubled.

I got a call from NCIS (Naval Criminal Investigative Service). They were conducting an investigation and asked me to come down for an interview to see if I had any information that would help.

When I arrived, one of the agents ushered me into a small interview room. He sat down and started asking me if I knew SSgt Wilson from Civil Affairs. I did in fact know him; I dealt with him almost daily, coordinating their air movements. The line of questioning started turning a little weird. The agent asked me about emails I got from the

Staff Sergeant and if they included pictures of women. Then he asked me why I was the first name on his email distro list. I didn't know but I guessed it was because my name started with A. I had gotten a few emails from SSgt Wilson that were kind of like internet memes but usually had scantily clad women. The questioning went on about the women in the pictures. Did I know any of them or did I know how old they were?

I slowly realized that I was a suspect in something and the agent was trying to figure out my involvement. I didn't know any of the models, nor did I know how old they were. I usually deleted the emails about as fast as I opened them. Evidently, SSgt Wilson was suspected of distributing underage porn. If I had temporary files on my computer, even if I had deleted the emails, was I complicit in underage porn? I was actually getting a little scared.

Then the NCIS agent started asking me about personal cameras. I knew there was nothing on my digital camera or my video camera. I didn't think I'd even used my video camera. I'd only used my digital camera for taking a few pictures around the base. I agreed to let them review/inspect my cameras and my personal computer. I wasn't sure about my office computer. It was classified but these guys all had US SECRET clearances, so I told them we could check with the IT guys.

The whole interview took about two hours. I felt like I had been through the ringer. When we were done, we walked over to my can and I laid out my phone, both cameras, and my laptop. I logged into my laptop and stepped back. One agent continued asking me cryptic questions while the other agent went through all my devices. When he finished with one, he would look up and nod to the other agent, then start on the next device. When he was done, we headed over to the office. The silent walk over to the office was uncomfortable.

When we got to the office building, I stuck my head in the IT office and asked the Sergeant on duty if there was any issue letting NCIS preview my work computer.

"No, no problem if you want to."

The way he said it made me think that I shouldn't be giving them permission, but I wanted to be done with this and cleared of any involvement. I was pretty sure that since I hadn't forwarded or saved anything, I wouldn't be considered a distributor. It sounded like that was what they were looking for. We went down to the office. Since it was midnight now, other than Sgt Belkin on watch, the office was empty.

I logged onto my computer and then moved back so the agent could sit down in front of it. The first agent asked me a few more questions while the agent on the computer ran some searches. It was all from the DOS prompt. He didn't open my email or even look through the photos folder. After a couple minutes, he nodded at the other agent and they thanked me for my cooperation. With that, they were gone. I was pretty sure that meant everything was good.

I told Drowsy about it the next morning when he came in. He was kind of miffed about it. As I had suspected, NCIS was supposed to notify someone in my chain of command before they pulled me in to grill me. Drowsy came back a few minutes later and told me there was nothing to worry about. He had called down to NCIS and they had nothing suspicious on me. I never did find anything out about the rest of it. I never did see SSgt Wilson again, either.

It was kind of strange to have a porn distribution investigation in a combat zone. It seemed like something that would be more likely back at home in a regular office setting. Other things like the Physical Fitness Test, Combat Fitness Test, and the Non-commissioned Officer (NCO) school made the environment in AFG seem like this was just another duty station back in the US. To me it raised a few questions. If we had the manpower to run all these things, maybe the numbers of personnel we deployed were a little bit high? Or maybe this was going to become just another duty station. I had heard about housing accommodations in some areas for married couples. It all seemed a bit strange. Maybe we were planning to be here longer than I realized.

A few weeks earlier I'd done a favor for the guys in UC-35 squadron. They flew Cessna Citation Vs for VIP transport. Afterwards, they told me, "If you ever need anything, anything from Qatar or wherever, let us know." I tried to think of what they could bring us that we couldn't already get. I had already ordered all kinds of stuff on Amazon. A few people in the building had plants in their offices and that was kind of cool. It was nice to see some green in the austere environment. I wanted something for the office that no one else had, something absurd to see in war-torn AFG. Then it came to me. A fish! A goldfish in a bowl would be awesome and definitely something no one else had!

I emailed them that I really wanted a goldfish. Surprisingly, they said no problem. They drove by a pet store almost every day on their way to the airfield in Qatar. Operation Goldfish was born.

Weeks went by and I forgot. Then one day I got a call from the UC-35 detachment operations officer.

"Barbie Jet is away, Code on Board."

Barbie Jet is the nickname they use for the UC-35 since it is so small. Code on Board means that there is a VIP on board. Usually that is a General or a congressman or something.

"You mean they got Chef?" Chef was my number two and had been in Qatar for a PR conference and I was trying to get him home.

"No, the code is Operation Goldfish!"

The sleek little gray jet pulled up ninety minutes later. The side door/stairs folded out and out came Chef with a bag on his back and a bright red cooler in his arms. He came trotting up, opened the lid to the cooler, and held it at arm's length for me to see. Inside was a plastic tank with three plastic bags, each containing a cup of water and a goldfish! Ha ha, I got my fish!

Walking back into the MEF security area, I was worried that the gate guard was going to give me a problem, but he didn't even ask to see inside the cooler.

Over the next few months, we had a lot of fun with the fish. People brought us stuff for our fish from everywhere. Soon I had ordered a better tank on Amazon with a light and a filter. They had plants and cool rocks and all kinds of stuff.

We started getting a lot of traffic through the office with people just wanting to watch the fish. We discovered we had to hide the fish food because everyone wanted to feed them. When I appointed Corporal Geyer official goldfish feeder, she lorded it over everyone.

I have to admit, I found it therapeutic to stare at the fish gently swimming between the swaying plants with the air bubbling up in the back.

Donna and I had decided that we wanted to live near one of our families when I retired. Comparing the quality of life and cost of living of north Florida and Northern California, we both agreed that we would move to north Florida near Donna's family.

There was a chain of small lakes less than a mile from her parents' house. When we would visit, that's where I would go for runs. I had been keeping track of the real estate on the lakes for the past six years. Now that the housing market was depressed, the houses on the lakes had fallen into our price range.

There was one house that Donna really liked so we made an offer. It was a bit odd trying to buy a house in Florida while I was deployed to Afghanistan, but with scanners and email it was actually pretty easy. By mid-December we owned lakefront! With the tax-free pay and extra combat pay I was getting, plus the savings we had been putting away for our retirement house, I was able to put 20 percent down and pay off another 10 percent. That was pretty exciting.

Christmas came and went. I prefer not to decorate or even acknowledge holidays when deployed. It's just another workday. When I decorated and did stuff, it just made me miss my family more.

In mid-February, we got a couple guys from II MEF in. They were our replacements and had planned a staggered turnover. Instead of having their whole crew come in at once, they were sending a few guys every two weeks. At the end of eight weeks, they would have responsibility for everything and we would head home.

I made double sure the new crew learned the routine for taking care of the fish. Soon they knew what kind of food to order and how often to change the water. Of course, we talked about the business at hand, too.

On the last day, I loaded my seabags on the baggage truck. I got my flight assignment and found my bus departure time. Then I headed back into the office, hoping to catch my replacement. He still wasn't in but I had a couple hours before my bus time, so I made my last coffee in the fancy coffeemaker I was leaving for them.

An hour before my bus departure time, I said goodbye to the fish and was just about to step out when my replacement, a LtCol, came stumbling in. He was still in the cammies he had been wearing for the last three days and needed a shave. But we still had about forty minutes for some turnover! I went through the turnover binder and hit the important stuff. I showed him some of the key stuff on the computer, bequeathed him my beloved office chair, and ran to catch my flight.

Chapter 39

Retirement

I had another eight months at Camp Pendleton before I would retire. The plan was for Donna and the kids to remain in Santa Cruz until school got out in three months, then move to the new house in Green Cove Springs, Florida. And then I would join them when I was done. It had been almost three years since I had really lived with my family. I was antsy to get us all together again.

I got the trailer out of storage and set up at an RV park near the beach. I had a few weeks left at MEF. I spent most of that time doing paperwork and putting a final revision on the orders and directives I had written for the Air shop. I MEF would be headed back to AFG in ten months so I needed to document everything I could to give the next crew the best head start possible. There were also fitness reports, awards, and various other routine documents to finish.

Once I was done at I MEF, I got signed out and headed back to MAG 39. After all, that is actually where I belonged. Mako (the HQ squadron CO) set me up with a good deal. I would become his executive officer for the HQ squadron. He understood that I was now going to be working on retirement proceedings, and the job would allow me the time to get everything sorted.

Preparing for retirement was almost a full-time job. There were online classes I had to do, plus two weeks of classroom instruction. Just filling out the request for a retirement date and getting it endorsed and submitted took a week.

There were several medical examinations to do, and the more health "issues" you have, the more there is to do. With the thickness of my health record, that meant I had a lot of appointments with various medical offices. The most noteworthy was Dental telling me I needed a dental implant and Ortho telling me that my knee still hurt because I needed another knee surgery. My requested retirement date had been approved, but those medical procedures couldn't be completed in the time I had left.

That meant both of them were deferred and would be completed by the VA after I retired.

As part of the preparation for retirement, one of the steps is to have a representative from a Service Organization (VFW, Marine Corps League, American Legion, DAV, etc.) review your medical records and help you file a disability claim. I sat down with a Marine Corps League representative and he thumbed through my thick medical record, taking notes along the way. After a few minutes, he shuffled some papers and started filling out the items on my VA disability claim. After he had listed about ten items, I had to say something.

"Uh, Sir, don't you think that is overdoing it? I mean, I can see filing for my knees and maybe the migraines, but all that?"

"Oh man, you have no idea. Don't worry about it. You need to file everything and take what you get."

"But filing for the scar on my face?"

"Oh yeah! Scars are a good disability." He leaned forward. "Here is what's going to happen: They aren't going to give you anything for the things that you think are obvious, like your knees or your back problems. They are going to downgrade those or maybe not consider them "service connected." It's tough to get things qualified as service connected. But they will give you 10 percent for flat feet and 10 percent for the scar on your face, things that you don't feel like you should file for. But it all comes out in the wash. If we get you all these little things and they don't give you anything for your back, it will come out about the same."

I thought I understood what he was saying but I wasn't totally comfortable with it.

He continued, "You know those things you told me about? Like going to the hospital in Iraq for your migraines? There isn't any entry in your record book. You probably won't get anything for migraines. You don't have any proof in here. All those times you didn't go to Medical because you were just dealing with it? Yeah, you screwed yourself. Now you don't have any proof."

What he was telling me was that all those sickbay warriors who went down to Medical for every little thing were the guys you saw parking in the handicap spot at the mall and then skipping into The Gap. They were getting 100 percent disability. The guys who just popped another Motrin and went back to work were lucky to get 20 percent disability.

The real surprise was when he showed me the charts. For multiple ratings, they discounted each one by the previous rating. For example, if you have five items that were 10 percent each, the total was not 50 percent disability. They got sequentially multiplied by the remaining "ability." It actually worked out to 43%, which then gets rounded down to 40%.

The percentages are simply a scale. It doesn't equate to a percentage of your pay grade. Ten percent means $135 a month, 20 percent was $260, 30 percent was $415, etc. If you were medically disabled at 100 percent, you'd get $2,973 a month. This percentage gets paid however you exit the military. So my buddy Tex, who was in a Cobra crash, broke his back and got medically retired, got a check for $2,973 a month. That was it.

If you get out of the military by retiring, the disability rate is deducted from your retirement pay. So you end up getting the same amount of retirement but your disability pay is tax-exempt.

I had done some homework on retirement pay and what my finances would look like, but this was all new to me. It was way more complicated than I'd ever imagined. As I left the office, the Marine Corps League rep told me he would expect me to see about 40 percent disability, which meant that $850 of my retirement check would be non-taxable. I thanked him and left, my mind whirling from all the new VA math.

Donna and the kids finished up the school year, so I took off ten days to get them moved out to Florida. Donna had been doing some freelance science writing and sending out resumes and had been offered a job in Gainesville at the University of Florida. I was excited she got a job already but a little disappointed there were still three months before we'd all be together again.

I was really "short" now in terms of how long it was before I'd retire. I had countdowns figured for just about everything: number of haircuts, number of uniform cleanings, number of physical training sessions, etc. Each morning when I'd walk into the Headquarters office, someone would ask me, "Hey, Hesty, how many haircuts left?" Everyone would chuckle.

The retirement prep had taken a lot of time, but I managed to get some things done as executive officer (XO), too. I'd put together a pretty good training plan and been getting a lot of stuff done for the junior Marines. I had overseen some barracks renovations and gotten some spaces cleaned out around the headquarters areas. Mako got my replacement in and we did some turnover so Cougar (the new guy) could pick up right where I left off. I unintentionally overheard Mako talking with Cougar about what to expect from the job once I left. It was a good feeling to hear the CO say that he hadn't expected much from me but that I had done some exceptional things for the unit and for the Marines while working on my retirement process.

My last actual day at work was anti-climactic. I made sure Cougar had full access to everything on the computer. Then I signed out in the ever-present green logbook in the admin section and turned in my active-duty ID. I already had my retired ID. I walked back out to my truck and sat looking at the static display Huey in front of the building. The MAG CO's name was on the right side door. I couldn't resist not leaving a mark of my own.

I grabbed a black paint pen from the back of my truck and painted my own name on the left side door. Beneath my name I added "Instructor Pilot." I was sure it would last a week at the most before the Colonel noticed and screamed at someone to "clean that shit off." I was pretty sure that the Marines who were ordered to go clean it off would be chuckling, though.

With that, I chirped the tires a little bit, leaving my last mark on Marine Corps property, and headed out the parking lot and out through the base gate. I had to take a picture of the gate in my rearview mirror as it faded behind me.

It was a bittersweet feeling. I had been a Marine since 1987 – all of my adult life. All of a sudden, that identity was gone, and I was a nobody again. But, I didn't have to meet all the crazy requirements that had been slowly increasing over the years. I could get up when I wanted to! I could walk around with something in my right hand or with my hands in my pockets! I could chew gum! I didn't have to shave or get a haircut! There were so many stupid little things now that I didn't have to worry about.

It was a good time for me to leave the Marine Corps. I had started to get a negative attitude about a lot of the new changes. I was getting a bit old to play some of the silly little games that never used to bother me, or the bigger political games that I really detested. It was good to leave on a high note.

There was a bit of fear and sadness though, too. As the base faded in the rearview, so did a lot of friends and brothers that I had shared time with. I did have some bitterness about a few things, but truth be told, I'd do it again. I might do a few things differently, but yes, I'd definitely do it again. I was proud of my service, proud of what I'd done and accomplished.

I drove long days and slept a few hours at a time at rest stops and made it to the new house in Green Cove Springs in three days. I was finally home in our new house. The kids had just started school. Vic was in fourth grade at the school half a mile away. Emily had just started high school and caught the school bus at the end of the street. Donna had to leave early in the morning to make the one-hour commute to Gainesville.

The first few days I unloaded the truck and tried to find spaces to put all my stuff. There wasn't much space in the new house, which felt kind of small, but whenever I saw the beautiful lake in the backyard, I knew it was worth it.

I started the day by making sure Emily got down to the bus stop on time. She was pretty good about getting up and getting ready on her own. Every time I saw her, I was a little shocked at what a young lady she had become. Then I'd make sure Vic was moving and getting some breakfast. I'd take the dog out for a potty break and get her some breakfast. When Vic was ready, I'd ride my bike with him to the front of the school. He'd branch off from there and I would go across the street to the coffee shop and get a real coffee. I'd stop and chat with the crossing guard for a few minutes, then ride back to the house. It was a great way to start the day.

I had two years' worth of projects at the house lined up already. I had to get some storage space built up in the attic. The master bathroom didn't have any doors and it really needed some pocket doors to work. The little boathouse wasn't big enough for our eighteen-foot boat so I needed to rebuild that. The dock was dilapidated and needed rebuilding. The back porch needed some work too. It was a sound house and very livable. With a bit of work it would be really cool.

Donna had signed Vic up for soccer with the local club. We had practice three days a week. This was a U10 team, meaning most of the kids were ten years old. The three coaches were active-duty Navy. They were all in the same squadron and rotated so that usually there were two of them at practice.

Since I waited there during practice anyway, I started helping out. After about a month, the head coach pulled me aside and asked me to take over coaching. Their squadron was deploying and all three of them were going. Just like that, I was coaching soccer again. Vic loved it, the other parents loved it, and I was surprised to be loving it. Originally I had been thinking of avoiding additional responsibilities, but the kids were great and it was fun to be outside and with Vic.

We had a fantastic season and the kids all got along really well so I hosted an end-of-season party at the house. I was on the back porch, grilling hot dogs and looking out over the yard and the lake. There were around twenty kids splashing and playing in the lake, having a great time while their parents relaxed and watched. This was my new domain. This was my new life. And life was good.

GOAT
(Glossary Of Acronyms and Terms)

ANGLICO: Air Naval Gunfire Liaison Company. A Marine unit that specializes in controlling supporting arms from mortars to cruise missiles.

AO: Area of Operations. Ground where a unit works.

AOR: Area of Responsibility. Ground that a unit is responsible for.

ASR: Alternate Supply Route. Military term for secondary roads. Usually has a code name. For example in Fallujah the east-west roads were female names and north-south roads where male names (See also MSR).

ATO: Air Tasking Order. An order from senior aviation authority to subordinate squadrons regarding what missions to fly, including some coordinating information. Similar to a flight schedule but infinitely more confusing.

Boot: Derogatory term meaning lack of experience or knowledge. Used to describe anyone who has one day less in the Marine Corps than you (or one day less of deployed time).

Brain Housing Group: Marine term referring to your mind, often used in a derogatory manner.

CAX: Combined Arms Exercise. Large-scale exercise involving grunts, Supporting Arms, and aviation units usually at a regimental level held in Twentynine Palms, California.

Clusterfuck: Total chaos; mission success is doubtful.

CP: Command Post. A generic term for any level of command headquarters location.

COC: Command Operation Center. Battalion and above hub of the Command Post. Usually full of communication devices (radios, computers, etc.) and where a commanding officer goes to control his forces. Pronounced *See-Oh-See* unless you are being negative, then its pronounced *cock*.

Contact: Verbal confirmation that you see a defined visual reference point. See also *Tally and Visual*.

Click: Kilometer. A favorite military abbreviation, generally only used in grunt units.

DASC: Direct Air Support Center. Group of Marines that procedurally controls and prioritizes aircraft flying support in a theater of operations.

Deck: Shipboard term that Marines use for whatever you are standing on – floor, ground, deck of a ship, floor of an aircraft, etc.

DI: Drill Instructor. Similar but better and more fierce than Army drill sergeants.

DOD: Department of Defense.

EGA: Eagle Globe and Anchor. Marine Corps' trademark. Marines put it on everything.

Escalation of Force: A rule of engagement that stipulates that you attempt to neutralize a threat with the smallest weapon system or action possible, then increase as necessary.

FAC: Forward Air Controller. The guy who controls the movement of an aircraft from the ground. Usually an officer, and most often a pilot who is sentenced to live with the grunts for a period.

FCT: Firepower Control Team. A small team of two to six Marines (and sometimes sailors) in ANGLICO that controls aviation and surface fires for the commander of a ground unit.

GOAT: Glossary of Acronyms and Terms. Just in case there weren't enough, let's make another to define how many we have. Similar to the list of lists.

Goatrope: Moderate level of chaos. May still achieve mission success but will be much more difficult than planned.

Gouge: Information or rumors. Also skinny, scoop, or skuttlebutt as in "give me the latest gouge."

Gunny: Shorthand for Gunnery Sergeant. Generally used affectionately, but often strikes fear in lower rank's hearts.

GWOT: Global War on Terror, also known as The Long War. Often used to refer to a significant plus up in funding for the DOD.

HA/HI: Hostile Act, Hostile Intent. Two distinct definitions but usually lumped together to satisfy a common rule of engagement threshold, allowing engagement with weapons.

LCpl: Lance Corporal. Lower rank, E-3; usually achieved in eighteen months. Not negative by definition but often implies newness, naivete, or lack of experience.

LOD: Line of Departure. Imaginary line usually with a visual reference, where forces begin a planned attack.

MAGTF: Marine Air Ground Task Force. The universal description of a typical Marine deployment unit. It generally contains a ground combat element, an aviation combat element, and a support element. It is overseen by a command element. It can be scaled as small as battalion-sized elements (this would be a MEU) or as large as division-sized elements (this would make a MEF).

MEPS: Military Entrance Processing Station. Regional facility that processes recruits for all branches of the military. Mostly medical screening. It is an in-depth (and often humbling) medical evaluation.

MOS: Military Occupational Specialty. A job or a job field in the military.

MOUT: Military Operations in Urban Terrain. Pretty much what it sounds like, fighting or operating in cities or developed areas.

MSR: Main Supply Route. Military term for primary(major) roads. Usually has a code name. In Iraq, they were state names for MSRs. Marines just like to rename everything (see also ASR).

MULE: Modular Universal Laser Equipment. Large, heavy piece of gear used by special operations type forces for laser designating targets. Can also have thermal or night vision modules attached.

NCO: Non-commissioned Officer. Generally the ranks of corporal and sergeant (in the USMC). Implies a higher level of trust and confidence and more responsibility.

PCI/PCC: Pre-combat Inspections/Pre-combat Checks. Self-checking and command checking of weapons and equipment before going on an operation or patrol.

PFT: Physical Fitness Test.

Proportionality: A confusing rule of engagement that stipulates you match a weapon system or action to a threat. You don't drop a nuke on a single sniper…unless that's all you have.

RBE: Remain Behind Element. Small detachment unit that remains at their home base when they deploy.

ROC/ROC walk: Rehearsal of Concept. A formal rehearsal of the plan for an attack, patrol, or other operation. Often includes using a model of the area.

ROE: Rules of Engagement. List of conditions that must be met before deadly force can be used.

S-1: Administrative department or the Admin officer.

S-2: Intelligence department or the Intel officer.

S-3: Operations department or the OPSO (Operations officer).

S-4: Supply and Logistics department or the Logistics officer.

S-6: Communications (and computer) department or the CommO (Communications officer).

S-10: We just made that up because my buddies, the LogO and CommO, shared a tiny office.

SANG: Saudi Arabian National Guard (basically the Saudi Army).

SJA: Staff Judge Advocate. This is a Marine Corps lawyer, a real one – not a barracks lawyer. Usually addressed by the nickname "Judge." They have a full law degree but are also full-fledged Marine Corps officers.

Snivel Gear: Extra gear that makes being in the field or deployed a little easier. Can actually be issued gear but often is civilian. Can be anything from nice socks to a tent heater. Usually revolves around staying warm in cold enviornments.

SOI: School of Infantry. The school that infantry Marines attend to earn their infantry MOS (0311).

Tally: Verbal response to indicate you see a bad guy or a bad guy position. Can be followed with a number to indicate how many you see (see also contact and visual).

TIC: Troops in Contact. DOD-wide term that indicates personnel in an actual fight with the enemy. This gives them priority for supporting assets.

TOC: Tactical Operations Center. Army version of the COC.

TOF: Time of Flight. How long it takes an artillery or mortar round to fly through the air and impact the target at a given range.

TTPs: Tactics, Techniques, and Procedures. Can be any method Marines use to do something that is not written down as doctrine. Generally means something you have learned by doing it a few times.

UAV: Unmanned Aerial Vehicle. Simply a drone. Used to be RPV for Remotely Piloted Vehicle

Unsat: Unsatisfactory, below par, not acceptable. Or it looks like shit.

Visual: Verbal response to indicate you see a friendly or friendly position. Can be followed with a number to indicate how many you see (see also *Tally and Contact*).

0300: Zero three. 3 a.m. Marines don't say "oh;" they say zero.

Acknowledgements

Andy:
First and foremost, deepest thanks to my wife Donna and children Emily and Vic. Thank you for enduring the research and writing phase but more significantly, putting up with the constant moves, long deployments, late nights, mood swings, and all that other stuff that goes with being a Marine family as we lived it! It has been a long haul. Thanks to the early readers, Brian King, Dee Dee Fitzpatrick, Mike Sheehan and James Couture: you all were key to us finding our "track" as we were developing the manuscript. Thanks to Stan Coerr and Andy Milburn for your time and advice. Working with Tara Moran and Harriet Fielding at Pen & Sword has been fantastic, thank you both. Thank you to Marco Einaudi for the fantastic maps! There has been a lot of support, encouragement, and advice from others along the way, thank you all. Finally, thanks to Rob. I spewed on the pages and you fashioned it into a coherent, readable story. Reminds me of that joke where the optimistic kid is handed a pile of poo but then molds it into a sculpture. Couldn't have gotten here without you bud!

Rob:
Thanks to my wife Suzie, my daughter Julia and my stepdaughter Etta for all your love and support. Thanks to my dad for drawing the maps, and for getting me obsessed with Vietnam War books at a young age. Thanks to my mom for cheering on my writing habit all these years. Thanks to the early readers of this manuscript: my brothers Fred and Andrew, James Couture and Mike Sheehan. Deep gratitude and admiration to the great John L'Heureux, an early proponent of this book. Thanks to our editor David Aretha, and to Tara Moran and Harriet Fielding at Pen & Sword. And many thanks to the rest of the folks who offered advice and encouragement along the way: Johannah Rodgers, John Coyle, Ben Sherman, Amy Smith Bell, Angie Ricketts, Mike Musto, John Talbot, Scott Anderson, and Nathaniel Fick. And finally, thanks to Andy for agreeing to this crazy project – probably a bit more than you bargained for!